The
UPGRADER'S
Guide

to Microsoft
Office
System
2003

D1447814

Mike Gunderloy
Susan Sales Harkins

QUE®

800 East 96th Street, Indianapolis, Indiana, 46240 USA

Upgrader's Guide to Microsoft Office System 2003

International Standard Book Number: 0-789-73176-2

Library of Congress Catalog Card Number: 2004104260

Printed in the United States of America

First Printing: June 2004

07 06 05 04   4 3 2 1

Trademarks

All terms mentioned in this book that are known to be trademarks or service marks have been appropriately capitalized. Que Publishing cannot attest to the accuracy of this information. Use of a term in this book should not be regarded as affecting the validity of any trademark or service mark.

Warning and Disclaimer

Every effort has been made to make this book as complete and as accurate as possible, but no warranty or fitness is implied. The information provided is on an "as is" basis. The authors and the publisher shall have neither liability nor responsibility to any person or entity with respect to any loss or damages arising from the information contained in this book.

Bulk Sales

Que Publishing offers excellent discounts on this book when ordered in quantity for bulk purchases or special sales. For more information, please contact

U.S. Corporate and Government Sales
1-800-382-3419
corpsales@pearsontechgroup.com

For sales outside of the U.S., please contact

International Sales
1-317-428-3341
international@pearsontechgroup.com

Associate Publisher
Greg Weigand

Acquisitions Editor
Michelle Newcomb

Development Editor
Laura Norman

Managing Editor
Charlotte Clapp

Project Editor
Sheila Schroeder

Production Editor
Megan Wade

Indexer
Mandie Frank

Proofreader
Suzanne Thomas

Technical Editor
Greg Perry

Publishing Coordinator
Sherry Lee Gregory

Interior Designer
Anne Jones

Cover Designer
Anne Jones

Contents at a Glance

Contents

About the Authors

Mike Gunderloy is an independent developer and author who has been working with computers for 25 years. His experience with Microsoft Office dates back to Office 4.3 which, despite the number, was the very first version of the integrated suite. In the intervening years, he has worked closely with the Office product team, participating in focus groups and even contributing some code to the finished product. Mike has written or contributed to more than 20 books on development topics. He's currently the editor of the weekly Developer Central newsletter. You can reach Mike at MikeG1@larkfarm.com or visit his Web site at http://www.larkware.com.

Susan Sales Harkins is an independent consultant with an expertise in Access. With Mike, Susan has written two Access books: *Absolute Beginner's Guide to Microsoft Office Access 2003* and *Absolute Beginner's Guide to Microsoft Access 2002*, both from Que. Currently, Susan writes for a number of technology-based publishers and magazines, including *Element K Journals*, *builder.com*, and *devx.com*. Her most recent books, also with Mike, include *Exam Cram 2 ICDL* and *ICDL Practice Questions Exam Cram 2*, both from Que.

Dedication

To all the folks at MCP Magazine.

—Mike Gunderloy

To the Black Knight.

—Susan Sales Harkins

Acknowledgments

It's always nice to finish another book—and one of the nice things is to be able to thank the people who helped make it happen. In our case, that includes Michelle Newcomb, Laura Norman, Greg Perry, Sheila Schroeder, Megan Wade, Mandie Frank, and Suzanne Thomas at Que, all of whom helped move the project along. They all did their best to make sure a fine book made it to the printed page and, if any mistakes remain, it's certainly not their fault.

Mike would also like to thank his family: Dana, who helps out with a million and one things around the farm from moral support to stacking firewood, with an eye toward minimizing chaos; and Adam and Kayla, who help in their own way by making life chaotic again. Thanks, too, to the understanding editors and customers who let me put off their projects for a little bit when there was a chapter to write or a galley proof to review.

Susan would like to thank the Que folks for continuing to support great book projects. Most especially, Susan thanks her family for supporting her decision to work from home in her pajamas so she can grow old with her granddaughter.

We Want to Hear from You!

As the reader of this book, *you* are our most important critic and commentator. We value your opinion and want to know what we're doing right, what we could do better, what areas you'd like to see us publish in, and any other words of wisdom you're willing to pass our way.

As an associate publisher for Que Publishing I welcome your comments. You can email or write me directly to let me know what you did or didn't like about this book—as well as what we can do to make our books better.

Please note that I cannot help you with technical problems related to the topic of this book. We do have a User Services group, however, where I will forward specific technical questions related to the book.

When you write, please be sure to include this book's title and author as well as your name, email address, and phone number. I will carefully review your comments and share them with the author and editors who worked on the book.

Email: feedback@quepublishing.com

Mail: Greg Weigand
         Associate Publisher
         Que Publishing
         800 East 96th Street
         Indianapolis, IN 46240 USA

For more information about this book or another Que Publishing title, visit our Web site at www.quepublishing.com. Type the ISBN (excluding hyphens) or the title of a book in the Search field to find the page you're looking for.

W elcome to *Upgrader's Guide to Microsoft Office 2003*! Our goal in this book is to smooth your transition to the newest and best version of Microsoft's business productivity software, the Microsoft Office System. You won't find endless discussions of features you already know and use here. Instead, we'll demonstrate the new and improved features, so you know how to take your Office skills to the next level.

Who This Book Is for

You should already be familiar with a previous version of Microsoft Office before you read this book. Because we focus solely on the new features, there are very few basic tutorials here. If a feature is entirely new to Office (such as the digital rights management features discussed in Chapter 12, "What's New in Rights Management," for example), we'll offer an in-depth discussion. But for features that have been around for a version or two (or more), we're assuming you already know how to use Office. This book is designed to help you learn the new bells and whistles in Office 2003 and apply them quickly.

We've focused on the differences between Office 2003 and Office XP (sometimes called Office 2002). You'll find this book most useful as you're deciding whether to upgrade to Office 2003 in your own organization. Our goal has been to provide you with a concise overview of the changes so you can decide whether it makes sense to upgrade now or to wait for the next version.

If you're currently using Office 2000, you'll still find our research useful, though, because there are not a lot of differences between Office 2000 and Office 2002. If the new features we discuss here look useful to you, you can upgrade straight from Office 2000 to Office 2003, skipping the intervening version.

What's in This Book

The book consists of 12 chapters, starting with an overview of the changes to Office 2003 overall and progressing through each individual application in the Office system as well as a few newcomers.

The first two chapters of the book provide an overview of the innovations and changes in Office 2003. Chapter 1, "What's New in Office 2003," introduces the major themes Microsoft is emphasizing for this release of Office. Chapter 2, "Shared Office Features," covers new task panes, sharing functionality, and other features that are shared by more than one application in the Office 2003 system.

The next several chapters cover the core Office 2003 applications, with one chapter for each:

- Chapter 3, "What's New in Outlook 2003"

- Chapter 4, "What's New in Word 2003"

- Chapter 5, "What's New in Excel 2003"

- Chapter 6, "What's New in PowerPoint 2003"

- Chapter 7, "What's New in Access 2003"

Each of these chapters discusses the differences between the 2003 and 2002 versions of these applications. You'll learn about new features, as well as about existing features that were changed and menu items that seem to have been inexplicably moved.

This book has a pair of chapters that also look at one application each. These are the applications that, although not in the box with the major editions of Office, are still used by many Office users:

- Chapter 8, "What's New in FrontPage 2003"

- Chapter 9, "What's New in Publisher 2003"

The final three chapters tackle the completely new parts of Office 2003. These are entire areas and applications that don't exist in Office XP. Chapter 10, "Introducing Microsoft OneNote 2003" and Chapter 11, "Introducing Microsoft InfoPath 2003," explain the basic use of these two new applications. Chapter 12 shows how Office 2003 fits into the digital rights management story Microsoft is beginning to explain. This is an area that we think will be increasingly important in coming years, and we're excited to be able to include a chapter on this technology.

You'll also find two appendixes to round out the book. Appendix A, "Office 2003 Version Guide," discusses the various ways in which Office 2003 has been packaged and which applications are included in each version. Appendix B, "Office 2003's Business Contact Manager," introduces the Business Contact Manager (BCM), an optional piece of software that works with Outlook 2003.

You don't need to be familiar with every single Office application to make good use of this book. We recommend that you first read Chapters 1 and 2, which provide overview material. After that, feel free to skip around from chapter to chapter, reading only the chapters on the applications you actually use.

Special Features

Throughout the book we've included some helpful features to ease your transition to Microsoft Office 2003:

 Find More notations point to related information in other chapters. For example, you might follow a Find More from the chapter on Word to the chapter on shared features.

! UPGRADERS BEWARE

Upgraders Beware paragraphs warn you of potentially confusing or damaging side effects to upgrading. This might be as simple as a new keystroke combination to learn or as dangerous as a new way to lose data.

EXPERT ADVICE

Expert Advice paragraphs offer our tips and tricks for making effective use of Office 2003. If you apply the knowledge from these paragraphs, we think you'll have a smoother upgrade experience.

MORE INFO

More Info paragraphs provide additional notes or background on Office 2003 features. These tidbits of information can help you understand what's going on when you upgrade or point you to additional resources when you want to learn more.

Contacting the Authors

One of the best things about writing a book is the opportunity to hear from readers. We can't upgrade Office for you, but we'd be happy to hear from you if something's not clear or if you just want to tell us how much you liked the book. You can email Susan at ssharkins@bellsouth.net or Mike at MikeG1@larkfarm.com.

What's New in Office 2003

W elcome to the Microsoft Office System 2003! With the release of this version, Microsoft is no longer referring to Office simply as a suite of applications that work together. Instead, Microsoft has upped the ante by referring to it as an entire *system*, including not just the personal productivity applications, but also some other programs such as Windows SharePoint server. In this chapter, we introduce some of the major themes of this version of Office. You'll explore the details of these areas (and other changes to Office) in the rest of the book.

The Office System

So, what is an Office *system*, anyhow? Other than being simply marketing-speak, we can see two reasons for the new designation:

> • The Office applications work more closely together than ever before, using XML (and other technologies) to move information back and forth.
>
> • Office workers can more easily use services such as Microsoft Office Online and servers such as Windows SharePoint Services as part of their routine work.

You'll find all these new features discussed throughout this book. But, to be honest, you won't see any sweeping changes in the way that functions are split up between Office applications as a result of Office being rebranded as a system. You'll still open Excel to work with numbers, or Access to deal with your database. The change between *suite* and *system* is more evolutionary than revolutionary. Indeed, if you were to dismiss the change as simply a marketing move, you wouldn't be far wrong.

Collaboration

We've mentioned SharePoint a couple of times already. Windows SharePoint Services (the new name of the product formerly known as SharePoint Team Services) is at the heart of Office 2003's new emphasis on collaboration. Of course, other ways of collaborating haven't gone away; Microsoft rarely removes a feature from Office. So you can still move Access data to Word or embed an Excel worksheet in a PowerPoint presentation, just as you've been able to do for many versions.

 MORE INFO

Two different products go under the generic name of SharePoint. Windows SharePoint Services is a free add-on for Windows Server 2003. SharePoint Portal Server is a more expensive, enterprise-ready upgrade for Windows SharePoint Services. The Office System works with either version, but when we refer just to *SharePoint* in this book we're talking about Windows SharePoint Services.

SharePoint itself is a browser-based collaboration product. You can use Internet Explorer together with a SharePoint site to track events and appointments, post announcements, and work with lists of all sorts. Figure 1.1 shows a SharePoint site open in the browser.

Although SharePoint itself is useful, it gains a whole new level of usefulness when coupled with Office 2003. That's because Microsoft built in hooks between the various Office applications and SharePoint. With these connections, you can work with data stored on a SharePoint server directly from an Office application rather than from the browser. Three Office features work directly with SharePoint:

- Word, Excel, and PowerPoint can create Document Workspaces that build collaboration on a document.

- Outlook can create a Meeting Workspace that lets you use SharePoint for meeting documentation such as agendas.

- Access can import, export, and link to data stored on a SharePoint server.

Figure 1.2 shows a Document Workspace in Excel 2003. It looks like an ordinary worksheet, but it is shared with other members of the team by being stored on a SharePoint server. The Document Workspace handles all the details of alerts, task-tracking, and other collaborative functions.

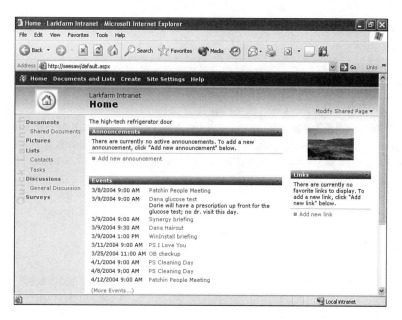

FIGURE 1.1   Using Windows SharePoint Services, you can easily collaborate with other Office users.

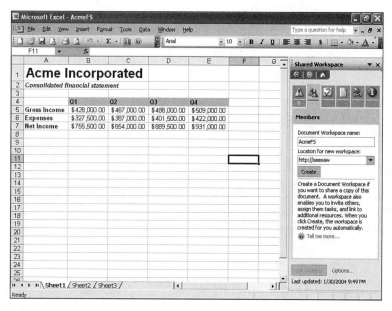

FIGURE 1.2   A SharePoint Document Workspace.

We'll discuss document and meeting workspaces in Chapter 2,"Shared Office Features."You can read more about Access and SharePoint in Chapter 7,"What's New in Access 2003."

! UPGRADERS BEWARE

Although Windows SharePoint Services is free, it requires you to install Windows Server 2003. If you haven't yet upgraded your network servers to this version, you need to count those costs into your Office upgrade plan (or give up these collaborative features). Corporations are likely to be the most important users of this new collaborative technology, at least for a while. Most home users, even net-worked home users, probably aren't candidates for SharePoint Services.

XML

Extensible Markup Language (XML) is a standard for creating documents that contain both data and metadata (data about data). For example, here's an extremely simple XML document:

```
<?xml version="1.0" encoding="UTF-8"?>
<Customer>
  <CustomerName>ABC Incorporated</CustomerName>
  <CustomerCity>Colfax</CustomerCity>
  <CustomerState>Washington</CustomerState>
</Customer>
```

The metadata in an XML document is in the form of *tags*—bits of information in angle brackets. Thus, by looking at the document, you can tell that Washington is the name of a state where a customer is located, and not a city or a person's name.

MORE INFO

A formal specification for XML is maintained by an organization called the World Wide Web Consortium (W3C). You can learn more by visiting http://www.w3.org/XML/, but you won't need to know most of the details to just use XML in Office 2003.

One of the major advances in Office 2003 is strong support for XML. This takes the form of improvements to the core Office applications as well as an entire new application, Microsoft InfoPath.

XML Support in Word, Excel, and Access

You'll find support for working with XML built right in to the core Office applications:

- **Excel**—Allows you to attach a custom XML schema to a workbook. You can then map elements from the schema to cells in the workbook and import and export XML data to the mapped cells.

- **Word**—Provides a full-fledged XML editor. You can base a document on a custom XML schema, and then the document will use tags only from that schema. Word also provides support for using XSL transforms when opening and saving documents.

- **Access**—Can export data to XML or import XML data to tables. You can use XSL transforms in either direction, and you can use XML schemas to specify the structure of the data.

In addition, Word and Excel can save any document to custom XML formats known as WordProcessingML and SpreadsheetML.

⇨ We'll cover the XML features of Word in Chapter 4, "What's New in Word 2003"; Excel in Chapter 5, "What's New in Excel 2003"; and Access in Chapter 7, "What's New in Access 2003."

InfoPath

Microsoft didn't limit the XML integration in Office 2003 to just improving existing applications. It also created an entirely new application—InfoPath 2003—that is centered on editing XML. Figure 1.3 shows InfoPath in action.

You might be wondering where the XML is in Figure 1.3. The answer is that it's all behind the scenes. Although InfoPath exists to edit XML files, it is designed to hide the XML from end users. InfoPath enables a two-step workflow for creating XML files:

1. A designer creates an InfoPath template, which is a file that dictates the XML that will be created and the user interface that will be used to create the XML.

2. An end user fills out a copy of the template to create the actual XML file.

InfoPath designers should know XML, but that knowledge isn't needed by those who fill out InfoPath forms. This makes it possible to use InfoPath to implement XML throughout your organization without the drawbacks of needing to teach a programming language to every employee.

⇨ Chapter 11, "Introducing Microsoft InfoPath 2003," is devoted to InfoPath.

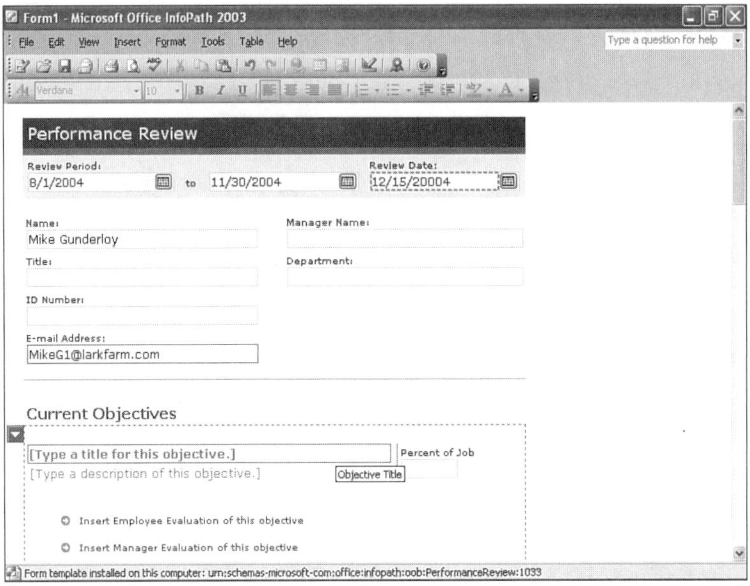

FIGURE 1.3   Editing XML with InfoPath 2003.

Rights Management

Rights management is another new area for Office in this release. *Rights management* refers to the ability of the creator of a file to limit the actions that other users can perform with that file. For example, if you're publishing electronic books, you might want to allow purchasers to buy and download copies but not to make other copies to send to their friends (without paying you!).

Rights management has been a hot topic in the press recently. Due to the rise of file-sharing networks that allow both legal and illegal trading of music and movies, more people are keenly aware of copyright issues than ever before. This awareness has extended to business settings as well. What would your company do if a critical memo on upcoming product strategies were to be emailed to your competition?

To deal with these issues, Office 2003 implements some basic rights management functionality under the name of Integrated Rights Management (IRM). The idea behind IRM is that you can assign rights to your documents without ever leaving Office. For example, if you're working in an Excel worksheet, you can specify a short list of users who can modify the worksheet and another list of users who can read the worksheet without modifying it. All other users are locked out entirely. In addition to protecting documents in Word, Excel, and PowerPoint,

IRM also allows you to create email messages that cannot be copied or forwarded. Although IRM does have some limits, it's a good first step in rights management.

➡ You'll learn more about IRM and related topics in Chapter 12, "What's New in Rights Management."

Servers, Services, and Solutions

Finally, many other Microsoft applications work with Office 2003 to complete the Office system. You won't necessarily need to install any of these applications to productively use Office, but if you do, you'll find that you can do more with Office than you can without them:

- **Windows Server 2003**—For the SharePoint-based collaboration features or the rights management features of Office 2003 to work, you need to have at least one Windows 2003 server on your network.

- **Windows SharePoint Services**—As already mentioned, this is a key piece of the Office 2003 collaboration story.

- **SharePoint Portal Server**—This upgraded version of SharePoint offers additional features for large networks and organizations.

- **Exchange Server 2003**—Outlook will work with nearly any email server, but some of its advanced features are available only if you use Exchange Server 2003 as an email server.

- **FrontPage 2003**—You might be used to thinking of FrontPage, the Microsoft Web design program, as a part of Office. In this version, though, it has been dropped from all the versions of the Office suite. We're sure there are many FrontPage users among our readers, so we'll cover its new features in Chapter 8, "What's New in FrontPage 2003."

- **Visio 2003**—Visio 2003, Microsoft's business diagramming solution, has the same general look and feel as the Office 2003 applications we discuss in this book. It also offers some interoperability with other Office applications through SharePoint and XML connectivity.

- **Project 2003**—Microsoft's project-planning application also shares the Office 2003 user interface style. It can interoperate with Office by importing and exporting data and by sharing tasks with Outlook.

Microsoft also provides plenty of help with using Office, ranging from simple tips and tricks through complex programming examples. A good starting point is the Microsoft Office Online Web site at `http://office.microsoft.com/home/default.aspx`. You should also check out all the Office 2003 books offered by Que Publishing at `http://www.quepublishing.com`.

Shared Office Features

Each program in the Microsoft Office System is a separate application—but they all share some common features. You can tell by looking at an Office application that it's part of the family, and you can depend on some things to work consistently in any Office application. In this chapter, we'll introduce some of the new common features you'll find across the Office 2003 line.

IN THIS CHAPTER

- The new look and feel of Office
- Task panes everywhere
- The new Office Help system
- The Research task pane
- Document and meeting workspaces

Touring the New Look and Feel of Office

With each new version of Office, Microsoft changes the user interface. In some cases the changes are made to help with ease of use or to make features more readily discoverable. In others, it seems to us, the changes are merely for the sake of change. Just as each new model year of an automobile changes its styling to seem new and exciting, so does each release of Office adjust the look and feel for much the same reason.

Icons, Menus, and Toolbars

A good place to start a tour of Office 2003 is with the very first thing you'll see: the icons Office uses for menu items and document files. Figure 2.1 shows some of the Office icons, with the Office XP (2002) versions at the top of the screen and the Office 2003 versions at the bottom. As you can see, Microsoft has gone for a softer, fuzzier look in the 2003 model year and added detail for users working with high-resolution screens. If you've seen the early screenshots of Windows Longhorn (the next major Windows release, currently slated for 2005 or 2006), you'll know that Microsoft user interfaces in general are moving in this direction.

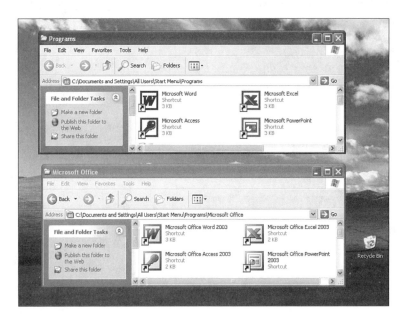

FIGURE 2.1 Office XP icons (above) compared to Office 2003 icons (below).

These changes carry through the whole Office user interface. Figure 2.2 shows Microsoft Word 2002, a part of Office XP. For comparison, Figure 2.3 shows the same part of the Word interface in Office 2003.

Inspecting these figures, you'll see a number of changes in the newer version:

- A blue and peach color scheme replaces the gray and blue-gray scheme as the Office default.

- Toolbars and the icon area at the left of menus get a more rounded, 3D look.

- Various parts of the user interface, such as the ends of toolbars and the panels in task panes, are rounded rather than squared off.

- The arrow for revealing hidden menu items on an IntelliMenu is easier to discern and rounder.

- Icons have more detail and 3D rendering. For example, compare the Save or Print toolbar buttons between the two versions.

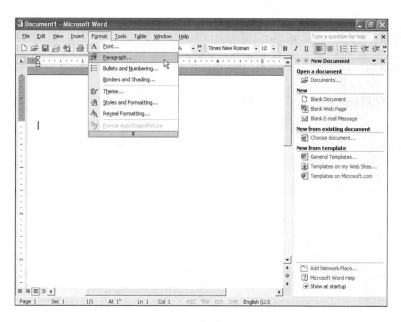

FIGURE 2.2   Microsoft Word 2002 demonstrates the Office XP user interface.

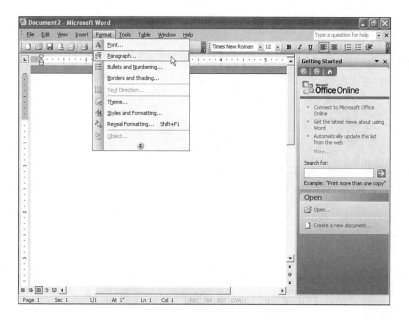

FIGURE 2.3   Microsoft Word 2003 demonstrates the Office 2003 user interface.

Does any of this have an impact on performance? Not a bit. You'll find that menus and tool-bars function just the same in this version of Office as they did in the previous version. But you can easily tell which version you're looking at just by glancing at the user interface.

Customizing the User Interface

Office has allowed customizing menus and toolbars for quite some time now. But Office 2003 gives you a more streamlined interface for making these changes. Right-click any toolbar or menu bar and select Customize to open the Customize dialog box, shown in Figure 2.4.

FIGURE 2.4   The Customize dialog box has one new option.

The Rearrange Commands button is new in this dialog box. Click Rearrange Commands to open the Rearrange Commands dialog box, shown in Figure 2.5.

FIGURE 2.5   The Rearrange Commands dialog box lets you customize menu bars and toolbars from a single unified interface.

When the Rearrange Commands dialog box is open, you can perform a number of actions:

- Use the controls at the top of the dialog box to select any menu bar or toolbar for customization, even if it's not currently visible in the user interface.

- Select a control (menu item or toolbar button) to work with by clicking in the Controls area.

- Move the selected control up or down in the menu bar or toolbar by clicking the Move Up and Move Down buttons.

- Add a new control by clicking the Add button.

- Delete the selected control by clicking the Delete button.

- Change the name, image, or style of the control, or assign a hyperlink or macro to the control, by clicking the Modify Selection button as shown in Figure 2.6.

- Reset all changes and return the toolbar or menu bar to its original state by clicking the Reset button.

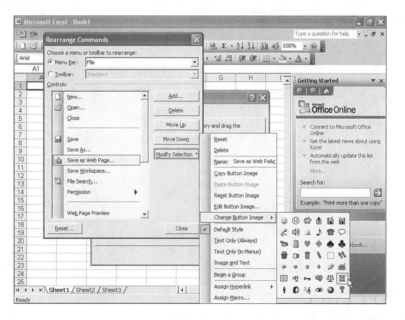

FIGURE 2.6   The Modify Selection button draws together all the ways to customize a toolbar button or menu item in one place.

 UPGRADERS BEWARE

Watch out for the Reset button! Although it's the easiest way to get back to the original menus if you make a mistake, it also removes *all* of your customizations and its effects can't be undone.

Tapping into Task Panes

Office 2000 introduced the task pane interface for grouping task-oriented controls together to the right of the workspace. Office 2003 adds many new task panes and refines the interface just a little bit. The net result is that you'll probably find yourself using task panes more often in the new version, and using them more effectively.

Figure 2.7 shows the New Workbook task panes from Excel 2002 (left) and Excel 2003 (right) together so you can see the differences more easily. Other applications have the new Getting Started task pane, which fills a similar purpose—giving you a good place from which to begin. The task pane is specific to the application, and we review it in subsequent chapters when appropriate.

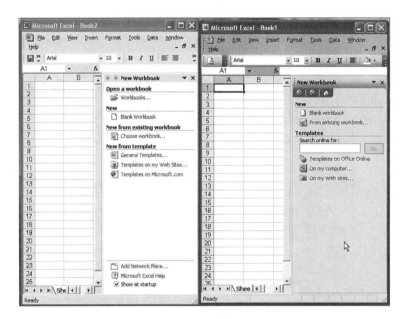

FIGURE 2.7   Office 2003 modifies and enhances the task pane interface.

Following is a list of the major task pane changes you should notice:

- The options on individual task panes have been streamlined and more tightly focused on a particular task.

- The forward and back buttons, which move between recently opened task panes, have been moved from the task pane title bar to a mini navigational bar. There's also a Home button on this navigational bar, which brings you back to the default task pane.

- Many task panes emphasize online links of one sort or another. For example, Help now retrieves information directly from Microsoft's Web site, instead of your computer, by default. We'll show you more specific links as we review the actual task panes.

- Task panes now have a grab handle on the title bar, which makes it more obvious that they can be undocked and moved.

⇨ Later in this chapter, we cover the new Research task pane in depth. For other task panes, refer to the product-specific chapters.

Several task panes are shared by many Office applications:

- **Search Results**—Read the "The Help Task Pane" section, later in this chapter, for a look at this task pane.

- **Help**—Review the "Using the New Office Help System" section in this chapter for a look at this new task pane.

- **Document Updates**—This task pane is part of the SharePoint collaboration feature.

- **Template Help**—This is an automated way to download template files.

- **ClipArt**—This organizes media files and options.

Although many applications share these new task panes, they might contain links and options that are application-specific. In addition, not every shared task pane occurs in each application.

Figure 2.8 shows the shared Document Updates task pane. This feature is available only if a copy of the document is also available in a Document Workspace.

⇨ Learn more about SharePoint Services and the Document Workspace task pane in Chapter 1, "What's New in Office 2003."

Templates come with their own Help files that are available when you work with a template. Figure 2.9 shows the Business Plan template with the Template Help task pane open in PowerPoint 2003. This task pane is available only when you're working with a template.

⇨ If the template has no corresponding help file, the Template Help item is disabled. Most templates have online help files you can download by downloading the online version of the template from http://office.microsoft.com/templates/.

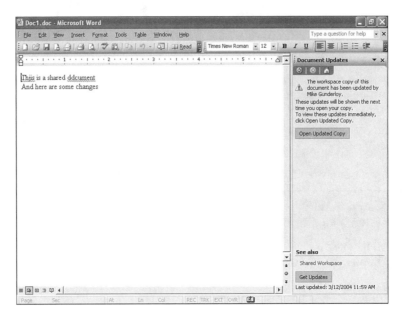

FIGURE 2.8   Use the Document Updates task pane to retrieve changes made by other members of a workspace.

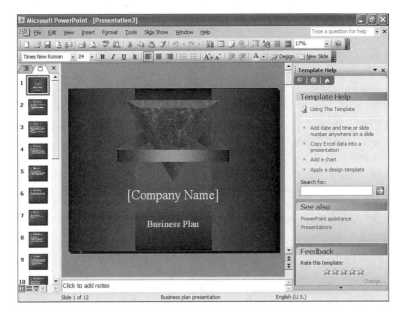

FIGURE 2.9   The Template Help task pane offers quick answers when you work with a template.

Working with clipart has never been easier now that you can work from the Clip Art task pane. Use this task pane to import media files stored on your system (or networked). After the files are imported, a simple click selects an individual clip (from numerous categories) and imports that clip into your document, as shown in Figure 2.10. This task pane (in Excel 2003) also offers a link to more online clips.

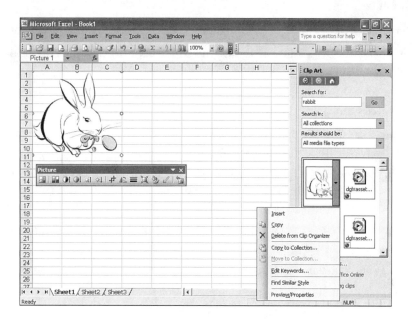

FIGURE 2.10   Use the Clip Art task pane to import image files.

Considering how much work this task pane does, it's simpler to use than you might think. First, enter a search string in the Search For control and initiate a search. Matching clip art files are returned below. To limit the search, use the Search In and Results Should Be controls.

Hovering the mouse over a file displays a drop-down arrow. Click this arrow to display a list. The next step is to click Insert; Excel 2003 then adds the clipart file to the worksheet and launches the Picture toolbar. It couldn't be simpler!

Using the New Office Help System

Help is another area where Microsoft just can't seem to leave well enough alone. The big innovation in Office 2003 is online help, but there are some small changes as well.

The Help Menu

The Help menu is more extensive in this version of Office than it has been in the past, perhaps reflecting Microsoft's attempt to offer different avenues of assistance. Here are the choices you'll find on the PowerPoint Help menu, which is typical of all the applications in the Microsoft Office System:

- **Microsoft Office PowerPoint Help**—Opens the PowerPoint Help task pane.

- **Show the Office Assistant**—Displays the famous but noisy paper clip (or other character of your choice) for friendlier help.

- **Microsoft Office Online**—Opens a browser window to display the Microsoft Office Online Web site.

- **Contact Us**—Opens a browser window to display a Web site where you can read about various options for getting more help.

- **Check for Updates**—Opens a browser window to the Office Update section of the Microsoft Office Online Web site, where you can find updates and patches for all current versions of Office.

- **Detect and Repair**—Checks your Office installation and repairs any problems.

- **Activate Product**—Connects to Microsoft over the Internet to activate your Office installation. You can use Office only a limited number of times without activation.

- **Customer Feedback Options**—Opens the Service Options dialog box to display information on the Customer Experience Improvement Program, as shown in Figure 2.11. This program automates the collection of error information from your computer to help improve future versions of Office.

- **About Microsoft Office PowerPoint**—Displays version and copyright information for the application, as well as buttons to compile diagnostic information.

The Help Task Pane

Even though the Help menu is full of changes, the real action is in the Help task pane, shown in Figure 2.12. When you're ready to actually get some assistance, this is where you'll be (assuming you're not the sort of person to use the Office Assistant, which is unchanged from Office 2002).

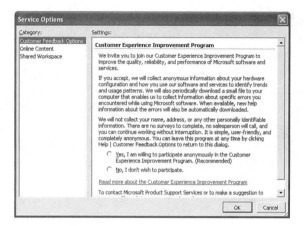

FIGURE 2.11 The Customer Experience Improvement Program collects anonymous information about your Office use and any errors that occur.

FIGURE 2.12 In Office 2003, Help options are collected into a task pane.

The task pane offers a number of choices for finding help. By picking out specific user assistance tasks to highlight here, Microsoft hopes to make it easier to discover the help you really need:

- The Assistance section of the task pane offers two methods to get into the traditional help. You can enter a search term and then click the arrow button to search the help, or you can click the Table of Contents hyperlink to display the contents for the entire help.

- The Microsoft Office Online section of the task pane offers targeted links to various parts of the Office Online Web site. For example, the Assistance link takes you to a page with a variety of tips for using Office effectively, whereas the Communities link takes you to the peer-to-peer discussion groups for Office.

- The See Also link takes you to other targeted help areas. These include a list of new features in the particular product, ways to contact Microsoft, and specific help on making the help itself more accessible to users with disabilities.

The final link in the Help task pane, Online Content Settings, opens another section of the Service Options dialog box, as shown in Figure 2.13.

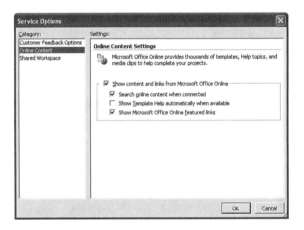

FIGURE 2.13   Office 2003 searches online help across the Internet by default.

This dialog box controls Office 2003's interactions with Microsoft's Web site while you're working with the help. By default, when you search for something in help, it searches both the help files on your local computer *and* help located on Microsoft's Web site.

 UPGRADERS BEWARE

The online Help features require an active Internet connection. If you're not connected to the Internet, the Help features default to the Help files stored locally.

This is a brand-new feature with Office 2003, and it's a mixed blessing for many users. On the one hand, by placing the help on its Web site, Microsoft can continually update the help and add more content, without requiring you to install service packs or patches to your local computer. On the other hand, searching the Internet is almost always going to be slower than searching files on your own computer. Unless you have a broadband connection to the Internet, you'll probably notice the delay when trying to get help.

 **EXPERT ADVICE**

If you're using a slow Internet connection, such as a dial-up connection, we recommend that you uncheck the Show Online Content When Connected option.

The online connection also allows Microsoft to include sample files and even marketing in your help results. Figure 2.14 shows the result of searching for "template" in the PowerPoint 2003 help, with online results included. Sample templates and a link to the Microsoft Office Marketplace, together with links to more traditional help topics such as "Save a presentation as a template," are shown.

FIGURE 2.14   Office 2003 search results, showing online content intermingled with local results.

 **EXPERT ADVICE**

Even if you leave the online content selected in the Service Options dialog box, you can limit any particular search to your local computer. To do so, select Offline Help in the drop-down list in the Search area of the Help task pane before searching.

Working with the Research Task Pane

Another new task pane is available across most of Office 2003: the Research task pane. This task pane is included in Word, Excel, Outlook, OneNote, PowerPoint, Publisher, and Visio. Figure 2.15 shows the Research task pane open in Publisher (which, for some reason, breaks the pattern of the rest of Office and shows its task panes on the left by default).

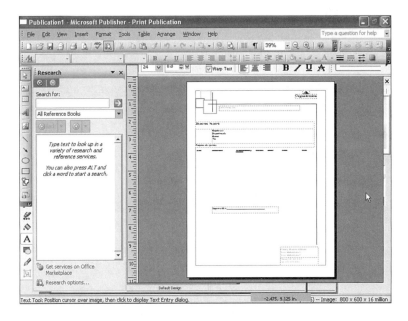

FIGURE 2.15   The Research task pane offers access to a variety of online reference sources.

The Research task pane lets you search for information across a variety of online reference sites. As we write this, the default sites that are available include

- **Reference books**—These include the Encarta Dictionary; U.S., French, and Spanish thesauruses; and a translation service.

- **Research sites**—These include eLibrary, Encarta Encyclopedia, Factiva, and MSN.

- **Business and financial sites**—These include Gale Company Profiles and MSN Money stock quotes.

This list will change over time because Office 2003 checks the Office Web site to learn whether new research services are available.

Figure 2.16 shows the result of performing a search with the Research task pane. Relevant results are retrieved directly to the task pane, with a title and short summary. Clicking the Read Now link displays the entire item in a browser window.

 UPGRADERS BEWARE

In some cases, you might find that you need to pay for a subscription to a commercial service to view the entire item. For example, both eLibrary and Factiva are commercial services. Microsoft unfortunately does not distinguish in the Research task pane which services are free and which require a subscription.

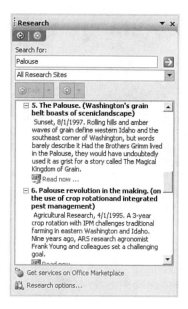

FIGURE 2.16 Use the Research Task pane to search for specific subjects on the Internet.

The two options at the bottom of the Research task pane that you can use to customize its operation are

- **Get Services on Office Marketplace**—This link takes you to a section of the Office Online Web site where you can read about additional commercial services you can add to the Research task pane.

- **Research Options**—This link opens the Research Options dialog box, where you can selectively enable or disable the various research services used by the task pane.

MORE INFO

If you're a developer, you can even build your own research service that integrates into the Research task pane. To do so, you need to be familiar with a development environment that can create Web services, such as Microsoft .NET. For details, refer to the Microsoft Office Research Service Software Development Kit, which is available online at `http://msdn.microsoft.com/library/en-us/rssdk/html/rsconAboutRSSDK.asp`.

Understanding Document and Meeting Workspaces

Some components of the Microsoft Office System don't ship in the Office box. One of these is SharePoint, Microsoft's collaborative services product. There are actually two versions of SharePoint: SharePoint Portal Server, which is a rather expensive product, and Windows SharePoint Services, which is a free add-on to Windows 2003 Server.

You can interact with SharePoint in several ways. Anyone can use SharePoint from a Web browser. But Office 2003 also offers deep integration with SharePoint directly from within Office products, using document workspaces and meeting workspaces.

MORE INFO

If you have Windows Server 2003 installed, you can download Windows SharePoint Services from `http://www.microsoft.com/windowsserver2003/techinfo/sharepoint/wss.mspx`.

UPGRADERS BEWARE

The SharePoint integration in Office 2003 requires the new version of SharePoint, either Windows SharePoint Services or SharePoint Portal Server 2003. If you have an older version of SharePoint on your network (such as SharePoint Team Services), you won't be able to use these features unless you upgrade.

Using Document Workspaces

A *document workspace* gives you a way to organize collaboration centered on a particular document (or group of documents). You can create a document workspace from Word, Excel, or PowerPoint.

To create a new document workspace, load your document and then access the Shared Workspace task pane, as shown in Figure 2.17. You need to supply a name for the workspace and a URL on your SharePoint server to hold the associated Web site.

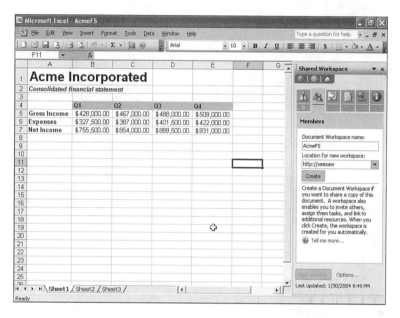

FIGURE 2.17   Creating a document workspace enables other members of your workgroup to collaborate with you.

After you create a new workspace, the Shared Workspace task pane displays a link to open the corresponding SharePoint Web site in a browser, as well as six tabs:

- **Status**—Displays any status messages for the workspace.

- **Members**—Displays the members of the workspace. You can use this tab to add new members to the workspace. You can also send email or instant messages or schedule a meeting with an existing member, all without leaving your document.

- **Tasks**—Displays the tasks in the workspace, together with the status of each task and who it is assigned to.

- **Documents**—Displays any additional documents that have been added to the workspace.

- **Links**—Displays any hyperlinks you have added to the workspace.

- **Document Information**—Displays the version history of the document, the user who last modified it, and any custom properties that have been added to the document.

Most of these tabs let you manipulate the information they display. For example, from the Tasks tab, you can add or delete tasks, mark them as completed, or edit the description of each task. You can also set an alert to cause SharePoint Services to email you when the status of a task changes. In some cases, a browser window enables you to complete an operation through SharePoint's Web interface. For example, Figure 2.18 shows the process of setting up a task alert. We've clicked the Alert Me About Tasks hyperlink in the Shared Workspace task pane, and SharePoint opened a browser window to allow us to complete the operation.

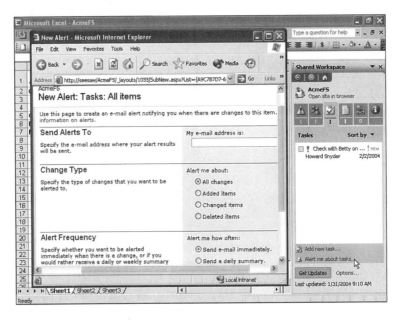

FIGURE 2.18   Document workspaces use the SharePoint Web interface for some operations.

Using Meeting Workspaces

A *meeting workspace* is very similar to a document workspace, but it is linked to a meeting in Outlook 2003 rather than to a particular document. To create a meeting workspace, you start by creating a meeting request (by selecting File, New, Meeting Request in the Outlook menus). After filling in the meeting details, click the Meeting Workspace button. This opens the Meeting Workspace task pane within the meeting request itself, as shown in Figure 2.19.

After you create the workspace, your meeting request contains a hyperlink to go to the workspace. Click the hyperlink to open the workspace in your browser. This workspace has a structure specifically designed for meetings, including objectives, an agenda, attendee information, and shared documents, as shown in Figure 2.20.

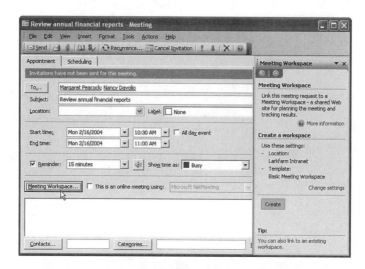

FIGURE 2.19   You can create a meeting workspace when you send a new meeting request from Outlook 2003.

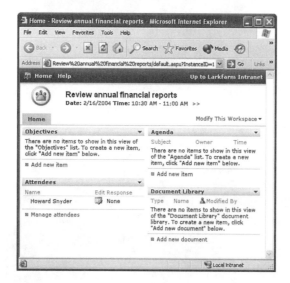

FIGURE 2.20   A meeting workspace is a SharePoint site with a structure designed for meetings.

When attendees receive your meeting invitation, it includes a hyperlink to the meeting workspace. You can also jump to the meeting workspace at any time from the meeting block on your Outlook 2003 calendar.

With the introduction of document workspaces and meeting workspaces, Microsoft has made it easier than ever to collaborate from within the boundaries of your Office applications. There's no need to open a separate collaboration application to share documents, send messages, organize meetings, or perform other collaborative activities.

What's New in Outlook 2003

Although most of the Office 2003 applications received only a few new toys, Outlook received an extreme makeover. Outlook looks new, has a number of new features—more than any other application in the suite—uses a new storage format and even connects to Microsoft Exchange Server differently. If you use Outlook frequently, the upgrade might be worth just this one application.

 UPGRADERS BEWARE

Standalone versions of Outlook 2003 don't offer as complete a package as does upgrading the entire Office suite. You can't use Word as the email editor and you'll also lose a few of the more advanced contact features. It kind of makes sense because any feature that relies on another Office application is going to get the boot in a standalone version of Outlook 2003.

New Look and Feel

Outlook's new user interface should definitely improve your outlook. Let's face it, Outlook was a bit clunky before. It still presents some very busy windows, but it's a busy business, so that's acceptable. Now, let's review the new ways you'll view all that data.

IN THIS CHAPTER

- **New look and feel**
- **Email management features**
- **Productivity enhancements**
- **Exchange Server and SharePoint integration**
- **Business Contact Manager**

UPGRADERS BEWARE

If you upgrade from Outlook 98 or Outlook 2000, Outlook 2003 won't import your password. The first time you attempt to send or retrieve mail, Outlook 2003 will prompt you for your password. Enter it and click the Save This Password in Your Password List option.

The New Menus

There are no changes to the File menu, but there are a few to the New command's submenu. There are two new commands: Search Folder and Internet Fax. The Navigation Pane Shortcut item replaces the Outlook Bar Shortcut item.

⇨ Read about search folders later in the "Search Folders Create Unique Views" section in this chapter.

There are a few changes to the Folder submenu. First, the Copy Folder Design command is gone. You'll find two new items: Customize This Search Folder and Sharing. The Sharing option lets you share Outlook data via SharePoint Services.

There's only one change to the Edit menu. The Clear command is gone.

The View menu has significant changes due to all the new views. First, Current View is replaced by Arranged By. Also, Go To is gone. There are three new items: Navigation Pane, Reading Pane, and Refresh.

There are lots of changes to the View menu's Current View submenu:

- New grouping categories include Date Folders, Size, Subject, Type, Attachments, E-mail Account, Importance, and Categories.

- The following items are gone: Messages, Messages with AutoPreview, Unread Messages, Message Timeline, Define Views, and Format Columns.

- Flag replaces By Follow-up Flag; Conversation replaces By Conversation Topic; From replaces By Sender; To replaces Sent To; and Custom replaces Customize Current View.

You'll find one new item on the Toolbars submenu. Selecting Task Pane displays the task pane. All four of the task panes available in Outlook 2003 are reviewed in Chapter 2, "Shared Office Features."

The Favorites menu is gone. Favorite items are now a more permanent feature in the Favorites section of the Navigation pane, which you'll learn about in the next section.

Figure 3.1 shows the new Go menu. All items are new to this version.

FIGURE 3.1   The Go menu is new.

The Tools menu has lost several items: Send/Receive Settings, Dial-Up Connection, Find Public Folder, Out of Office Assistant, and Recover Deleted Items. Sending, receive, and connection items have been moved to the Send/Receive submenu. The Advanced Find item has been moved to the Find command's submenu. Rules and Alerts replaces the previous Rules Wizard command, and Tools on the Web has been moved to the Help menu.

The Find All command is missing from the Actions menu. Also gone are Accept, Tentative, Decline, Propose New Time, and Check Calendar. The Microsoft Outlook (HTML) item on the New Mail Message Using submenu has been replaced by Microsoft Office Word 2003 (HTML). The Microsoft Office submenu now includes a Microsoft Publisher Publication item.

The Junk E-mail submenu has all new commands: Add Sender to Blocked Senders List, Add Sender to Safe Senders List, Add Sender's Domain (@example.com) to Safe Senders List, Add Recipient to Safe Recipients List, Mark As Not Junk, and Junk E-mail options.

> Changes to the Help menu are standard throughout all the Office applications. Read more about these changes in Chapter 2.

Three Panes—Lots of Options!

The first thing you'll notice when you open Outlook 2003 for the first time is the new three-paned window, shown in Figure 3.2. Now, you can more easily control what you see and what you don't.

Outlook 2003's new Reading pane is based on Microsoft's eReader technology. As a result, the window resembles a regular piece of paper. Reading email is more like reading a real letter or memo now, as you can see in Figure 3.3.

The larger window is a great improvement over its predecessor, which displayed only a few lines of each email message. The only way to read the entire message was to scroll through it.

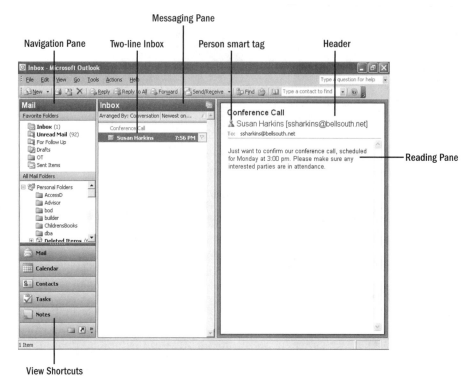

FIGURE 3.2   Outlook now sports three panes of information.

FIGURE 3.3   The new Reading pane resembles a traditional letter or memo.

The new Reading pane eliminates a lot of scrolling because most of the time the pane displays the entire message. In addition, the Inbox displays the same details about each message that it used to, but those details are arranged in two lines instead of one (you can change back to the old one-line view via View, Arrange By, Current View, Customize Current View). Microsoft claims the new arrangement displays 40% more email than Outlook 2002's window.

 EXPERT ADVICE

Change is often a little uncomfortable, but give the new layout a little time. If you still decide you don't like it, you can return the Reading pane to the bottom of the screen. To do so, select Reading Page from the View menu and then select Bottom. Or, right-click the gray border around the Reading pane and select the Bottom option. This context-sensitive menu contains other customizing options, such as changing the text size and marking mail items.

The Reading pane's default view includes several changes:

- The message header at the top displays the message's subject text and the sender's name. The recipient is listed just below the sender's name and email address.

- The Person SmartTag icon, just to the left of the sender's name, lets you know the sender's current online status (using Microsoft Instant Messenger or MSN Instant Messenger). A gray icon means the sender doesn't have an online contact. Right-click this icon to perform a variety of tasks, such as schedule a meeting, add the sender to your Messenger contacts, send email, send an instant message, and so on.

- The InfoBar tells you whether you've replied to the message and when. When the message contains a meeting request, you can accept or decline in the InfoBar. None of our figures show this information, but it would be just above the sender's name.

 EXPERT ADVICE

You can turn off the header information in the Reading pane and thereby view even more of the message. To do so, right-click the gray border that surrounds the Reading pane and deselect the Header Information option.

The Navigation pane reduces clutter by exposing just the elements you need, when you need them. Simply click one of the view shortcuts—Mail, Calendar, Contacts, and so on—to update the current data accordingly. These buttons replace the Outlook bar from earlier versions.

The Date Navigator in the Calendar Navigation pane has a new home. Previously, this pane was to the right of the Calendar folder and by default was displayed by the TaskPad. In Outlook 2003, it's no longer a default and it's in the Navigation pane, as shown in Figure 3.4.

Date Navigator

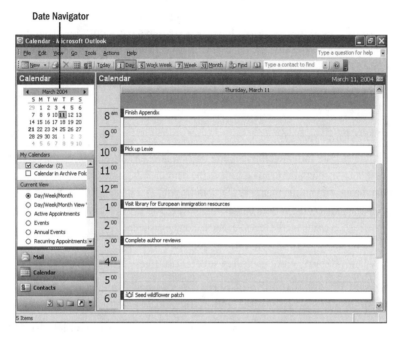

FIGURE 3.4   Look for the Date Navigator in the Navigation pane.

 **EXPERT ADVICE**

Most views are customizable now. Simply right-click anywhere in the view window and select Customize Current View. The resulting list offers a number of options, but only appropriate options are enabled. We won't walk you through each one—it's enough to know the capability now exists. Just spend a little time looking and experimenting so you don't miss something useful.

Interacting with the Date Navigator updates the Calendar view. For instance, Figure 3.4 shows the entire current day so Outlook displays the Day view. If you select a range of days, Outlook updates the Work Week view to display only those days selected in the Date Navigator.

 **EXPERT ADVICE**

If you prefer working with the TaskPad in Calendar view, select TaskPad View from the View menu. Doing so launches the TaskPad and moves the Date Navigator to the right.

The Calendar view options are the same, but there are a few new features you'll find useful. First, views indicate the current time and day by displaying an orange bar across the top of the current day's square, as shown in Figure 3.5.

Available Calendar folders

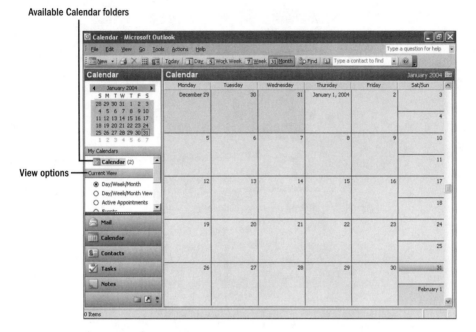

View options

FIGURE 3.5   The current day and time are indicated by an orange bar.

A variety of Calendar view options are available in the Navigation pane; the options aren't new, but their placement in the Navigation pane is—saving you the trouble of drilling down through several menu layers to get at the same options. All Calendar folders are displayed in the Navigation pane. The Tasks window presents its own context-sensitive list of views.

Quick Access to Favorite Folders

With all the new views, you'd think everything would always be right at your fingertips in whatever order you want, but that won't always be the case. Chances are you work with a lot of user-created folders and, in Mail view, you might not be able to see all those folders in the My Mail Folders list. That's why Outlook 2003's Navigation pane has a new Favorite Folders list. By default, this list contains the Inbox, Sent Items, and two search folders (Unread Mail and For Follow Up).

> ➪ You learn more about search folders later in this chapter. Look for the topic in the "Search Folders Create Unique Views" section.

Store your most frequently used folders in the Favorite Folders list so they're quickly accessible, as shown in Figure 3.6. Instead of scrolling through the list of folders in the All Mail Folders list, just click a folder in Favorite Folders.

Click often-used folders here...

...or browse through the list to find a folder

FIGURE 3.6   The Favorite Folders list offers a quicker route when you have lots of folders.

To add a folder to your Favorite Folders list, right-click the folder and select Add to Favorite Folders. You can remove a folder from the Favorite Folders list by right-clicking the folder and selecting Remove from Favorite Folders. (Folders in the Favorite Folders list are copies; the original folder remains in its default position.)

Using Outlook As a Personal Information Manager

A growing business is great, but it requires more resources to track all those new contacts and appointments. That's what a personal information manager (PIM) is for, and despite what you've heard, they don't have to be complex.

Outlook 2003 isn't really a PIM, but you can put its features to work for you just the same. The goal is to make information easy to access and easy to manipulate.

Quick Flags for Recognition

You've always been able to flag messages for future follow-up, but the feature was a tad bland. Outlook 2003's Quick Flag feature lets you flag a message with one quick click, as shown in Figure 3.7.

FIGURE 3.7   One quick click flags a message for follow-up.

Six flags are now distinguished by the following colors: red, blue, yellow, green, orange, and purple. The default flag is red. To select a flag other than the default, right-click the Quick Flag column and select a different-colored flag. To change the default, right-click the Quick Flag column, select Set Default Flag, and select the new color. When you're done with a message, simply click the Complete column. To clear a flag, right-click the Quick Flag column and select Clear Flag.

Search Folders Create Unique Views

Quick flags are at their best when combined with search folders, another new feature in Outlook 2003. These virtual folders display information from any folder after running a search for all items that meet specific criteria. In other words, you can find it quickly in one of these search folders, regardless of where a message is actually stored.

You probably have a number of unread messages scattered throughout a number of folders. Using search folders, you can use one virtual folder to view all unread messages. In fact, Outlook 2003 provides a default search folder—Unread Mail—for just that purpose. All unread mail is available through the Unread Mail folder. (Messages in these folders aren't copies; they're just views of the original messages.)

There are two more default search folders: Large Messages and For Follow Up. All flagged messages are available through the For Follow Up folder. They're even grouped by flag order for quick recognition, as shown in Figure 3.8.

To create a custom search folder, right-click an existing search folder or on the search folder item in the All Mail Folders window. Select New Search Folder to launch the Search Folder Wizard, shown in Figure 3.9. Select one of the predefined criteria or scroll down to the bottom of the list and click the Create a Custom Search Folder option.

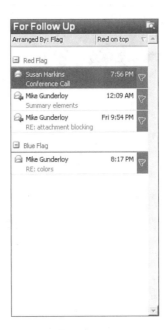

FIGURE 3.8   The For Follow Up folder groups messages by flag color.

FIGURE 3.9   Create your own search folder.

Suppose you want to create a search folder for all mail received from a specific client. To do so, you'd follow these steps:

1. Select the Mail from and to Specific People option under the Mail from People and Lists section.

2. Enter the client's email address by clicking the Choose button at the bottom of the dialog box to open the screen shown in Figure 3.10.

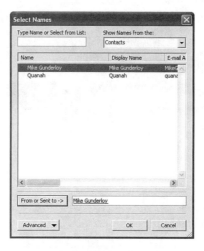

FIGURE 3.10   Select an email address.

3. Select the client, and click OK. (You can choose more than one email address.) When you return to the previous dialog box, Outlook 2003 copies the address to the Show Mail Sent and Received From control, as shown in Figure 3.11. You can enter the email address yourself, but choosing it avoids typos.

FIGURE 3.11   Outlook 2003 copies the selected email address for you.

4. After you've added the name (or names), click OK to create the search folder shown in Figure 3.12.

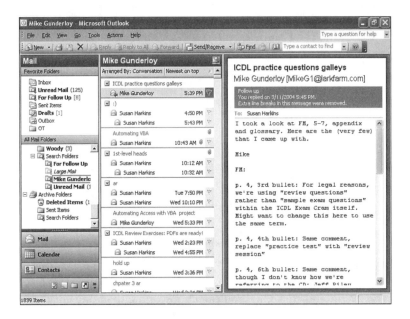

FIGURE 3.12   Outlook 2003 displays all the messages from or to Mike Gunderloy grouped by flag color.

 UPGRADERS BEWARE

Search folders aren't "real" in the sense of folders that store actual files or messages, but the items you view are real. You're seeing the real items in a special view. If you delete an item in a search folder, Outlook 2003 deletes the real message.

Intelligent Grouping

All views benefit from intelligent grouping, another new feature in Outlook 2003. Groups aren't new to Outlook 2003, but they are more flexible and logical. For instance, date groups were fairly useless because Outlook considered the time as well as the date and consequently created a group for every message. Grouping by date in Outlook 2003 produces a more reasonable set of groups: Today, Yesterday, Two Days Ago, Last Week, Last Month, and Older. Figure 3.13 shows a few of those groups. Keep in mind that if you have no items that fulfill a group, the group doesn't exist in the view until you gain an item that does.

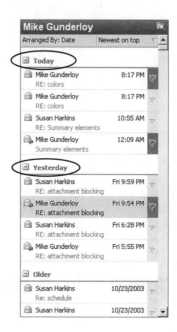

FIGURE 3.13   More intelligent grouping creates more relevant groups than in previous Office versions.

This newer, improved grouping feature is utilized by new arrangements. *Arrangements* are predefined sorts that arrange items in sensible ways. Select Arrange By from the View menu to see the context-sensitive list of arrangements shown in Figure 3.14. Some views include an Arranged By header so you can bypass the menu. The pane shown in Figure 3.13 is based on the Date option.

Picturing Your Contacts

Identifying contacts takes on a new meaning now that Outlook 2003 supports pictures. To associate a picture with a contact, click the Contacts view shortcut in the Navigation pane and double-click the appropriate contact to view that contact's information.

FIGURE 3.14 There are several predefined arrangement options.

Then, click the Add Picture button—that's the button to the left of the email address shown in Figure 3.15. When Outlook 2003 displays the Add Contact Picture dialog box, use the Look In drop-down to locate the picture file, and then click OK.

FIGURE 3.15 Click the Add Picture button to add a picture of the current contact.

From here on, everything is fairly automatic. The picture sizes itself and displays as shown in Figure 3.16 without anymore input from you. Just remember that sending the contact record to another user also sends the picture. In addition, as you might expect, the picture file increases the contact file size a bit. Be sure to click Save and Close before closing the dialog box if you want to save the picture.

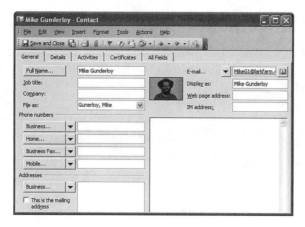

FIGURE 3.16   It's easy to display a picture of a contact.

Email Management Features

Most of us receive a lot of email these days—it has become a favored way to communicate. That means you probably receive a lot of it and ultimately that means more work for you. Outlook 2003 makes managing your email easier than ever.

Improved AutoComplete

AutoComplete's not new to Outlook 2003, but it's better. The AutoComplete feature is a convenient tool that finishes your email address based on just a few characters. In earlier versions, you had to type enough characters for Outlook to find a unique entry. Now, Outlook 2003 displays a pop-up box that displays all entries that match the current characters, similar to the one in Figure 3.17. For instance, enter `mi` and the pop-up box displays all the names that begin with the letters *mi*. Using the arrow key, you can select the appropriate entry and press Enter—saving yourself several keystrokes and the possibility of typos.

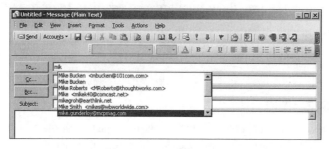

FIGURE 3.17   Select the appropriate email address from the list of available addresses in AutoComplete's new pop-up box.

Intuitive Arrangements

Several predefined view arrangements are new to Outlook 2003, which we discussed briefly in the "Intelligent Grouping" section, earlier in this chapter. One arrangement bears mentioning: The By Conversation arrangement presents a much more intuitively displayed group, with indented replies, as shown in Figure 3.18.

FIGURE 3.18   Conversations are easier to follow in this arrangement.

Every thread has at least one message, but not all are shown. You can tell at a glance which conversations have read or unread messages. If all messages have been read, only the latest message is displayed. When there are unread messages, only those are displayed.

The small arrows to the left of the message title can be your best clue:

- If the arrow points down, there are more messages than those displayed in that thread.

- If there's no arrow, all messages are there.

- An arrow that points up simply means the thread is expanded. Click it to collapse it.

 **EXPERT ADVICE**

To arrange messages, select Arrange By from the View menu and then choose from the predefined options. Or, click the Arranged By button in the Messaging pane's title bar.

Dynamic Distribution Lists

A *distribution list* includes multiple addresses; you use such a list to send the same message to a number of people at the same time. Outlook 2003 lists are more flexible than they were in previous versions. Now you can remove members temporarily—for one message—without removing that member from the original list.

To temporarily remove a member from a distribution list, you create an email and specify the list in the To field as you normally would. Then, expand the distribution list by clicking the plus sign (+) to the left of the list, as shown in Figure 3.19. Click OK when Outlook warns you that you can't collapse the list again.

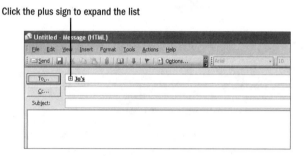

FIGURE 3.19   Expand a distribution list in the email.

Outlook expands the list so you can see all the members, as shown in Figure 3.20. (Larger lists are displayed in a pop-up box.) Select the member you want to delete and then press Delete.

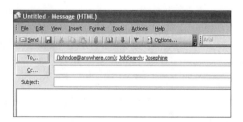

FIGURE 3.20   Expand the list to show all the members.

Filtering Junk Email

Outlook 2003's junk mail filter is based on four levels of protection. To set a filter, select Options from the Tools menu and click the Junk Email option on the Preferences tab to display the filtering levels shown in Figure 3.21.

FIGURE 3.21   Choose from the new junk email filtering levels.

Select the appropriate option for you:

- **No Automatic Filtering**—No filtering for junk email.

- **Low**—Moves the most obvious junk email to the Junk E-mail folder. Check it occasionally, but you probably won't find too many messages that don't belong there.

- **High**—Catches most junk email but also tags some valid messages. In the latter case, add the sender to your Safe Senders list and the filter will let mail from that sender through.

- **Safe Lists Only**—This is the most restrictive setting because it filters out everything that isn't explicitly allowed. The sender must be in your Contacts folder or in your Safe Senders list.

> Information rights management (IRM) helps you deal with sensitive and confidential information that's shared via email. IRM gives the author control over her content by preventing an email from being forwarded, printed, copied, or distributed. Learn about IRM in Chapter 12, "What's New in Rights Management."

Multiple Signatures

Most of us have more than one persona. For instance, you probably don't sign mail to your spouse and your clients in exactly the same way. That's why the capability to specify different signatures for each account is a welcome improvement. Of course, that means you'll also have to use different accounts when conversing with different people, but many do just that.

To configure an account signature, select Options from the Tools menu and click the Mail Format tab. Choose an account from the Select Signatures for Account drop-down list.

Identify the appropriate signature for both new messages as well as replies and forwards. For instance, Figure 3.22 points to the signature file for Susan Sales Harkins for new messages on Susan's email account. (Click the Signatures button to create a new signature.) It's that simple—wonder why it took them so long to add this feature.

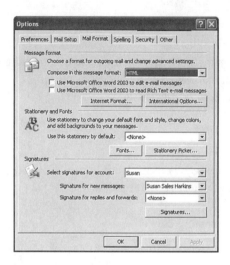

FIGURE 3.22 Set up signatures for multiple accounts.

Attachment Freedom—Sort of...

Big Brother is alive and well at Microsoft—but he's beginning to respond to customer demand. If you've used Outlook before, you know that it totally blocks dangerous attachments. There's nothing you or your administrator can do about it. You can't have those files.

That's good for Microsoft because that serious limitation makes Outlook more secure (from viruses). What's good for Microsoft isn't always good for you—do you really want Microsoft deciding what you can receive and can't receive?

Outlook 2003 offers a bit of a compromise—it's not the easy-to-use switch most of us would like, but it's better than nothing. Earlier versions of Outlook had one level of attachment security—everything dangerous was blocked, period. Outlook 2003 expands that to three levels of attachments:

- **Level 1**—These files are completely blocked. You can't save, delete, open, print, or access these attachments.

- **Level 2**—You must save these attachments before you can open them.

- **Level 3**—Outlook allows you to open these attachments.

Outlook 2003 brands 52 file types as Level 1 offenders. For a complete list of types, search Help for "Attachment file types blocked by Outlook." The trick is to change Level 1 files to Level 2 by changing the Registry. To do so, close Outlook 2003 and then launch the Registry Editor by selecting Start from the Windows taskbar, selecting Run, typing **regedit** in the Open control, and then clicking OK.

UPGRADERS BEWARE

Before modifying the Registry, back it up in case something goes wrong. For more information on this subject, refer to Microsoft Knowledge Base article 256986, at `http://` `support.microsoft.com/?kbid=256986`.

EXPERT ADVICE

You don't have to modify the Registry. There's an add-in available at `http://` `www.slovaktech.com` that modifies the Registry for you.

In the Registry, find the following key:

`HKEY_CURRENT_USER\Software\Microsoft\Office\11.0\Outlook\Security`

If this key doesn't exist, you must create it. To do so, locate this key:

`HKEY_CURRENT_USER\Software\Microsoft\Office\11.0\Outlook`

If the key does exist, skip to the next list. To create the key, follow these steps:

1. Select Edit, New, Key.

2. Type **Security** and press Enter.

3. Select the Security key.

To alter the key, do the following:

1. Select Edit, New, String Value.

2. Type **Level1Remove** as the value name, and press Enter (see Figure 3.23).

3. Right-click the `Level1Remove` entry and then click Modify.

4. Type the file type extensions that represent those files you want to move to Level 2, and click OK. Use a semicolon to separate multiple extensions, as shown in Figure 3.24.

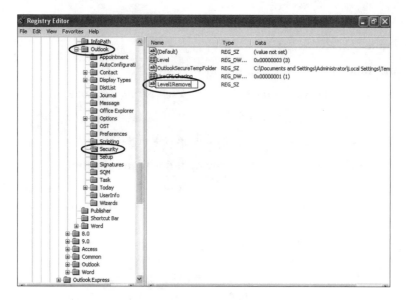

FIGURE 3.23   Create a new key value named `Level1Remove`.

FIGURE 3.24   Separate multiple extensions with a semicolon.

5. Close the Registry Editor.

6. Reboot your computer. You'll still have to save the attachments before you can open them, but at least you can control what you are able to receive.

Rules Rule!

Most of the time, rules just mean interference, but Outlook 2003's new Rules and Alerts Wizard is the exception to the rule. Use this wizard to create rules that corral your incoming mail and notify you when incoming mail meets certain conditions.

In previous Outlook versions you used predefined rules in the Organize pane to help Outlook correctly deliver your mail as it arrived. The Rules and Alerts Wizard is a bit more complicated, but it's worth getting to know. To launch the wizard, select Rules and Alerts from the Tools menu.

The Rules and Alerts dialog box offers several options:

- **New Rule**—Creates a new rule.

- **Change Rule**—Modifies an existing rule.

- **Copy**—Copies an existing rule so you can use it as the basis of a new rule.

- **Delete**—Deletes an existing rule.

- **Up Arrow**—Repositions a rule, moving it up one at a time.

- **Down Arrow**—Repositions a rule, moving it down one at a time.

- **Run Rules Now**—Runs a rule and subsequently moves, copies, or otherwise acts on the specified messages accordingly. This is a good way to move messages to a new folder you've just created.

- **Options**—Imports and exports rules from a previous version of Outlook.

Not all rules and alerts run while Outlook is closed—even if you use Microsoft Exchange as your email server. That's because Outlook stores some rules and actions on the client side. Consequently, if a message arrives at the server but the associated rule or action is on the client, Outlook 2003 can't apply the rule or execute the action because it isn't open. The rule or action is acted on when you open Outlook 2003, but not until then. The following rules and actions are stored on the client side:

- With specific words in recipient's address

- With specific words in senders' address

- Flagged for action

- Assigned to a category

- With specific words in the subject or message

- Notify Me Using a Specific Message

- Flag Message for Action

- Flag Message with a Colored Flag

- Start Application

- Run a Script

- Display a Specific Message in the New Item Alert Window

- Display a Desktop Alert

- Clear the Message Flag

- Assign It to a Category

- Play a Sound

- Move It to the Specified Folder

- Move a Copy to the Specified Folder

- Reply Using a Specific Template

- Perform a Custom Action

➪ You can learn more about alerts in "Exchange Server 2003 and SharePoint Integration," later in this chapter.

Productivity Enhancements

Most enhancements and new features increase productivity, but they're more specific to a specific area of use, so they appear in other areas of this chapter. All changes and new features are supposed to make you productive. However, the new file format is one change you might not even notice.

More Storage Room

Outlook 2003 personal folders are huge—chances are you'll never run out of space. That's because Outlook 2003 offers a new compressed file format, Unicode. Personal folders that use this format are capable of storing terabytes of data. Earlier versions were limited to 2GB.

 UPGRADERS BEWARE

The Unicode format has one major drawback: Older versions can't read Unicode formatted data. If you need to share data files with older versions of Outlook, don't use this format. The previous format is still available. When you create a new personal folders file, Outlook 2003 lets you select between the two formats.

 EXPERT ADVICE

A large personal folders file won't perform as well as you like. For optimum performance, keep your files at 5GB or smaller or things might slow down a bit.

Exchange Server 2003 and SharePoint Integration

Outlook 2003 is used by some single users, but its strength is in its client/server capabilities. Enhancements to the way Outlook 2003 works with Exchange Server 2003 and SharePoint make it a more dependable and resourceful email client.

Working Offline Using Cached Exchange Mode

Exchange Server users know that connectivity is a sensitive issue—the loss of a high-quality connection unleashes a number of error messages you have to endure until they finally stop because it's out of your control. More often than not, even if the connection is restored, you still have to restart Outlook.

Cached Exchange Mode keeps a copy of your messages on your local computer. That way, if the connection fails, Outlook can still find and—more importantly—work with the stored messages, which Outlook 2003 stores in the Offline Folders file. In addition, Cached Exchange stores a copy of all your messages on your computer. If you lose the connection, you can still work with what you've got.

What this all means is that your mail is still accessible, offline. To toggle between offline and online, select Work Offline from the File menu.

Let Me Check Your Calendar

Exchange Server users are only a few mouse clicks away from sharing calendars with everyone. This capability can be very important to the busy office—meaning almost instant collaboration. Outlook 2003 lets you view a full day, week, work week, or month for multiple users in your Calendar window.

In Calendar view, click the Open a Shared Calendar link in the Navigation pane. Outlook 2003 prompts you to identify the contact; select a contact, and click OK.

Corporate-Level Filtering

Individual users can use filters to limit the amount of junk mail they have to sift through. Exchange Server 2003 has its own junk mail filter. Employing filters at this level filters junk mail before it ever reaches the Outlook client. The advantage is a decrease in storage requirements because the message isn't stored on the server until it's downloaded by the client and it's never downloaded to the client.

Even better, Exchange administrators can configure Exchange servers to work together with Outlook to identify and trap junk mail. The administrator can use the Exchange Intelligent Message Filter to assign a numeric rating to new incoming messages indicating the probability that they're spam. Outlook in turn can use this rating to decide whether to route an incoming message to the user's Inbox or her Junk Mail folder.

Managing SharePoint Alerts

You learned about SharePoint in Chapter 2, "Shared Office Features." Specifically, you learned how to create a new meeting workspace and alerts that notify you (or others) when certain conditions are met. You can create, manage, and delete an alert from Outlook 2003. For instance, you might create an alert that notifies you if a meeting time is changed.

To configure a SharePoint alert, select Rules and Alerts from the Tools menu. Next, click the Manage Alerts tab, which displays existing alerts. You must be part of a SharePoint Server 2003 to configure alerts from the resulting window shown in Figure 3.25. Select New Alert to launch the Rules Wizard. Or, modify or delete an existing alert rule.

FIGURE 3.25 Manage SharePoint alerts from inside Outlook 2003.

Planning Meetings

A SharePoint *meeting workspace* is actually a Web site that manages information and materials for a meeting, such as an agenda document. The first step is to create the meeting workspace. To do so, select Calendar view, select a meeting date from the Date Navigator, and then select New from the File menu and then select Meeting Request. In the resulting window, enter the attendees (the To control), a subject, the location of the meeting, and reminder specifics as shown in Figure 3.26.

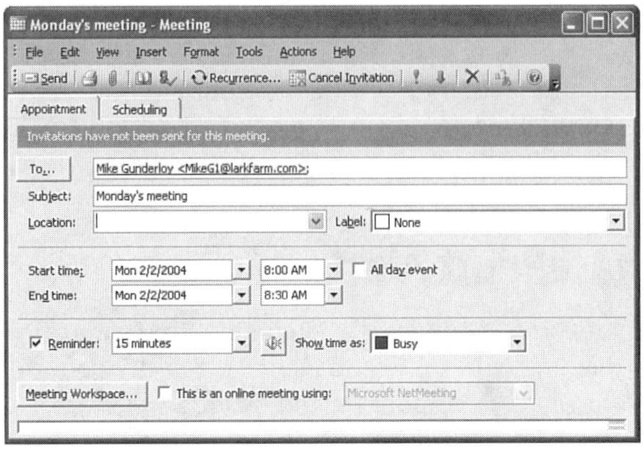

FIGURE 3.26   Set up a SharePoint meeting.

When you've entered all the appropriate meeting information, click the Meeting Workspace button to open the Meeting Workspace task pane shown in Figure 3.27. If Outlook 2003 prompts you for server and default template selections, enter the choices and click OK; then click Create to create the request shown.

FIGURE 3.27   Open the meeting workspace task pane.

To visit the workspace, click the link in the meeting request. Here, you can upload documents, create an agenda, create action items, and enter meeting objectives. Attendees can propose new meeting times, and you can update the subject, invite new people, or change the location.

Business Contact Manager

Business Contact Manager (BCM) is a new add-on for Outlook 2003 that contains forms, reports, and views that should help you manage customers, accounts, leads, prospects, and activities, all in one spot. BCM makes you more productive and efficient—that's its purpose in a nutshell.

We won't show you how to install the product or even use it right here, but there are a few interesting things you'll want to know before deciding whether you want to try it:

- Right now the product is still a bit limited. There's no PDA support and it's meant for the single user. You can't integrate or share information.

- BCM installs the .NET Compact Framework on your system.

- BCM stores data in a Microsoft SQL Server Desktop Engine (MSDE) database that BCM installs locally.

- BCM supports multiple profiles for those organizations in which more than one person uses the same system.

⮞ Appendix B, "Outlook 2003's Business Contact Manager," offers a more in-depth look at using the BCM.

For the Developer

Security features in previous versions of Outlook that were meant to prevent the spread of viruses actually complicated Outlook development. Without getting into the nuts and bolts of the conflict, it suffices to say that it was difficult to run code behind an Outlook form that sends messages without setting off a cascading event of prompts to which the user had to respond.

Outlook 2003 is less restrictive in that any COM add-in you install in Outlook is automatically trusted. Consequently, Outlook 2003 bypasses all those security prompts. That means any code written in Outlook's VBA editor is also trusted. The object model supports the new properties, methods, and events listed in Table 2.1.

TABLE 2.1   Supported Properties, Methods, and Events

Object	Name	Property or Method	Description
MailItem	FlagIcon	Property	Sets a quick flag for a mail or meeting item.
MeetingItem	FlagIcon	Property	Select from the following constants: olNoFlagIcon, olPurpleFlagIcon, olOrangeFlagIcon, olGreenFlagIcon, olYellowFlagIcon, olBlueFlagIcon, and olRedFlagIcon
AppointmentItem; MeetingItem	MeetingWorkspaceURL	Property	Returns the URL of the meeting workspace currently attached to the item.
ContactItem	HasPicture	Property	Determines whether a contact item has a picture (Boolean).
ContactItem	AddPicture(ByVal PicturePath As String)	Method	Adds a picture to the contact, replacing an existing picture (if any).
ContactItem	RemovePicture	Method	Removes an existing picture from a contact item.
MailItem; MeetingItem; PostItem	SenderEMailAddress	Property	Returns an email address from a mail message, meeting item, or post.
Namespace	ConnectionMode	Property	Indicates the current connection mode: olOffline, olLowBandwidth, or olOnline.
MAPIFolder	ShowItemCount	Method	Displays the total number of items for a folder instead of the number of unread items.

This is certainly good news for the Outlook developer because the process is much simpler, without violating the system's security measures.

What's New in Word 2003

For the most part, the changes in Word 2003 are evolutionary, not revolutionary—with one major exception. That exception is XML support, where Word 2003 adds significant value over older versions. In this chapter, you'll learn about those new features, as well as some other changes you'll find when you upgrade.

User Interface Changes

Of course, Word sports the same rounded, shaded user interface as the rest of Office 2003. But there are some other changes you might not be expecting in this area:

- A few menu items have been added, removed, or altered.

- There's a new Reading Layout view, designed for times when you just need to read rather than edit a document.

- The new side-by-side comparison feature helps you find differences between two versions of a document.

We'll look at each of these changes in turn.

Menu Changes

It seems like the Office menu designers can never leave well enough alone. Things always move around between versions, and Word 2003 is no exception. Most of the changes in this area are new additions, but there are some other surprises lurking as well.

For starters, on the File menu, Search has been renamed to File Search. Our guess on the renaming would be that during some usability test people tried to use that menu item to search for text in the current file, but there are also some minor changes in the feature. Figure 4.1 shows the old and new task panes side by side.

FIGURE 4.1   The Word 2003 File Search task pane (left) offers some incremental improvements over the Word 2002 version (right).

As you can see, the See Also items have been moved up from the bottom of the screen, where they were easy to overlook. There's a new link for the Research task pane. Otherwise, everything works the same as it did in Word 2002, although the new eye candy makes the 2003 version look more impressive.

On the File menu, you'll also find a new Permissions menu. This leads into the new *Integrated Rights Management features (IRM)* (assuming you have the Enterprise edition of Office to work with).

➪ You'll find more information about the IRM features of Office 2003 in Chapter 12, "What's New in Rights Management."

The View menu includes an item for the new Reading Layout, which you'll read about in the next section. On the Tools menu, you'll find Research and Shared Workspace items to lead into those features. The Tools on the Web item has been removed from the Tools menu, but the Microsoft Office Online item on the Help menu provides the same functionality.

UPGRADERS BEWARE

Office Online is the one case where you'll need to memorize a new keyboard shortcut in Word 2003: Instead of the old Alt+T+B, it's now Alt+H+M.

Also new is the Compare Side By Side items on the Window menu (why isn't this on the View menu?). You'll learn more about ths side-by-side comparison feature later in this chapter. Finally, the Help menu has been rearranged, as you've already learned.

➪ We covered the new Help menu in Chapter 2, "Shared Office Features."

All in all, the menu system in Word 2003 should be comfortable for experienced users. Now it's time to turn to some of the other new user interface features.

The New Task Panes

Apparently, users like the task panes because almost all the Office 2003 applications have a lot of new ones. Several are shared by all the Office 2003 applications. We reviewed those task panes—Help; Search Results, which replaces Search; Research; Shared Workspace; and Document Updates—in Chapter 2.

You'll probably start a lot of new documents with the Getting Started task pane shown in Figure 4.2. This task pane contains a few links for opening blank files, templates, and existing documents.

FIGURE 4.2 You might want to begin at the Getting Started task pane.

Figure 4.3 shows the new Protect Document task pane. It's fairly self-explanatory if you've worked with document protection before. It simply pulls protection features together into one convenient location.

FIGURE 4.3   Use the Document Protection task pane to quickly identify protected areas.

⇨   The XML Structure task pane offers the same options you'll find in the Templates and Add-ins dialog box. Learn more about using XML in Word 2003 later in this chapter.

Reading Layout

Microsoft says the new Reading Layout view "optimizes the reading experience." In practice, that means three things:

- Simplifying the visual clutter by eliminating most toolbars, as well as elements like the status bar and task panes

- Making the screen look like one or two sheets of paper

- Automatically turning on Clear Type font smoothing

You can switch any document to Reading Layout view by:

- Clicking the Read toolbar button on the Standard toolbar

- Selecting Reading Layout from the Tools menu

- Clicking the Reading Layout button at the bottom left of the Word interface

- Pressing Alt+R

Figure 4.4 shows a document open in Reading Layout view.

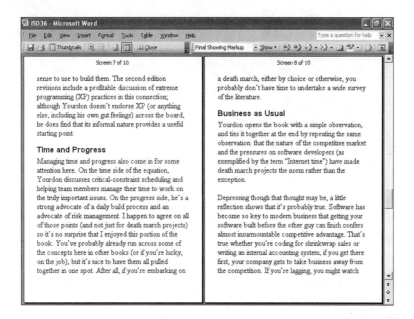

FIGURE 4.4   Reading Layout view hides most of the usual screen clutter and divides your document into synthetic pages.

You'll notice that Reading Layout view numbers its contents as *screens* rather than *pages*. That's because these screens are made up artificially by Word to maximize screen space. If you like, you can use the Actual Page toolbar button on the Reading Layout toolbar to see real pages instead of these artificial ones; however, if you then try to change the text size, you'll be right back to screens instead of pages again.

 UPGRADERS BEWARE

When you're in Reading Layout view, resizing the text doesn't resize text in tables. This makes Reading Layout view a poor choice for documents that contain many tables.

You can also use toolbar buttons to display either of a pair of navigation aids (but not both at once): document map or thumbnails. The document map hasn't changed in this version of Word. With thumbnails open, Reading Layout view is eerily reminiscent of Adobe's Acrobat reader, as you can see in Figure 4.5. But Reading Layout view isn't static like Acrobat; you can edit, highlight, and otherwise change text right in this view. In fact, Reading Layout view displays the Revisions toolbar to make marking up drafts easy.

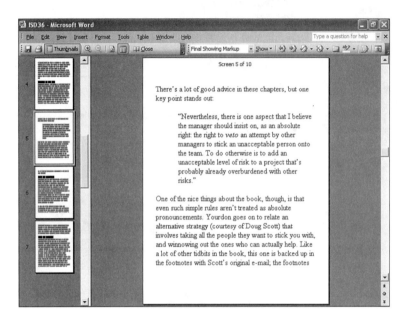

FIGURE 4.5   Thumbnails provide an overall sense of where you are and what your document looks like.

 **EXPERT ADVICE**

Word 2003 uses Reading Layout view by default when you open a Word document attached to an email message. If this behavior drives you nuts, you can turn it off. Select Tools, Options, General and uncheck Allow Starting in Reading Layout.

Compare Side by Side

The other major user interface innovation in Word 2003 is Compare Side by Side. This feature is aimed at those who need to compare multiple versions of documents without the benefit of revision marks. Perhaps a customer changed a contract draft and you're not sure where the changes are. That's an ideal use for this feature.

To compare two documents, open both documents in Word 2003 and select Compare Side by Side With from the Window menu. If you have exactly two documents open, each refers to the other on this menu (for example, DocumentA has the menu item Compare Side By Side

With DocumentB, whereas DocumentB has the menu item Compare Side By Side With DocumentA). If you have more than two documents open, the menu item is simply Compare Side By Side With and selecting it opens the Compare Side by Side dialog box shown in Figure 4.6.

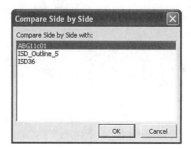

FIGURE 4.6 If you have more than two documents open in Word 2003, you can compare the current document with any other open document.

After you select the appropriate comparison document, click OK. Word tiles the two documents horizontally on your screen. It also synchronizes their scrolling, so that moving around in one document automatically moves the other as well. The Compare Side by Side toolbar, shown in Figure 4.7, automatically appears when you enter this mode. It offers three options:

- **Synchronous Scrolling**—This turns on and off the synchronous scrolling feature.

- **Reset Window Position**—You might want to maximize one of the documents to edit it. If you do, this button returns the windows to the side-by-side arrangement when you're done.

- **Close Side By Side**—This exits this mode.

 MORE INFO

The Compare Side by Side toolbar isn't available through the usual View, Toolbars menu. However, you can add its buttons to any other toolbar by opening the toolbar's Customize dialog box and selecting the All Commands category, or by using the Rearrange Commands dialog box.

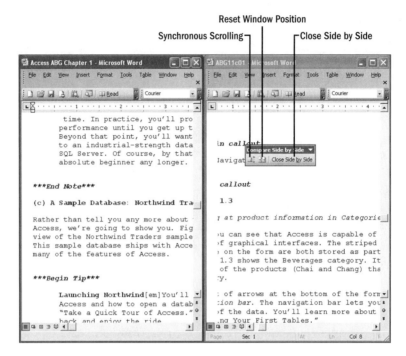

FIGURE 4.7   The Compare Side by Side toolbar lets you toggle synchronous scrolling between a pair of documents.

Using Word As an XML Editor

The changes we've discussed so far are really pretty minor. For Word 2003, the development team apparently chose to put most of their efforts toward one major feature: XML support. They've succeeded in bringing far-reaching XML capabilities to Word, including

- Direct editing of XML documents
- Using XML schemas to validate documents
- Support for XSL Transformations
- Saving Word documents as XML in the WordProcessingML format

In this section of the chapter, we'll show you how to use Word 2003 as your XML editor and demonstrate how you can integrate XML data into your Word documents. With XML increasingly becoming the standard format for interchanging data between applications and organizations, this is a useful set of skills to master.

UPGRADERS BEWARE

Word's XML features are available only in the Professional and Enterprise editions of the Office 2003 System and in the standalone Word 2003 product. If you have one of the less-expensive suites (such as Office Standard) or Word bundled into another package (such as Microsoft Works), it won't include these features.

 MORE INFO

Although Word's XML capabilities are impressive compared to the few bits of XML support in previous versions of Office, they're far from covering all the interlocking standards that make up the XML universe. If you find yourself frustrated by the limits of Word's support, consider a dedicated XML editor such as XMLSPY (`http://www.xmlspy.com`) or Xselerator (`http://www.marrowsoft.com/`).

Editing an XML Document

To demonstrate the use of Word as an XML editor, we'll start with a very simple XML document, `P01.xml`:

```xml
<?xml version="1.0" encoding="UTF-8"?>
<PurchaseOrder>
  <PONumber>K-1482</PONumber>
  <CustomerName>Elton and Jasperson Inc.</CustomerName>
  <CustomerCity>Endicott</CustomerCity>
  <CustomerState>WA</CustomerState>
  <Items>
    <Item ItemNumber="1202" Quantity="5"/>
    <Item ItemNumber="B18" Quantity="7"/>
    <Item ItemNumber="MM-428" Quantity="22"/>
  </Items>
</PurchaseOrder>
```

This document represents a purchase order—or at least a simplified sketch that might some day be built up into a purchase order! We're not going to try to teach you XML in this book, but we will point out that the document is built up of *elements* and *attributes*. In this document, PurchaseOrder, CustomerName, and Items are some of the elements. ItemNumber and Quantity are attributes. As you can see, elements can be nested and any element can have attributes. Elements in XML are marked out by either matching start and end tags (such as <CustomerName> and </CustomerName>) or a self-closing tag (such as <Item />).

MORE INFO

For a thorough introduction to XML, check out *Sams Teach Yourself XML in 21 Days, Third Edition* (ISBN: 0672325764, Sams Publishing 2003).

Loading an XML Document

To get started with the XML document in Word, select Open from the File menu, click the Open toolbar button on the Standard toolbar, or use any other normal method of opening a file. If you leave the Files of Type set to All Word Files, Word automatically shows you XML files, as you can see in Figure 4.8.

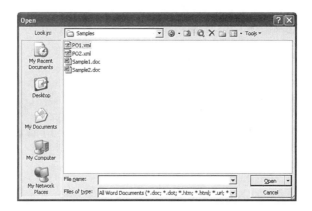

FIGURE 4.8   Word 2003 views XML documents as a type of Word document.

When you open an XML document in Word, it shows you both the tags and the content of the document, as shown in Figure 4.9. By default, Word displays the XML Structure task pane alongside the document. We'll discuss data views later in the chapter, in the "Using XSL Transformations" section.

If you inspect the view of the document in Figure 4.9, you'll notice that it displays element names and values but not attributes. Even though the original file has attributes in all the Item elements, they're not displayed by Word. To see them, you can right-click any element and select Attributes. This opens the Attributes for *Element Name* dialog box shown in Figure 4.10.

If you select an attribute in the Assigned Attributes box, you can edit its value in the Value box.

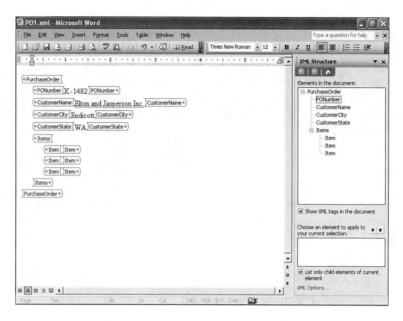

FIGURE 4.9 An XML document in Word 2003, showing tags and content.

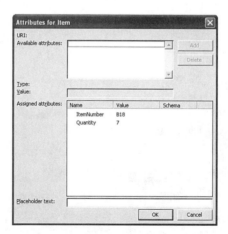

FIGURE 4.10 Word uses a separate dialog box to view and edit the attributes of an XML element.

UPGRADERS BEWARE

The Attributes dialog box does not indicate with which element you're working. The caption of the dialog box includes the name of the element, but if there are multiple instances of this element (as there are with the Item element in the sample we're working with), you can't tell them apart. We suggest highlighting the element before opening the Attributes dialog box so you don't forget with which element you're working.

 MORE INFO

Word can add new attributes to an XML document, but only if the XML document has an assigned XML schema. We discuss XML schemas in the next section of this chapter.

Setting XML Options

Word offers a few options that control its handling of XML—but they can be a bit difficult to find. To locate the XML Options dialog box, follow these steps:

1. Select Templates and Add-Ins from the Tools menu.

2. Select the XML Schema tab in the Templates and Add-Ins dialog box.

3. Click the XML Options button on the XML Schema tab to open the XML Options dialog box, shown in Figure 4.11.

 EXPERT ADVICE

There's an alternative path to the XML Options dialog box: Open the XML Structure task pane and click the XML Options hyperlink at the bottom of the task pane.

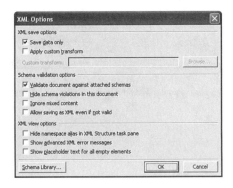

FIGURE 4.11   Setting Word's XML options.

Unlike some other options in Word, these options are set on a per-document basis. When you make changes here, you're changing things only for the current document. If you open another XML document, it reverts to the default option settings.

The XML Options dialog box gives you two choices when saving your XML document. If you select Save Data Only (the default), Word saves the pure XML data. The other choice, Apply Custom Transform, lets you specify an XSL Transform to be applied to the data before it is saved. If you select this choice, any data that's not used by the transform is discarded when you save the document.

Four of the options apply to XML schemas, which you'll see in the next section of the chapter:

- **Validate Document Against Attached Schemas**—When checked (the default), this tells Word to validate your work continuously, to ensure that your edits conform to the document's schema.

- **Hide Schema Violations in This Document**—This option doesn't disable validation, but it hides the wavy lines Word otherwise uses to show schema violations. This option is off by default.

- **Ignore Mixed Content**—This option lets you apply formatting to XML elements without saving the formatting. This option is off by default.

- **Allow Saving As XML Even If Not Valid**—This option lets you save the document even when there's a schema violation.

Finally, there are three options that control the XML view, all of which are off by default:

- **Hide Namespace Alias in XML Structure Task Pane**—If you have multiple schemas attached to a single document, Word automatically shows you which elements come from which schema. This option disables those hints.

- **Show Advanced XML Error Messages**—Generally, Word attempts to condense error messages down to something simple and friendly. This option discards the friendly messages in favor of displaying the full details.

- **Show Placeholder Text for All Empty Elements**—This option is useful when you're asking unsophisticated users to fill in XML document templates. It shows fill in the blank text wherever the user needs to type.

⇨ If you're trying to build an XML document to be filled in by beginning users, you should take a look at Microsoft InfoPath as an alternative to Microsoft Word. Read more in Chapter 11, "Introducing Microsoft InfoPath 2003."

Editing the XML Document

Of course, Word wouldn't be much of an XML editor if it didn't allow you to edit the document. Fortunately, there's full support for editing your XML documents. To get started, use the drop-down list at the top of the task pane to display the XML Structure task pane, as shown in Figure 4.12.

FIGURE 4.12   The XML Structure task pane.

In Figure 4.12, we've unchecked the List Only Child Elements of Current Element check box; by default it's checked. When you're editing an XML document that does not have an associated XML schema, you'll find that changing this setting makes for easier editing.

To change existing data in an XML document, type over the data, just as you would in any other Word document. You can continue to use features such as Word's spell-checker and search and replace without worrying about whether the document is XML instead of a native document.

Similarly, you can delete data from the XML document by using the Delete key. If you want to delete an element, highlight everything from the start tag to the end tag of the element and then press the Delete key. Remember to include the tags (which Word shows in maroon outlines) if you want to delete the entire element. Deleting only the contents results in an empty element.

To add a new element to the document, use the lower pane of the XML Structure task pane. Position your cursor where the new element should go and then click the name of the element. This inserts new start and end tags for the element, with the cursor positioned between them.

Without an XML schema, you can't add a new attribute to an element in Word.

XML Schema Support

We've mentioned several cases where Word requires an XML schema for full functionality. An *XML schema* is a special type of XML file that describes the structure of other XML files. For example, here's a possible XML schema for the purchase order file we were just examining:

```
<?xml version="1.0" encoding="UTF-8"?>
<xs:schema targetNamespace="http://www.larkware.com/POschema"
    xmlns:xs="http://www.w3.org/2001/XMLSchema"
    xmlns="http://www.larkware.com/POschema"
    elementFormDefault="qualified" attributeFormDefault="unqualified">
  <xs:element name="PurchaseOrder">
    <xs:complexType>
      <xs:sequence>
        <xs:element name="PONumber" type="xs:string"/>
        <xs:element name="CustomerName" type="xs:string"/>
        <xs:element name="CustomerCity" type="xs:string"/>
        <xs:element name="CustomerState" type="xs:string"/>
        <xs:element name="Items">
          <xs:complexType>
            <xs:sequence>
              <xs:element name="Item" maxOccurs="unbounded">
                <xs:complexType>
                  <xs:attribute name="ItemNumber" type="xs:string"
                      use="required"/>
                  <xs:attribute name="Quantity" type="xs:integer"
                      use="required"/>
                </xs:complexType>
              </xs:element>
            </xs:sequence>
          </xs:complexType>
        </xs:element>
      </xs:sequence>
    </xs:complexType>
  </xs:element>
</xs:schema>
```

Once again, we won't describe the structure of an XML schema file in any depth. But you can see that it lists all the elements and attributes that are allowed in the purchase order document. It also contains information on the acceptable type of data (for example, the Quantity attribute must be an integer) and the relationships between the various elements. In this case, for example, the PONumber, CustomerName, CustomerCity, CustomerState, and Items elements must appear in precisely that order because they're part of a sequence. Also note that the Item element can occur any number of times (maxOccurs="unbounded"); the default is for each element to appear precisely once.

Any XML document can contain a reference to the applicable XML schema. For example, here's another purchase order file, this one identified with a schema:

```
<?xml version="1.0" encoding="UTF-8"?>
<PurchaseOrder xmlns="http://www.larkware.com/POschema"
    xmlns:xsi="http://www.w3.org/2001/XMLSchema-instance"
    xsi:schemaLocation="http://www.larkware.com/POschema
    M:\Mike\Que\UpgradersOffice\CHAPTE~1\Samples\PO.xsd">
  <PONumber>K1898</PONumber>
  <CustomerName>Bruce Williams</CustomerName>
  <CustomerCity>Cremona</CustomerCity>
  <CustomerState>GA</CustomerState>
  <Items>
    <Item ItemNumber="HY71" Quantity="12"/>
    <Item ItemNumber="M8" Quantity="4"/>
  </Items>
</PurchaseOrder>
```

The xsi:SchemaLocation attribute in the root PurchaseOrder element indicates the associated schema for this document. Note that this lists both the uniform resource identifier (URI) for the schema as well as its location on the local file system. Word can use this information to automatically load the schema when you open this file. Before it can do so, though, you need to tell Word about the schema. Follow these steps to add the schema to Word's schema library:

1. Select Templates and Add-Ins from the Tools menu.

2. Select the XML Schema tab.

3. Click the Schema Library button.

4. Click the Add Schema button.

5. Browse to the schema file and click Open.

6. Click OK twice to dismiss the dialog boxes.

Figure 4.13 shows the new file loaded into Word.

As you can see, having a schema associated with the document changes the user interface slightly. The XML Structure task pane now shows the schema name along with the element name for each element. Also, the lower pane shows (by default) only those elements that can be legally inserted into the document at the current position. Because the cursor is currently in the Items element, only Item elements are legal.

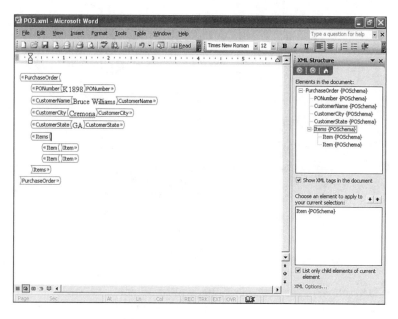

FIGURE 4.13   An XML document with an associated schema.

When you insert an element with attributes into an XML file with an associated schema, the Attributes dialog box shows the proper elements and lets you fill in their values.

 EXPERT ADVICE

Having an associated XML schema makes editing XML documents in Word more functional and pre-vents mistakes in editing. Whenever possible, make sure your XML documents have schemas.

Word can also create an XML document from scratch using a schema. To do this, select New from the File menu. In the New Document task pane, select the XML document. Click the Templates and Add-Ins link in the XML Structure task pane to go to the Templates and Add-Ins dialog box, shown in Figure 4.14. Here you can browse to a schema and check its box to associate it with the newly created document. Then the XML Structure task pane shows all the tags you can use to build the new document according to the selected schema.

 UPGRADERS BEWARE

If you're going to use your XML documents in tools other than Word, you might prefer to create them with a native XML editor rather than with Word. That's because Word inserts a variety of Microsoft-proprietary tags into XML documents it creates. For example, it stores the document properties and the styles used in the document. These tags both bloat the document and make it harder to read in other tools.

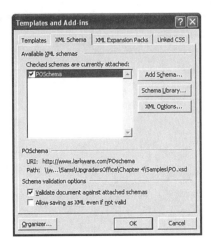

FIGURE 4.14   Selecting a schema for a new XML document.

Because an XML schema is itself an XML file, you could edit an XML schema in Word. However, as you've already seen, Word's interface isn't very friendly toward attributes, and schemas keep almost all their settings in attributes. You're better off using a dedicated XML editor such as Altova's XMLSPY (http://www.altova.com), or even Notepad, for schema work.

 UPGRADERS BEWARE

Although Word can associate a schema with an existing document, the results are likely to be less than satisfactory. That's because Word assigns an arbitrary namespace abbreviation to the schema but the existing elements aren't tagged with this abbreviation, so the schema doesn't apply to the data that's already in the document.

Using XSL Transformations

An *XSL transformation* is yet another variety of XML file; in particular, it's an XML file that specifies a way to rearrange and edit another XML file for particular presentation needs. As an example, here's an XSL transform to convert the purchase order XML files we've been working with into HTML documents:

```
<?xml version="1.0" encoding="UTF-8"?>
<xsl:stylesheet version="1.0" xmlns:xsl="http://www.w3.org/1999/XSL/Transform"
xmlns:n1="http://www.larkware.com/POschema" xmlns:xs="http://www.w3.org/2001/
    XMLSchema">
    <xsl:template match="/">
        <html>
```

```
<head />
<body>
    <xsl:for-each select="n1:PurchaseOrder">
        <xsl:for-each select="n1:CustomerName">
            <h1>
                <xsl:apply-templates />
            </h1>
        </xsl:for-each>
        <br />
        <xsl:for-each select="n1:CustomerCity">
            <xsl:apply-templates />
        </xsl:for-each>, <xsl:for-each select="n1:CustomerState">
            <xsl:apply-templates />
        </xsl:for-each>
        <br />Purchase Order #<xsl:for-each select="n1:PONumber">
            <xsl:apply-templates />
        </xsl:for-each>
        <br />
        <br />Please send the following:<br />
        <br />
        <xsl:for-each select="n1:Items">
            <table border="1">
                <thead>
                    <tr>
                        <td>
                            <span style="font-weight:bold; ">
                             ItemNumber</span>
                            <span style="font-weight:bold; "></span>
                        </td>
                        <td>
                            <span style="font-weight:bold; ">
                             Quantity</span>
                        </td>
                    </tr>
                </thead>
                <tbody>
                    <xsl:for-each select="n1:Item">
                        <tr>
                            <td>
                                <xsl:for-each select="@ItemNumber">
                                    <xsl:value-of select="." />
                                </xsl:for-each>
                            </td>
```

```
                            <td>
                                <xsl:for-each select="@Quantity">
                                    <xsl:value-of select="." />
                                </xsl:for-each>
                            </td>
                        </tr>
                    </xsl:for-each>
                </tbody>
            </table>
        </xsl:for-each>
    </xsl:for-each>
        </body>
    </html>
    </xsl:template>
</xsl:stylesheet>
```

You can think of an XSL transform as a set of instructions to a processor. For example, this particular XSL transform instructs, among other things, that every instance of the CustomerName element should be copied to the output surrounded by <h1> tags to turn it into header text. To see how you can use Word to process the XML document with this XSL transform, follow these steps:

1. Open the XML file in Word.

2. Select Add-Ins and Templates from the Tools menu to open the Add-Ins and Templates dialog box.

3. Select the XML Schema tab.

4. Click the Schema Library button to open the Schema Library dialog box, shown in Figure 4.15.

5. Select the schema being used by the document in the upper list in the Schema Library dialog box. Word associates transforms with particular schemas.

6. Click the Add Solution button.

7. Browse the XSL transform file you want to use and click Open.

8. Assign an alias (a friendly name) such as PO to HTML to the transform file in the Solution Settings dialog box (shown in Figure 4.16) and click OK.

9. Click OK twice to close the dialog boxes.

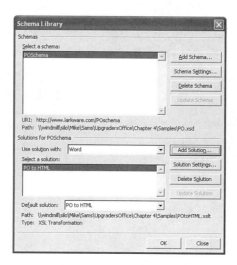

FIGURE 4.15   The Schema Library dialog box manages both schemas and transforms.

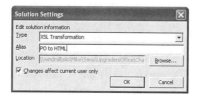

FIGURE 4.16   Assigning an alias to a transform in the Solutions Settings dialog box.

After associating a transform with the schema, you'll see that transform as a choice in the XML Document task pane when you open documents associated with that schema. Figure 4.17 shows the purchase order XML file with the PO to HTML transform applied.

Understanding WordProcessingML

One other piece of XML capability is included in Word 2003, and it's in all editions of Word: You can now save your Word documents in a native XML file format called WordProcessingML. Microsoft developed this file format to make Word data available to any other application that can read XML files. It provides a full-fidelity way to store a document; that is, a Word document of any complexity can be saved to WordProcessingML without losing either its data or its structure.

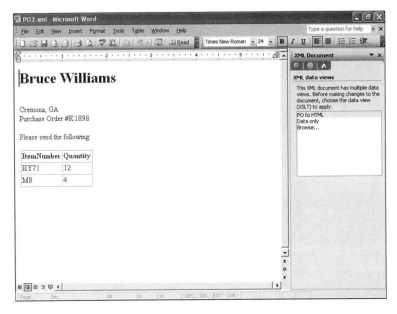

FIGURE 4.17 An XML file transformed to HTML by applying an XSL transformation.

To save a Word document in the WordProcessingML format, select Save As from the file menu and then select XML Document in the Save As Type drop-down list in the Save As dialog box. Your document is then assigned the .xml file extension—rather than Word's native .doc file extension—and the contents of the file are valid XML (although very complex valid XML).

In general, there's no need to save a Word document as XML unless you want to access it from some other application that reads and writes XML files. You might, for example, use this capability to integrate a Word document with a Web service that accepts purchase orders submitted as XML. Alternatively, you could use an environment that creates XML files (such as Microsoft .NET) to create Word documents by building WordProcessingML files from scratch.

Of course, there are already many, many applications that can read and write XML files. Many business systems such as Customer Relations Management (CRM) or Enterprise Resource Planning (ERP) systems can use XML to communicate. Web services, too, package their messages as XML. Other Microsoft products, including BizTalk Server 2004 and SharePoint Portal Server, make heavy use of XML. To a large extent, XML has become the common language of applications.

MORE INFO

Microsoft has published the Office 2003 XML Reference Schemas, which includes the complete schema for WordProcessingML. You can download a copy from `http://www.microsoft.com/downloads/details.aspx?familyid=fe118952-3547-420a-a412-00a2662442d9&displaylang=en`. These schemas are indispensable if you plan to actually write code that integrates with Word's XML format.

Other New Features

Word 2003 includes a few other miscellaneous changes, which we'll mention here for the sake of completeness:

- Support for handwritten annotations if you have a Tablet PC or other ink-enabled device

- The ability to lock part of a document against editing while allowing the rest to be edited

- Support for additional Unicode characters

- Faxing directly from Word, using a subscription-based Internet faxing service

You'll find more information about these new features in Word's help file.

What's New in Excel 2003

M ost of Excel 2003's enhancements and new features are behind the scenes—you won't notice a lot of interface changes. Most users will benefit from Excel lists and the easy-to-use new task panes. Developers will like smart documents that help users do their job and the enhancements to Extensible Markup Language (XML) support.

Changes to the User Interface

Most of the user interface changes to Excel 2003 come in the form of a new softer look, which you read about in Chapter 2, "Shared Office Features," and the addition of several new task panes. A few menu commands have been added or moved.

The New Menus

The one thing you can always depend on with any new version is that some of your favorite menu commands won't be where they used to be. In addition, you'll find some new commands, and you might even learn that some commands are gone. In this section, we'll review new commands and show you where to find old friends:

- New menus include Permission, Research, Shared Workspace, List, XML, and Side by Side.

- File Search replaces Search, and Microsoft Office Online replaces Tools on the Web.

- The List toolbar is new.

IN THIS CHAPTER

- **Changes to the user interface**
- **Extensible Markup Language support**
- **Productivity**
- **SharePoint integration**
- **For the developer**

Starting with the File menu, you'll find two changes. First, the Search command is now called File Search. You read about that change in Chapter 4, "What's New in Word 2003." The information is basically the same on this particular command from one application to another. The Permission menu is another new shared item; it supports the new Digital Rights Management feature.

> ⇨ You can learn more about the File Search and Permissions commands in Chapter 4's "Menu Changes" section.

> ⇨ You can learn more about the Permission command in Chapter 12, "What's New in Rights Management."

There's nothing new on the View menu, but following the View, Toolbars path, you'll find a new toolbar listed, called List. This toolbar complements the new Excel List feature, which you'll learn more about later in this chapter.

The Research and Shared Workspace items are new to the Tools menu. The Shared Workspace menu opens the Shared Workspace task pane, which offers options for creating collaborative documents. The Tools on the Web menu is gone, but you'll find the same functionality on the Microsoft Office Online item on the Help menu. Just as in Word, the keyboard shortcut for this item is now Alt+H+M.

> ⇨ You can learn more about the Research pane in Chapter 2.

Two new items on the Data menu probably create the most stir in the new features category. The List and XML items make quick work of manipulating data—any data. Both new features are covered in this chapter.

The Window menu offers the new Compare Side by Side item that displays two instances of Excel side by side, automatically. You'll read about this new feature later in this chapter. Finally, the Help menu has been completely rearranged—items are gone, items are renamed, and new items have appeared.

> ⇨ You can learn more about the new Help menu's changes in Chapter 2.

New Look and Feel

Other than a few new task panes, you won't notice too many interface changes. You'll adapt right away to using Excel 2003. Almost everything's the same as before, except for the subtle graphic updates to individual menus and tool buttons. The new task panes provide a centralized location from which to perform a number of related tasks.

> ⇨ Chapter 2 discusses the graphical changes to the interface in great depth.

The New Workbook Task Pane

This new task pane appears to the right of the worksheet and is kind of a jack-of-all-trades, enabling you to initiate several common tasks from one spot. There are three ways to access the task pane shown in Figure 5.1:

- Select Task Pane from the View menu.

- Press Ctrl+F1.

- Select New from the File menu.

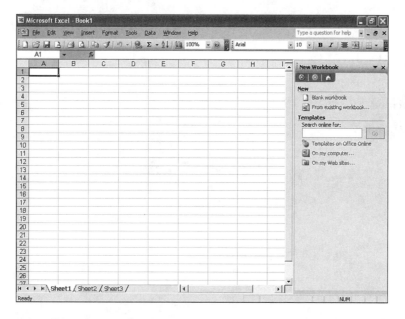

FIGURE 5.1   Excel 2003's New Workbook task pane offers a click point for a number of common tasks.

 **EXPERT ADVICE**

The New Workbook task pane is actually a toolbar. Although you won't dock it in the traditional toolbar manner, the task pane is available via the Toolbars menu. Select View, Toolbars, Task Pane. Or, select Tools, Customize, Toolbars.

Use the New Workbook task pane to create a new blank worksheet or base a new worksheet on a template. The template can be on your computer, on your Web site, or even online at Microsoft's site. Use the Back and Forward arrows just below the title bar to navigate back and forth between the task panes you've used.

Use the Other Task Panes control—the down arrow to the left of the task pane's Close button to display links to several other task panes, as shown in Figure 5.2:

- **[NEW]** • Getting Started
- **[NEW]** • Help
- • Search Results—was Search
- • Clip Art—was Insert Clip Art
- **[NEW]** • Research
- • Clipboard
- • New Workbook
- • Template Help
- **[NEW]** • Shared Workspace
- **[NEW]** • Document Updates
- **[NEW]** • XML Source

FIGURE 5.2   Click the arrow to access several other task panes.

 The new Help task pane is a shared Office feature. You can learn more about this new task pane in Chapter 2.

EXPERT ADVICE

The Clipboard Viewer isn't new to Excel 2003, but you can display the Clipboard Viewer by selecting Office Clipboard from the Edit menu or by pressing Ctrl+C twice. You'll find a new item—Show Office Clipboard When Ctrl+C Pressed Twice—on the viewer's Option menu. You can disable the Ctrl+C shortcut by unchecking this option.

⇨ You can learn more about using the new Research task pane in Excel 2003 in Chapter 2.

⇨ The new Shared Documents task pane is discussed in "List Integration with SharePoint" later in this chapter. You can also learn about SharePoint in Chapter 2.

⇨ Learn about the new XML Source task pane in the "Extensible Markup Language Support" section in this chapter.

Side-by-Side Workbooks

You've always been able to view multiple worksheets within the Excel window. Now, you can display multiple workbooks side-by-side. To accomplish the same feat in earlier versions, you must resize the entire Excel windows for both workbooks; now Excel does that for you.

In either workbook, select Window, Compare Side by Side with *workbook*, where *workbook* represents the other opened workbook. Figure 5.3 shows the results. Notice that *workbook* is beneath the original workbook.

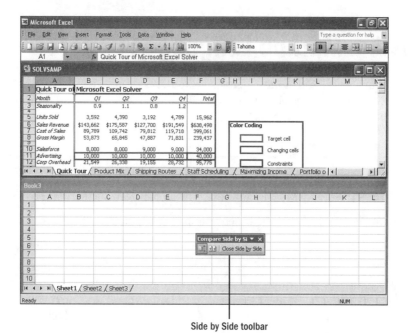

Side by Side toolbar

FIGURE 5.3   Excel displays two workbooks in the same window.

At the same time, Excel 2003 also launches the Side by Side toolbar. Click Synchronous Scrolling to scroll through both workbooks at the same time. Use the Reset button to return to the previous side-by-side display if you change the display by resizing a window. To return to just the original workbook, click Close Side by Side.

If more than two workbooks are open, Excel 2003 displays the Compare Side by Side dialog box shown in Figure 5.4, which lists all the open workbooks. Simply select the one you want to display along with the current workbook, and click OK.

FIGURE 5.4 Choose a workbook to compare.

Extensible Markup Language Support

Without a doubt, Excel 2003's most impressive addition is the expanded Extensible Markup Language (XML) support. Excel 2002 lets you save workbooks in an XML spreadsheet format, but that's about all you get in the way of XML.

Excel 2003's XML features are extensive:

- You can open XML data files into a new workbook.
- You can input XML data into existing spreadsheet calculation models.
- You can map custom XML schema to existing data.
- You can incorporate XML data from a Web service into an existing worksheet.

In a nutshell, all this support means you can seamlessly import and export XML data into and out of Excel. What you once thought was impossible, or what was once very difficult, is easily accomplished using XML.

 **MORE INFO**

The XML features in Excel are available only in Microsoft Office Enterprise Edition 2003, Microsoft Office Professional Edition 2003, and Microsoft Office Excel 2003.

What's XML?

XML is a platform-independent markup language for structured documents. If you're new to XML, that doesn't mean much to you. So, think of XML as a fairly new technology that makes sharing data easy because the file format no longer matters. Forget the days of finding a third-party product compatible with both the original file format and the target application with which you're sharing that data. Now, you just save the original data as an XML file and that's it.

XML produces a text file that contains data and what's known as *tags*, which identify the data. For instance, a tag might contain the name of a column heading in your worksheet. Following that tag would be all the entries in that column. You can share that XML file with almost any application.

To properly view imported XML data, you need a *schema file*, or an XSD file. The term *schema* simply means structure. An XML schema file describes the documents structure and the data. Most of the time the schema information is an automatic feature. However, the additional file does lend a lot of flexibility toward importing the data just the way you want it by applying a custom schema file to the imported data.

Another type of XML file you might run into is an Extensible Stylesheet Language (XSL) file. These files specify how the contents of an XML document are formatted.

Opening an XML File

What makes Excel 2003's XML integration so unique and powerful is that most of it is fully automated. You don't really need to understand what's going on behind the scenes to benefit. All you need to know is that you can add an XML schema and data to a workbook, regardless of or even in spite of where the data originated. The source just doesn't matter. If the original source can spit out an XML document, Excel 2003 can use it in one of three ways:

- You can create an XML list inside Excel from XML data.

- You can import XML data into a read-only workbook.

- You can import XML data into an Excel workbook and interact with it as you would any other data.

To open an XML file from Excel, do the following:

1. Select File, Open.

2. Select XML Files (*.xml) from the Files of Type control's drop-down list.

3. Using the Look in control, navigate to the XML file you want to open and click Open to display the Open XML dialog box shown in Figure 5.5.

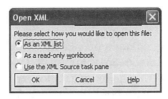

FIGURE 5.5   Select how you want to open the XML file.

4. Select the appropriate option in the Open XML dialog box, and click OK. Table 5.1 defines each option. (Excel 2003 might warn you that no schema exists and that it will create one. Click OK to this message to continue.)

TABLE 5.1   Open XML Options

Option	Explanation
As an XML List	Excel 2003 creates a list from the data. An XML list is similar to an Excel list in that it's a range of data you can manage and analyze independently of other data.
As a Read-only Workbook	This option lets you view data, but you can't manipulate it in any way. Excel 2003 displays the data in a static grid.
Use the XML Source Task Pane	This creates a map to link or bind a cell to an element in the XML file. Importing the file populates the cells with the bound data.

 EXPERT ADVICE

An XML *map* is an object added to a workbook when you add an XML schema. Excel 2003 uses an XML map to create mapped ranges and manage the relationships between the mapped ranges and the actual elements in the XML schema. A workbook can contain many XML maps, but each element can be mapped to a cell or range only once. If you try to open a previously mapped XML file, Excel 2003 opens a new instance of Excel 2003.

Importing XML into an Excel List

Figure 5.6 shows an XML file imported as an XML list. An XML list is basically the same in appearance and functionality as an Excel list. However, an XML list is mapped to one or more XML elements and each column represents an XML element.

➪ Excel lists are also new to Excel 2003. To learn about the functionality of this new feature (and also XML lists), see "Excel Lists" later in this chapter.

	A	B	C	D
1	Title	Artist	Track	Label
2	Meisner Darrell	Meisner Darrell	When The Saints Go Marching In	
3	Meisner Darrell	Meisner Darrell	On The Sunny Side Of The Street	
4	Meisner Darrell	Meisner Darrell	Ain't Misbehavin'	
5	Abbas Syed	Abbas Syed	Dreams	
6	Abbas Syed	Abbas Syed	5150	
7	Cencini Andrew	Cencini Andrew	Once upon a time in the west	Southridge Video
8	Cencini Andrew	Cencini Andrew	Expresso love	Southridge Video
9	Cencini Andrew	Cencini Andrew	Romeo and Juliet	Southridge Video
10	Entin Michael	Entin Michael	Alpine valley	Contoso Ltd.
11	Entin Michael	Entin Michael	Plains of joy	Contoso Ltd.
12	Entin Michael	Entin Michael	Waitin' guitar	Contoso Ltd.
13	Baker Mary	Baker, Mary	Subdivisions	Lucerne Publishing
14	Baker Mary	Baker, Mary	Time Stand Still	Lucerne Publishing
15	Baker Mary	Baker, Mary	Mystic Rhythms	Lucerne Publishing
16	Kane Lori	Kane Lori	Eine kleine Nachtmusik:Allegro	
17	Kane Lori	Kane Lori	Piano Concerto in A major, K 488: Adagio	
18	Kane Lori	Kane Lori	Flute Concerto in D major, K 314: Allegro	
19	Zimmerman Marc	Zimmerman Marc	via Medina	Proseware Inc.
20	Zimmerman Marc	Zimmerman Marc	Ewiva 'o Rre'	Proseware Inc.
21	Zimmerman Marc	Zimmerman Marc	Tempo di cambiare	Proseware Inc.
22	*			

FIGURE 5.6   Import an XML file as an Excel list.

At this point, you might be wondering how Excel 2003 knew just what to do with all that data. The original data was saved as an XML file, which used field names or column headings to create the following tags: <Title>, <Artist>, <Track>, and <Label>. When Excel 2003 opens the file, it uses these tags as column headings and maps the bound data to the corresponding worksheet column. You can identify XML data by the blue, nonprintable border Excel 2003 displays around a mapped cell or region.

 EXPERT ADVICE

By default, Excel 2003 surrounds XML lists with a border. You can turn off the border by clicking List on the Data menu and then clicking the Hide Border of Inactive Lists option. This option controls the borders around all Excel lists, XML lists, and single-mapped cells in the workbook. You can't hide the border for just one XML list or cell.

! **UPGRADERS BEWARE**

You can change the way Excel 2003 displays XML data using any of the formats you normally use. However, you can't export those formats when you export the data as XML data, unless the display format is Text. Excel 2003 exports only the mapped numeric data.

Adding an XML Map to a Workbook

In the last section, you created an XML list; you can also map an XML file to a workbook and use the data as you would any other data—without the list functionality. Use the File, Open menu method reviewed earlier, except select the Use the XML Source Task Pane option (refer to Figure 5.5).

To add an XML map to a worksheet, select File, Open and then select XML File from the Files of Type control. Locate the XML file in the Look in control and then click Open. Check the Use the XML Source Task Pane option in the Open XML dialog box. At this point, Excel 2003 might warn you that the schema doesn't exist. Click OK to clear the message and continue.

Figure 5.7 shows the results of opening the same file using the XML Source Task Pane option instead of the XML List option. Doing so not only creates the XML map, but also opens the XML Source task pane.

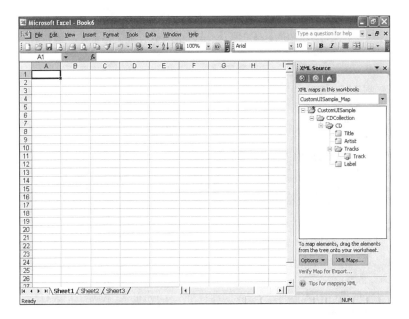

FIGURE 5.7   The XML Source Pane option maps the XML file but doesn't automatically import the data.

Were you expecting to see data in the worksheet? This option maps the file but doesn't automatically import the data. Instead, you can drag nodes from the task pane to the worksheet to customize the data you import.

Anytime you open an XML file, Excel 2003 creates an XML map, which you can view via the XML Source task pane. Whether you're working with an existing map or importing one, you can use the XML Source task pane to manipulate the XML data in your worksheet. The point is, after the map is in Excel 2003, you can map any of the elements to your worksheet.

Following the current example, drag the CD Collection node from the XML Source task pane to the worksheet to map all four columns at one time, as shown in Figure 5.8. After you map the elements, you can display the mapped data by selecting Data, XML, Refresh XML Data (see Figure 5.9) .

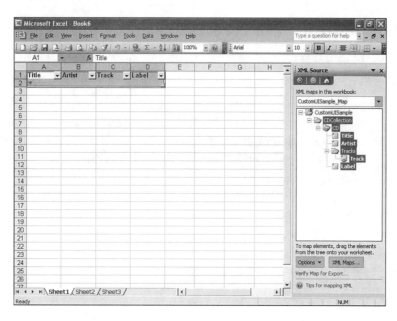

FIGURE 5.8   Drag mapped elements to the worksheet.

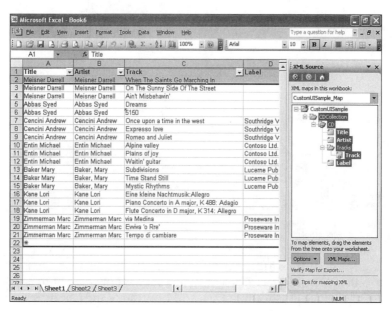

FIGURE 5.9   Display the mapped data.

About Repeating XML Elements

Excel 2003 works with two types of elements in an XML map:

- **Single**—Single, or nonrepeating, elements occur only once in any given XML file.

- **Repeating**—These elements can repeat any number of times in the same XML file.

Following the CD example, that means each artist and title can have more than one track (refer to Figure 5.9). The CD collection example data contains both types of elements.

When you map a repeating element, as shown in Figure 5.10, Excel 2003 displays the entire list, as you might expect. (If you're following the examples, you must delete the previous map or open a blank worksheet. You can't map the same elements twice.)

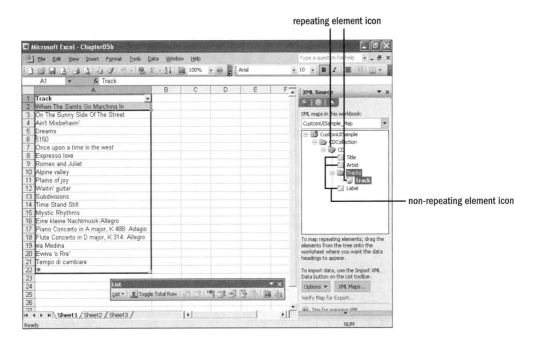

FIGURE 5.10   Map a repeating element.

Map a single element, such as Title or Artist, as a separate list. By that, we mean you don't map it next to the repeating Track element. When a list is not adjacent to another list, Excel 2003 displays the unique list shown in Figure 5.11 instead of the repeating list you saw earlier (refer to Figure 5.9).

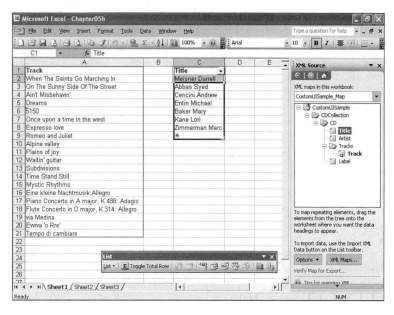

FIGURE 5.11 Map a single element as a lone list.

Now, watch what happens when you map a single element adjacent to an existing element. Figure 5.12 shows the Title single element mapped right next to the repeating Track element. Excel 2003 automatically incorporates the Artist element into the Track list and displays each Track item's corresponding Artist value. If you place the Artist element a few columns away, Excel 2003 displays a unique list of items, just as it did earlier when mapping the Title repeating element.

MORE INFO

XML is a huge topic, and we've provided just an introduction to using XML data in Excel 2003. For more information, search the Excel 2003 Help files for "XML support."

⇨ InfoPath lets you export a form to Excel, or you can open a form as an XML file within Excel. For more information on working with InfoPath in Excel 2003, read Chapter 11, "Introducing Microsoft InfoPath 2003."

UPGRADERS BEWARE

After a worksheet is mapped to an XML file, which you can easily track using the XML Source task pane, you can drag elements from the task pane to the worksheet. You can change these headings. However, if you plan to reimport the data from the same source or export the XML list data, Excel 2003 uses the XML element names.

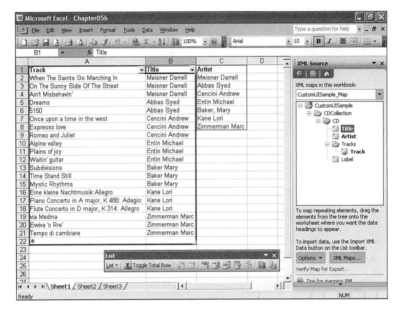

FIGURE 5.12   Map a single element adjacent to a repeating element.

More About the XML Source Task Pane

The XML Source task pane displays each XML map and its elements in a hierarchical structure. You can set a number of options for viewing XML data in this task pane by clicking the Options button and choosing one of the following options:

- **Preview Data in Task Pane**—Displays sample data in the element list if you have imported XML data associated with the XML map in the current session

- **Hide Help Text in the Task Pane**—Hides the help text displayed below the element list

- **Automatically Merge Elements when Mapping**—Automatically expands XML lists when you drag an element to a cell adjacent to the XML list

- **My Data Has Headings**—Uses existing data as column headings when you map repeating elements

- **Hide Border of Inactive Lists**—Hides list borders when working outside the list

Open this task pane by adding an XML map to the workbook. Or, select View, Task Pane and then select XML Source from the task pane's drop-down list.

About SpreadsheetML

SpreadsheetML is an XML dialect that represents information in an Excel spreadsheet. Microsoft defined this XML dialect to allow for easy interoperability between Excel and other applications.

The root element for an XML spreadsheet is the Workbook element. That element can, in turn, contain multiple Worksheet elements. The following is a simple XML spreadsheet file:

```
<?xml version="1.0"?>
<?mso-application progid="Excel.Sheet"?>
<Workbook
    xmlns="urn:schemas-microsoft-com:office:spreadsheet"
    xmlns:ss="urn:schemas-microsoft-com:office:spreadsheet">
<Worksheet ss:Name="Sheet1">
</Worksheet>
</Workbook>
```

This file produces a simple workbook with one sheet named Sheet1.

To save an Excel document in the SpreadsheetML format, select File, Save As and then select XML Document in the Save As Type drop-down list in the Save As dialog box. Your document is assigned the .xml file extension—rather than Excel's native .xls file extension—and the contents of the file are valid XML (although very complex valid XML).

 MORE INFO

Microsoft has published the Office 2003 XML Reference Schemas, which includes the complete schema for SpreadsheetML. You can download a copy from http://www.microsoft.com/downloads/details.aspx?familyid=fe118952-3547-420a-a412-00a2662442d9&displaylang=en. These schemas are indispensable if you plan to actually write code that integrates with Excel's XML format.

Productivity

Everyone wants to work more quickly and accurately. In truth, almost all new features and enhancements could be said to increase productivity, but a few features stand out in this area.

Document Recovery

There's nothing quite as frustrating as losing several minutes of work due to a crash while rushing to complete a project. Excel 2003 has a feature known as *document recovery* that automatically saves unsaved work when a file is corrupted or Excel crashes. After the recovery process, Excel 2003 prompts you to save the original file or the recovered file using the Document Recovery task pane. When this happens to you, just follow the advice listed in the task pane.

Excel Lists

Although Excel lists are new to Excel 2003, some of their functionality might seem familiar to you. You'll use them to organize, group, and analyze data when you don't want to consider adjacent data. In other words, you can manipulate the data in a list without affecting the surrounding cells or data. Figure 5.13 displays a typical Excel 2003 list.

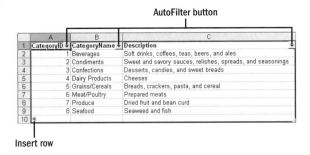

FIGURE 5.13   Excel 2003 lists manipulate related data.

Creating an Excel List

To create an Excel list, complete the following steps:

1. Highlight the data you want to turn into an Excel list.

2. Select Data, List, Create List. The Create List dialog box shown in Figure 5.14 displays the selected range. If you didn't select the range first, do so now or enter the cell references that identify the range in the Create List dialog box.

3. If the selected data has headers, select the My List Has Headers option.

4. Click OK.

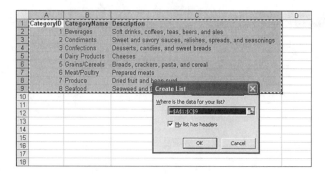

FIGURE 5.14 Identify the range that contains the data you want to turn into a list.

Working with Excel Lists

Excel highlights the specific range and surrounds it with a blue border. If you didn't select the My List Has Headers option in step 3, Excel adds generic header text at the top of the list. If Excel 2003 doesn't display the List toolbar, select View, Toolbars, List to launch it.

Also notice that Excel 2003 enables an AutoFilter drop-down list for each column in the list. That's right; a list doesn't have to consist of a single column. While working outside a list, the AutoFilter buttons aren't visible and the borders are not as thick and bright (refer to Figure 5.12). The AutoFilter buttons provide the same functionality as in earlier versions of Excel. Use these lists to sort and filter the data.

The asterisk character in the bottom-left cell (or the row above the totals row) indicates an insert row. Use this row to enter new data so that Excel 2003 incorporates that new data into the list.

You can quickly add a totals row to the bottom of a list by selecting the list and then clicking Toggle Total Row on the List toolbar. Excel 2003 inserts a row and then displays the sum of the values in the rightmost column in the last cell in that column, as shown in Figure 5.15. If that column doesn't contain numeric data, Excel 2003 counts the items in the column.

 **EXPERT ADVICE**

To quickly resize a list, select it and then drag any of the selection handles appropriately. Not every border displays a handle because you can't extend a list over existing data.

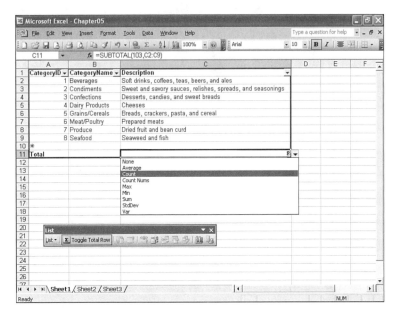

FIGURE 5.15   Add an aggregate function to evaluate list data.

Collaboration Improvements

SharePoint Services makes collaborating on shared documents easy. Excel 2003 enhancements include publishing Excel lists, creating Document Workspaces from inside Excel 2003, and restricting sensitive information.

➪ Information Rights Management (IRM) lets you restrict who views your documents. This feature goes a long way toward protecting your confidential and sensitive data. To use this feature, you must install the Windows Rights Management client. Learn all about this feature in Chapter 12.

List Integration with SharePoint

A shared workbook allows several people to edit the same data simultaneously. You don't have to share the entire workbook to share the contents of an Excel list:

1. Select the worksheet that contains the list you want to share (that worksheet must be active).

2. Select Data, List; then click Publish List.

3. In the resulting Publish List to SharePoint Site dialog box, shown in Figure 5.16, enter the appropriate SharePoint Web site URL in the Address control.

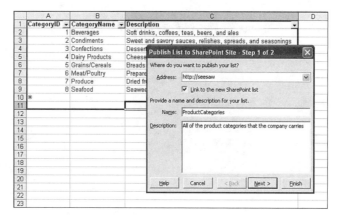

FIGURE 5.16 Identify where you want to publish the Excel list.

4. To create a dynamic link between the original Excel link and the published list, select the Link to the New SharePoint List option. The SharePoint version of your list automatically shows changes to the Excel list in your workbook, and vice versa.

5. Give the list a name and enter a description. (Both are optional.)

6. Click Next.

7. Examine the data types listed for each column, as shown in Figure 5.17, carefully. Click Finish to publish the Excel list and, if everything goes as expected, Excel 2003 displays the message shown in Figure 5.18. Notice that the message includes the URL for the shared list. Clear the message by clicking OK. Excel 2003 adds an ID column, like the one shown in Figure 5.19, to the first column of a linked Excel list. This column is read-only and can't be removed until you unlink the list.

FIGURE 5.17 Check the data types when publishing an Excel list.

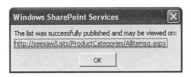

FIGURE 5.18 Excel 2003 confirms that the list has been published.

	A	B	C	D
1	ID	CategoryID	CategoryName	Description
2	1	1	Beverages	Soft drinks, coffees, teas, beers, and ales
3	2	2	Condiments	Sweet and savory sauces, relishes, spreads, and seasonings
4	3	3	Confections	Desserts, candies, and sweet breads
5	4	4	Dairy Products	Cheeses
6	5	5	Grains/Cereals	Breads, crackers, pasta, and cereal
7	6	6	Meat/Poultry	Prepared meats
8	7	7	Produce	Dried fruit and bean curd
9	8	8	Seafood	Seaweed and fish
10	*			
11	Total			8

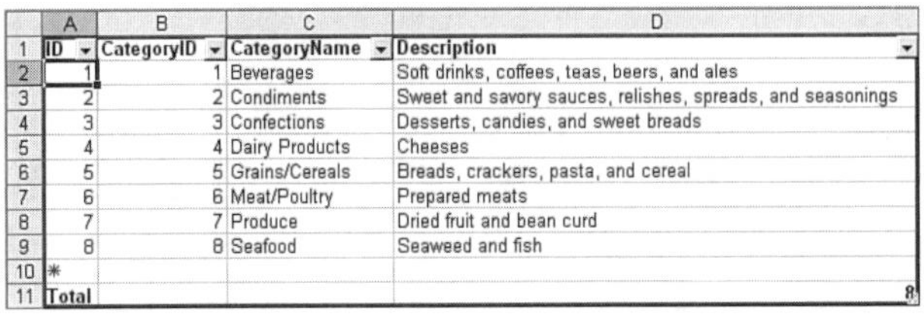

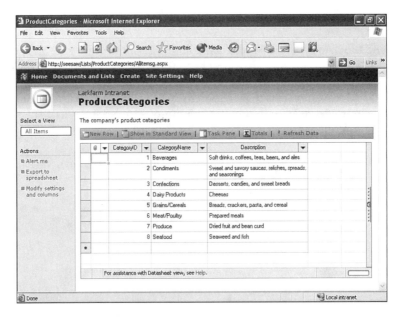

FIGURE 5.19 Excel 2003 adds an ID column to a published list.

8. To view the shared list shown in Figure 5.20, use your Web browser to navigate to the shared URL.

FIGURE 5.20 Use a Web browser to access the shared list.

UPGRADERS BEWARE

If anything goes wrong with the publishing process, you get an error message stating that the server cannot be contacted at this time. You get this message even if the actual error is something else (for example, an illegal character in your proposed Web site name).

After publishing an Excel list, you can view the published version. First, display the List toolbar if necessary. Select the Excel list, click List on the List toolbar, and click View List on Server.

➪ Document Workspaces is a Windows SharePoint feature that simplifies the process of collaborating on documents in real time. By creating a document on a Document Workspace, you and anyone else you allow to can modify the document. For more information on this feature, see Chapter 2.

What's New in PowerPoint 2003

PowerPoint is a big plus to the Office family; it's one of the easiest to use and most powerful presentation packages available. Cradle all that within Office's familiar interface and you have a winner that's sure to please a large variety of users, from the novice to the expert. If you've never used PowerPoint before, don't worry, because it'll seem like an old friend to anyone who is already at home with the Office products.

Changes to the User Interface

PowerPoint 2003 has had few changes to its interface beyond the whole new look you'll see throughout Office 2003. In this section, we'll cover the few menu changes and new task panes:

- New menu commands include Permission, Research and Thesaurus, Shared Workspace, and Schedule Meeting.

- Search replaces File Search, and Package for CD replaces Pack and Go.

- Tools on the Web and What's This are gone.

- New task panes include Getting Started, Help, Research, Template Help, Shared Workspace, and Document Updates.

- The Clip Art task pane replaces Insert Clip Art, and Slide Design replaces Slide Design – Design Templates.

IN THIS CHAPTER

- Changes to the user interface
- Viewer and Package for CD improvements
- Multimedia support

The New Menus

Like all the Office applications, PowerPoint 2003's menus are a little different. In this section, we'll tell you what's new, what's gone, and how to find what has been moved.

The File menu shares a few changes with all the other applications. The Search command is now the File Search command. In addition, the Permission menu is another shared menu that's shared with other Office applications.

⇨ Chapter 4, "What's New in Word 2003," reviews the new File Search menu. For information on the Permissions menu item, see Chapter 12, "What's New in Rights Management."

PowerPoint 2003 replaces the Pack and Go command with Package for CD. This enhanced feature lets you copy presentations to CD-ROM so you can later run them on systems running Windows 98 Second Edition (or later). You'll learn more about this feature later in this chapter.

 UPGRADERS BEWARE

The Package for CD feature requires Microsoft Windows XP. Windows 2000 users can package a presentation to a folder and then use a third-party writing application to copy a presentation to CD-ROM.

The Edit menu is the same, but the View menu has one small change. If you select Toolbars from the View menu, you'll see that the Revisions Pane has been renamed to just Revisions.

Subcommands on the Insert menu's Picture command have been rearranged. Look for Organization Chart at the bottom of the list.

PowerPoint 2003's Tools menu has several changes. First, the Research and Thesaurus items are new. The Research command (Alt+click) opens the new Research task pane. The Shared Workspace item is new and opens the Shared Workspace task pane, which assists in creating collaborative documents.

The Online Collaboration menu on the Tools menu has a new item, Schedule Meeting. Use this command to create a Microsoft Outlook Meeting request. This item replaces the Meeting Minder item in earlier versions. In addition, the Tools on the Web item is gone, but you can find the same functionality on the Help menu in the form of the Microsoft Office Online item (Alt+H, M).

⇨ You can learn more about the new menus in Chapter 2, "Shared Office Features."

PowerPoint 2003's Help menu has undergone substantial changes. There are several new items and the What's This? item is gone. Unlike some other Office applications, PowerPoint 2003 does not offer the new Side By Side comparison feature.

New Look and Feel

Anyone familiar with PowerPoint 2002 or earlier will have little trouble adjusting to PowerPoint 2003. It won't take long to learn the new features, and the interface is essentially the same. The task panes provide a centralized location for executing common tasks.

Display the task pane by either selecting Task Pane from the View menu or pressing Ctrl+F1. PowerPoint 2003 defaults to the new Getting Started task pane, whereas earlier versions default to the New Presentation task pane. Several new task panes are available from the task pane interface:

- **[NEW]** • Getting Started
- **[NEW]** • Help
- • Search Results, which replaces Search
- • Clip Art, which replaces Insert Clip Art
- **[NEW]** • Research
- • Clipboard
- • New Presentation
- **[NEW]** • Template Help
- **[NEW]** • Shared Workspace
- **[NEW]** • Document Updates
- • Slide Layout
- • Slide Design, which replaces Slide Design – Design Templates
- • Slide Design – Color Schemes
- • Slide Design – Animation Schemes
- • Custom Animation
- • Slide Transition

The Getting Started Task Pane

There are six new task panes. The Getting Started task pane is just what it suggests: a place to begin your work in PowerPoint 2003. Use the task pane shown in Figure 6.1 to create a new presentation, open an existing presentation, or get news on PowerPoint 2003 from the Web.

⇨ Many new task panes are actually shared Office components: Help, Research, Shared Workspace, Template Help, and Document Updates. Chapter 2 thoroughly covers each of these new task panes.

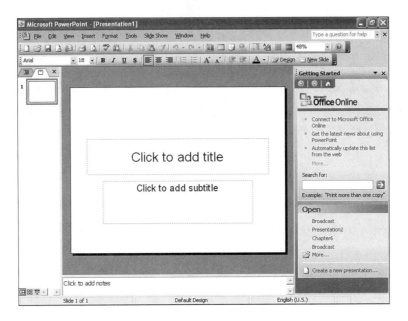

FIGURE 6.1   Use the Getting Started task pane to access presentations.

Productivity Enhancements

Most of the enhancements and new features will make you more efficient and productive. A few, such as the thesaurus and smart tags, have been around for a while, just not in PowerPoint.

 **EXPERT ADVICE**

The Thesaurus isn't new to Office, but it is new to PowerPoint 2003. It works like the thesaurus in any other Office application by listing synonyms.

Downloading New Templates

New templates are available all the time and now they're just a click away. To see what's new, select Slide Design from the Format menu to open the Slide Design task pane. (Or select Slide Design from the task pane's drop-down list.) Scroll to the bottom of the list of design templates until you see the Design Templates on Microsoft Office Online thumbnail shown in Figure 6.2.

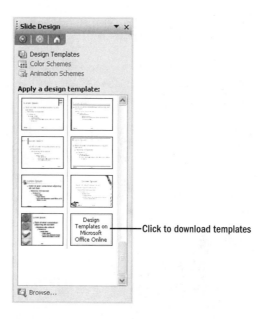

FIGURE 6.2   Click the Design Templates on Microsoft Office Online to download new templates.

Clicking this thumbnail launches your default browser and accesses the PowerPoint Design Templates site where you can browse, preview, and download templates.

Using Ink to Mark a Presentation

PowerPoint 2003 enables you to mark a slide with the mouse pointer while delivering a presentation. This feature probably works best if you have a pen input device or a Tablet PC, but the mouse works well enough.

In this context, the term *ink* simply refers to a free-style drawing tool. There are three kinds of ink:

- **Ballpoint pen**—Draws a thin line

- **Felt tip pen**—Draws a medium line

- **Highlighter**—Draws a fat colored bar that appears behind the text and objects

Use either pen to draw shapes or objects—such as circling an important term or number—to draw attention to that information during the presentation. You use the highlighter to actually highlight text and objects.

The pen feature is pretty easy to use. With the slideshow in progress, right-click the background and select Pointer Options from the context menu shown in Figure 6.3. Then, select one of the ink options.

FIGURE 6.3 Use one of these three ink options to mark a slide during a presentation.

If you choose a pen, the cursor becomes a small dot. When you select the highlighter, the cursor becomes a colored bar. When you see either cursor, just click and hold the mouse button while you drag the cursor to mark the slide.

To change the ink color for the current pen, right-click the slide's background, select Pointer Options, select Ink Color, and then select one of nine colors: black, white, red, green, blue, cyan, magenta, yellow, and gray.

Ink markings aren't permanent. To erase an ink mark, right-click the background and select Pointer Options, Eraser. The mouse pointer changes to a small eraser. Click an ink marking to erase it. You can erase all the markings at the same time by right-clicking the background and selecting Pointer Options, Erase All Ink on Slide. When you close the presentation, click Yes to save any markings along with the presentation.

UPGRADERS BEWARE

If you utilize this feature, you'll quickly learn that trying to write with a mouse or trackball is difficult. Most likely you'll use the mouse to emphasize certain points using the highlighter or by circling elements. If you do a lot of public presentations, you can also buy specialized wireless pointing hardware that makes it easier to draw by just moving your hand in the air.

 MORE INFO

If your organization hosts a SharePoint Web site, you can share PowerPoint 2003 presentations with other users via the document workspace. To take advantage of this connectivity feature, you use the Shared Workspace task pane. To learn more about this feature, read Chapter 2.

Smart Tags

Smart tags appeared in most Office applications in either Office XP or Office 2002. They're just now making it into PowerPoint 2003. Smart tags let you do things, such as viewing your Outlook schedule and reading the weather forecast, that you might have previously relied on other programs or Internet services to do for you.

To access smart tag options, select AutoCorrect Options from the Tools menu and then click the Smart Tags tab. The first step is to enable smart tags in the current presentation by checking the Label Text with Smart Tags option shown in Figure 6.4.

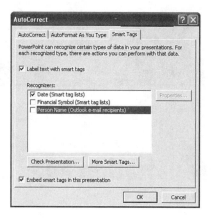

FIGURE 6.4 Enable smart tags in your presentation.

Three smart tags are available by default:

- **Date**—Use this smart tag to link to Microsoft Outlook so you can quickly schedule meetings and view your calendar.

- **Financial Symbol**—This smart tag links to MSN Money (over the Internet) where you can view the most current financial information, such as stock quotes.

- **Person Name**—These tags appear for your Outlook contacts.

 UPGRADERS BEWARE

If you want to save smart tags, be sure to check the Embed Smart Tags in This Presentation option at the bottom of the dialog box. Otherwise, PowerPoint 2003 discards all the smart tags when you close the presentation. If you forget and discard them, click the Check Presentation button the next time you open the presentation to get them back.

Figure 6.5 shows the Date smart tag at work. After enabling this smart tag, enter a date (in a text box) in any slide. PowerPoint 2003 recognizes the date data type and displays the smart tag icon. Click the drop-down list to see the options available.

FIGURE 6.5   The Date smart tag gives you quick access to your Outlook calendar and schedule.

Packaging a Presentation and PowerPoint Viewer

You can run a presentation on a computer other than the one you used to create it. For that reason, PowerPoint helps you copy a presentation to disk or email it. PowerPoint 2003 offers a few enhancements to this capability:

- You can now write your presentation to a CD-ROM.

- You can include the PowerPoint Viewer, which enables you to play a presentation on a system that doesn't have PowerPoint.

- You can instruct the presentation to launch automatically when the CD is inserted.

- You can copy the presentation to a folder for archiving purposes.

- You can include all the linked files and any TrueType fonts the presentation uses.

In addition, PowerPoint 2003 includes the PowerPoint Viewer in case the system you're using to run the presentation doesn't have PowerPoint installed. Previously, the PowerPoint Viewer was available only as a Web download.

Packaging a Presentation

The process of packaging a presentation is simple, but a tad lengthy, and you'll need to choose a number of options. Because the process isn't new, we won't review the entire feature at length, but we will review what's new.

Packaging a Presentation to CD-ROM

To package a presentation to CD-ROM, follow these steps:

1. Open the presentation.

2. Select Package for CD from the File menu to open the Package for CD dialog box. PowerPoint 2003 displays the current presentation's filename in the Files to Be Copied section.

3. Enter a name for the presentation in the Name the CD control, as shown in Figure 6.6.

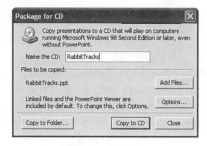

FIGURE 6.6   Name the current presentation package.

4. Click the Options button to display the options shown in Figure 6.7. Select the appropriate options and click OK to return to the previous dialog box.

FIGURE 6.7   These options help you set up a presentation.

5. Enter a password to open and modify the presentation, if required.

6. Click Copy to Folder if you want to create a folder that contains everything you need on your hard drive, a network folder, or to the CD-ROM. When prompted, enter the folder's path, as shown in Figure 6.8, and click OK. PowerPoint 2003 creates the new folder and copies everything you need to it.

FIGURE 6.8   Identify the folder where you want PowerPoint 2003 to copy the presentation.

7. Alternatively, place a CD-ROM in your CD-R or CD-RW drive and click Copy to CD in the Package for CD dialog box. PowerPoint 2003 writes the entire presentation (as determined by your settings) to the CD-ROM.

8. When the first CD is done, PowerPoint 2003 opens the drive and asks whether you want to create another CD. Click Yes or No, accordingly.

Packaging Multiple Presentations to the Same Location

PowerPoint 2003's Package for CD feature lets you package more than one presentation into the same folder or onto the same CD-ROM. To package multiple presentations, click the Add Files button in the Package for CD dialog box (refer to Figure 6.6). In the resulting Add Files dialog box, locate the additional presentation and click Add. The resulting Add Files dialog box is similar to any other Open dialog box. Use the Look In field to locate the presentation, and click Add to return to the Package for CD dialog box.

When you package more than one presentation, the Package for CD dialog box changes to accommodate multiple presentations. Figure 6.9 shows a package that includes two presentations.

FIGURE 6.9   Using PowerPoint 2003, you can package multiple presentations to the same location.

Use the arrows to the left of the presentations list to change their order. This is the order PowerPoint 2003 will refer to when playing the presentations automatically.

Using the PowerPoint Viewer

Use the PowerPoint Viewer to view a presentation when the system you're using doesn't have PowerPoint installed. The new and improved viewer has high-fidelity output and supports PowerPoint graphics, animations, and media.

 UPGRADERS BEWARE

If your presentation was created in PowerPoint 95 or earlier, open it in PowerPoint 2003 and save it. Otherwise, the PowerPoint Viewer won't run it.

 EXPERT ADVICE

The PowerPoint Viewer is freely distributable without any license fee, so there's no reason not to take full advantage of it. Anytime you're not in full control of the presentation environment, package the viewer along with the presentation. Even if the folks in charge of equipment have promised the system will have PowerPoint, there's just no guarantee. Having the viewer on hand might save the show, and the account!

To run the PowerPoint Viewer, do the following:

1. Using Windows Explorer, double-click `pptview.exe` (PowerPoint Viewer).

2. In the Microsoft PowerPoint Viewer dialog box, use the Look In control to locate the presentation.

3. Select the presentation, or enter the name in the File Name control.

4. Click Open to start the presentation.

5. When the show's over, click Cancel to close the Microsoft PowerPoint Viewer dialog box.

 UPGRADERS BEWARE

The PowerPoint Viewer is a great tool, but it has one limitation. It won't display linked and embedded objects and scripting, so be sure that your presentation doesn't contain these things before suggesting the use of the PowerPoint Viewer.

Multimedia Support

Running video and audio clips is more flexible than before. PowerPoint 2003 supports more file types, and the Online Broadcasting feature has a few new options:

- More media support
- New online broadcasting options
- Full-screen playback

Supported Media Formats

PowerPoint has supported video files for a while, but now that support is broader. When Microsoft Windows Media Player version 8 or later is installed, PowerPoint 2003 supports several media formats: ASX, WMX, M3U, WVX, WAX, and WMA in addition to earlier formats such as AVI, MOV, QT, MPG, and MPEG.

New Online Broadcasting Options

Online broadcasting hasn't changed a lot, but you're no longer restricted to the Windows Media Server. Now you can use a third-party Windows Media service provider—but only with a live presentation. This option is available when recording and saving a broadcast on the Broadcast Settings Advanced tab.

Full-Screen Playback

Now you can view a movie using the entire screen while in Slide Show view. In earlier versions, the movie ran in a small rectangle within the slide. To access this option, right-click the movie object, select Edit Movie Object, and check the Zoom to Full Screen option in the Display Option section.

What's New in Access 2003

IN THIS CHAPTER

- The new look and feel
- Productivity
- Enhanced XML support
- Changes to security
- SharePoint integration

At first glance, Access users and developers might not think that many improvements have been made to Access 2003. The core Access database objects—tables, queries, forms, and reports—are largely unchanged from Access 2003. But that doesn't mean the Access team was idle. Rather, they concentrated on improving two major features in this version: XML integration and SharePoint integration. We'll cover these changes, as well as more minor updates, in this chapter.

Changes to the User Interface

Access is more object-orientated than Excel and Word; therefore, Access users might notice that the new look is scattered about more. Despite the way it might appear, there's nothing new in Access 2003 (visually speaking) that isn't visible in the other applications; there are just more opportunities to view the changes:

- A look at the new menus
- The new task panes

The New Menus

Access 2003 has a few menu changes—new commands, moved commands, and missing commands. First, let's review the Office-wide change made to the Search command on the File menu. In Office 2003 applications, that command is now File Search.

In addition, the File menu has a new command, Back Up Database. This feature makes automatically backing up the current database easy. You'll learn more about this feature later in this chapter.

⇨ Read Chapter 4, "What's New in Word 2003," for a more in-depth review of the changes made to the File menu's Search command.

The Edit and Insert menus remain unchanged. The View menu has one new command, Object Dependencies, which you'll learn more about later in this chapter. The Tools on the Web command is missing from the Tools menu. In addition, the Database Utilities submenu also offers the new Back Up Database command.

The Window menu is unchanged, and it's worth noting that Access 2003 doesn't offer the new side-by-side window comparison now offered in a few other Office 2003 applications.

⇨ The Help menu has been substantially changed in all Office 2003 products. Read about these across-the-suite changes in Chapter 2, "Shared Office Features."

The Help menu has several new commands, but one that's unique to just Access is the Access Developer Resources item. Selecting Access Developer Resources from the Help menu launches your default browser and accesses the Access-specific page at the Microsoft Office Developer Resources site (you must have a live online connection for this to work).

The New Task Panes

The New File task pane isn't new, but selecting other task panes from it is. Click the drop-down arrow in the task pane's title bar to quickly access one of the following task panes:

- Getting Started
- Help
- Search Results
- File Search—Replaces Search
- Clipboard
- New File
- Template Help
- Object Dependencies

These task panes provide a centralized place for you to execute common tasks. Display the task pane by selecting Task Pane from the View menu or pressing Ctrl+F1.

The Getting Started task pane is a good place to begin. From this task pane, shown in Figure 7.1, you can check online information, open a recently opened database, or create a new one.

FIGURE 7.1 Use the Getting Started task pane to get the ball rolling.

⇨ Many task panes are shared throughout Office. You can learn more about the Help, Search Result, and Help Template task panes in Chapter 2. You can also read about the Template Help task pane in Chapter 2.

⇨ The new Object Dependencies task pane displays a list of objects that depend on the selected item. To select an item, right-click it in the Database window and select Object Dependencies. This subject is covered in-depth in the next section.

Productivity

Most of the new features in Access 2003 seem to push toward collaboration, but several new or enhanced features will help you work more efficiently.

Viewing Object Dependencies

Changing something as simple as a property setting can have far-reaching and unintended consequences. That's because so many Access objects are bound to another and inherit many of the underlying object's properties.

View an object in the new Object Dependencies task pane, shown in Figure 7.2, to ascertain that object's dependencies *before* you change a property or design feature (that might affect other objects). Almost all objects depend on, or support, another. So you'll probably find this a useful new feature.

FIGURE 7.2   The Object Dependencies task pane shows objects that depend on one another.

As you can see in Figure 7.2, the Employees table (a table in the Northwind sample database that comes with Access) has several dependencies, and those dependent objects are presented in a tree view. The task pane can handle up to four levels of dependencies.

To see an object's ancestors—the objects on which another object depends—click the Objects That I Depend on option at the top of the task pane and Access reverses the picture by showing you any objects on which the selected object depends. Figure 7.3 shows the objects on which the Employees table depends.

This new feature is useful but has a few limitations:

- By default, Access 2003's Track Name AutoCorrect Info feature is enabled. If this option is disabled, you can't view the Object Dependencies task pane. Instead, Access prompts you to change the setting.

- The task pane doesn't display dependencies for union queries or queries that contain subqueries.

- Be sure to save changes before viewing dependencies because the task pane doesn't reflect unsaved changes for an open object.

- Security can interfere. You must have permission to view an object in Design view to view that object's dependencies.

FIGURE 7.3   Display all the objects on which the selected object depends.

 **EXPERT ADVICE**

To disable or enable Track Name AutoCorrect Info, select Tools, Options and click the General tab. Then, check the Track Name AutoCorrect Info option in the Name AutoCorrect section.

Smart Tags

Smart tags aren't new to Office 2003, but they are new to Access 2003. If you use Excel or Word, you're probably already familiar with them.

Technically, a smart tag reacts dynamically to a term. In other words, you can use smart tags to automate tasks you'd normally use another program to do.

Access 2003 comes with a couple of built-in smart tags:

- Error checking flags form and report errors and offer possible solutions.

- Propagating field properties warns you when you attempt to change a property that has dependent objects.

The Error Checking Smart Tag

The new error checking smart tag points out form and report errors and offers possible solutions. This tag recognizes several types of errors:

- **Unassociated Label and Control**—This error occurs when you select an unassociated control and label on a form or report.

- **New Unassociated Labels**—This error occurs when you add an unassociated label to a form or report.

- **Keyboard Shortcut Errors**—This error occurs when you select a form control that has an invalid shortcut key. For instance, an unassociated label can't have a shortcut key.

- **Invalid Control Properties**—This error occurs when you select a control with an invalid property value on a form or report.

- **Common Report Errors**—This error occurs when a report has an invalid sorting and grouping scheme or a group section is wider than the selected paper.

If an object has more than one error, Access 2003 displays the error indicator (the tag icon) until you correct or choose to skip all the errors. To ignore an error, select Ignore Error on the Error Checking Options indicator's drop-down list shown in Figure 7.4. The tag tells you that the label doesn't have an associated control. You can choose to associate it with an existing control or ignore the error.

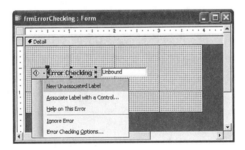

FIGURE 7.4   The error checking smart tag warns you when a problem exists.

 **EXPERT ADVICE**

To turn off error checking, select Tools, Options and then click the new (to 2003) Error Checking tab. Disable the feature by unchecking the Enable Error Checking option. Or, disable individual checks by specifying the appropriate setting in the Form/Report Design Rules options.

The Property Update Options Smart Tag

If you make a change that could affect a dependent object, the Property Update Options smart tag warns you and gives you an opportunity to also change the dependent property. For instance, open the Employees table in Design view, select the CustomerID row, and delete the Input Mask setting. When you attempt to leave the property, Access displays the Property Update Options tag shown in Figure 7.5.

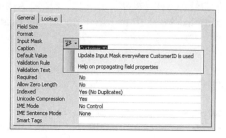

FIGURE 7.5   This smart tag's appearance means you've changed a property that has dependencies.

 UPGRADERS BEWARE

Neither the Object Dependencies task pane nor the Property Update Options smart tag is available in an Access data project (ADP) or data access page (DAP).

 EXPERT ADVICE

Other smart tags are available. In fact, Access 2003 comes with three that you must enable to use. To enable or download other smart tags, open the table or form to which you're adding the smart tag in Design view. Then, click the Builder button to the right of the Smart Tag property field to open the Smart Tags dialog box. Check a smart tag to enable it in the current table. Or, click the More Smart Tags button to find available tags online.

 MORE INFO

If you're interested in developing your own custom Smart Tags, download the Microsoft Office 2003 Smart Tag Software Development Kit (SDK) from `http://www.microsoft.com/ downloads/details.aspx?FamilyID= c6189658-d915-4140-908a-9a0114953721&DisplayLang=en`.

Automatic Backup

Backing up your work used to mean using the Windows Explorer (or some other third-party tool) to make a copy of your database. Access 2003 lets you back up the current database from inside Access.

To back up the current database, select Back Up Database from the File menu (or select Tools, Database Utilities, Back Up Database). Use the resulting Save As Backup dialog box as you would the familiar Save As dialog box. To restore a database, locate the backup file and rename it.

Local Linked Tables

Linked tables are slow because Access has to retrieve data from an external source. Access 2003 lets you work with a local copy of a linked table, which means the data's pulled over and Access 2003 works with the data locally. Consequently, Access 2003 responds more quickly when using that data.

To create a local copy of a linked table, link the table as you normally would. Then, select the linked table in the Database window and select Edit, Copy. Next, select Edit, Paste. In the Paste Table As dialog box, select the Structure and Data (Local Table) option shown in Figure 7.6; then click OK. Remember to update the local table often to ensure you're working with the most current data.

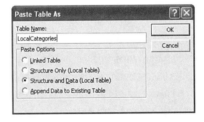

FIGURE 7.6   Create a local linked table.

Sorting Control Lists

The one shortcoming of earlier versions of the combo and list box controls is that you can't sort the list without resorting to Visual Basic for Applications (VBA). Access 2003 includes a wizard that takes the work out of sorting these lists.

To enable this easy sort feature, you must use the control-creating wizards. These wizards are available when you have a form or report open in Design view. Make sure that the Control Wizards button in the Toolbox is toggled on (depressed), and then create a new list box or combo box control to see this feature in action. The wizard's fourth pane, shown in Figure 7.7, presents four sorting levels.

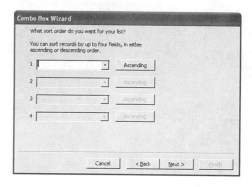

FIGURE 7.7   Sort a control's list.

 **EXPERT ADVICE**

Unfortunately, a property still isn't available that lets you directly specify a sort order. However, if the Row Source is a SELECT statement, you can always add an appropriate ORDER BY clause.

New Service Options

A new button on the Options General tab provides a bit of control for all the new online connectivity that comes with Access 2003. To access these options, select Tools, Options and click the General tab. Then, click the new Service Options button at the bottom. In the resulting pane, select the Online Content item in the Category list to display the new options shown in Figure 7.8. Check the items from Microsoft Office Online that you want to have available within Access.

 **EXPERT ADVICE**

Access 2003's Table Analyzer Wizard fixes some old bugs. If you'd given up on the wizard, try it again. You'll find it more reliable than before.

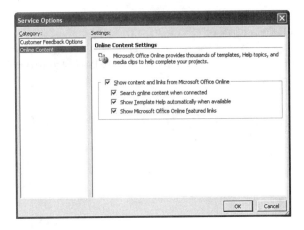

FIGURE 7.8   There are a few new general options.

Enhanced XML Support

XML integration isn't new to Access 2003, but Access 2003 offers much better support for XML than Access 2002 did. Access 2003 lets you export related tables to a single XML file and keeps any relationships and related data intact. Access 2003's XML support includes the following XML standards:

- **XML**—The standard for formatting structured files
- **XSLT**—Lets you change the structure of XML data being imported or exported
- **XML Schemas**—A way to describe a database structure in XML

Exporting and Importing Relationships

Using Access 2003's enhanced XML feature, you can export related data into a single XML file and then reimport that XML file into multiple Access tables with just a few clicks. We'll run through a quick example to illustrate this enhancement:

1. Using Northwind, open the Employees table and select one or more of the employee records. If you want to export the entire table, don't open it; just select it in the Database window. (We'll select Leverling and Peacock for our example.)

2. Select Export from the File menu.

3. Select XML (*.xml) from the Save As Type control's drop-down list, as shown in Figure 7.9.

FIGURE 7.9   Save the data in XML format.

4. Enter a name for the file and click Export All.

5. Click More Options in the resulting dialog box. The Data tab in the resulting Export XML dialog box displays the Employees table and any related tables in a tree view. Figure 7.10 shows that tree view expanded to display even indirect relationships.

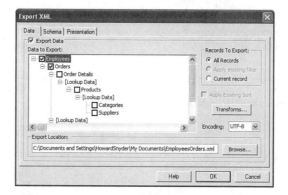

FIGURE 7.10   When exporting to XML, you can select to include related tables.

6. The Employees table is already checked. Check the Orders table, but don't check the Order Details table or any other tables. This selection exports the selected Employees and their related order records.

7. Click the Current Record in the Records to Export section if you selected records in the Employees table. If you don't, Access 2003 exports all the data in the Employees table, instead of just the records you selected.

8. Click OK to export the data.

You can open the XML file in Internet Explorer, but the format won't make much sense to you. Figure 7.11 shows `EmployeesOrders.XML` (the XML file we just exported) in Internet Explorer. If you look closely, you'll see that the file contains only the data for the selected employees (Leverling and Peacock) and their orders. If you exported the entire table, data for all the employees appears in the file. The thing to remember is that one file contains employee data and corresponding related records.

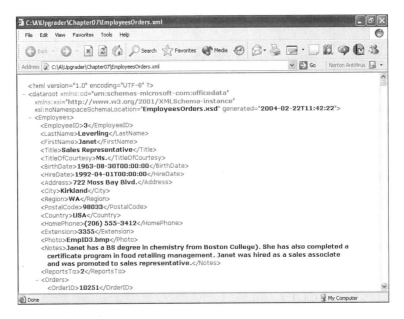

FIGURE 7.11   The XML file doesn't present the data in a readable format.

Now, let's import the XML file with related data back into Access 2003. Here's how to do so:

1. Open a blank database.

2. Select Get External Data from the File menu, and select Import.

3. Select XML (*.xml; *.xsd) from the Files of Type control's drop-down list. Then use the Look in control to locate the XML file you created in the last exercise.

4. Click Import and in the resulting dialog box, click the Options button.

5. Select Structure and Data.

6. Click OK twice to import the data.

Access 2003 creates two tables for the imported data: Employees and Orders. If you selected employee records instead of importing the entire table, these tables contain a subset of the original data, which might not be the subset you expected (see Figure 7.12).

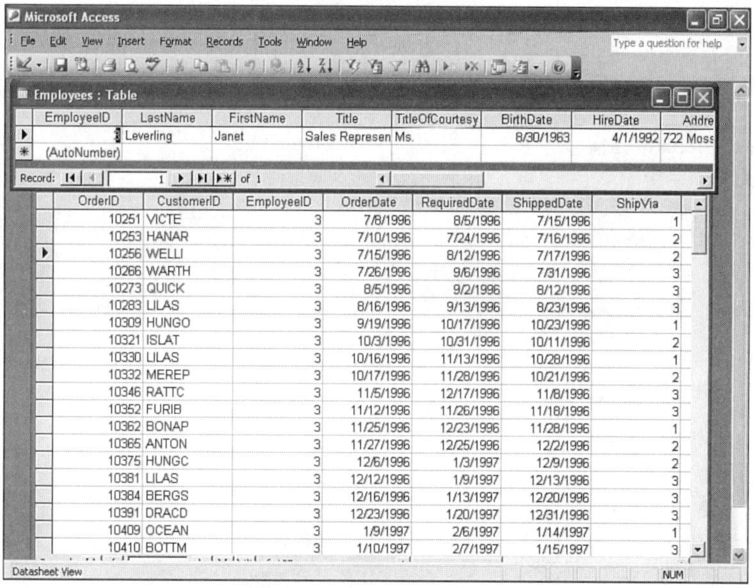

EmployeeID	LastName	FirstName	Title	TitleOfCourtesy	BirthDate	HireDate	Addre
	Leverling	Janet	Sales Represen	Ms.	8/30/1963	4/1/1992	722 Moss
(AutoNumber)							

OrderID	CustomerID	EmployeeID	OrderDate	RequiredDate	ShippedDate	ShipVia
10251	VICTE	3	7/8/1996	8/5/1996	7/15/1996	1
10253	HANAR	3	7/10/1996	7/24/1996	7/16/1996	2
10256	WELLI	3	7/15/1996	8/12/1996	7/17/1996	2
10266	WARTH	3	7/26/1996	9/6/1996	7/31/1996	3
10273	QUICK	3	8/5/1996	9/2/1996	8/12/1996	3
10283	LILAS	3	8/16/1996	9/13/1996	8/23/1996	3
10309	HUNGO	3	9/19/1996	10/17/1996	10/23/1996	1
10321	ISLAT	3	10/3/1996	10/31/1996	10/11/1996	2
10330	LILAS	3	10/16/1996	11/13/1996	10/28/1996	1
10332	MEREP	3	10/17/1996	11/28/1996	10/21/1996	2
10346	RATTC	3	11/5/1996	12/17/1996	11/8/1996	3
10352	FURIB	3	11/12/1996	11/26/1996	11/18/1996	3
10362	BONAP	3	11/25/1996	12/23/1996	11/28/1996	1
10365	ANTON	3	11/27/1996	12/25/1996	12/2/1996	2
10375	HUNGC	3	12/6/1996	1/3/1997	12/9/1996	2
10381	LILAS	3	12/12/1996	1/9/1997	12/13/1996	3
10384	BERGS	3	12/16/1996	1/13/1997	12/20/1996	3
10391	DRACD	3	12/23/1996	1/20/1997	12/31/1996	3
10409	OCEAN	3	1/9/1997	2/6/1997	1/14/1997	1
10410	BOTTM	3	1/10/1997	2/7/1997	1/15/1997	3

FIGURE 7.12 Access 2003 imports related data into multiple tables.

If you remember, we selected two employees—Leverling and Peacock—but only one record made it back into Access. That's because Access 2003 exported only one record: the first record in the selection. To export more than one record, you must apply a filter (using the Apply Existing Filter option). Access 2003 ignored the record for Peacock.

UPGRADERS BEWARE

When importing an XML file that contains related data, Access knows to import that data into separate tables. However, Access doesn't create the actual relationship between the newly imported tables.

Applying Transforms

You can apply *transformation files* to imported and exported XML data to further customize the data. For instance, you might use a transform to limit the XML data you actually import. Or, you might use a transform to export data differently to different recipients.

The first thing you need is an XSL file, which you can create using almost any text editor. The following XSL code limits the employee and order data from the previous exercise:

```
<?xml version="1.0" encoding="UTF-8"?>
<xsl:stylesheet xmlns:xsl="http://www.w3.org/1999/XSL/Transform" version="1.0">
<xsl:output method="html" version="4.0" indent="yes" />

<xsl:template match="dataroot">
        <html>
            <body>
                <table>
                        <xsl:apply-templates select="Employees"/>
                </table>
                <table>
                        <xsl:apply-templates select="Employees/Orders"/>
                </table>
            </body>
        </html>
</xsl:template>

<xsl:template match="Employees">
    <Employee>
            <LastName><xsl:value-of select="LastName"/></LastName>
            <FirstName><xsl:value-of select="FirstName"/></FirstName>
            <Region><xsl:value-of select="Region"/></Region>
    </Employee>
</xsl:template>

<xsl:template match="Employees/Orders">
    <Order>
            <OrderID><xsl:value-of select="OrderID"/></OrderID>
            <CustomerID><xsl:value-of select="CustomerID"/></CustomerID>
            <OrderDate><xsl:value-of select="OrderDate"/></OrderDate>
            <ShipRegion><xsl:value-of select="ShipRegion"/></ShipRegion>
    </Order>
</xsl:template>

</xsl:stylesheet>
```

Specifically, this file, which we named RegionalOrders.XSL, imports only the first and last names and each corresponding region—even if the XML file contains more data. From the order data, the transform imports only the order ID, order date, and shipped region.

 **EXPERT ADVICE**

You can use Notepad to create the accompanying XSL file. Just be sure to select All Files from the Save As Type control in the Save As dialog box, and then enter the XSL extension as part of the file-name.

To import the same XML file as before using the previous transform, do the following:

1. Open an empty database.

2. Select File, Get External Data, Import.

3. Select XML (*.xml; *.xsd) from the Files of Type control's drop-down list and use the Look in control to select RegionalOrders.XML.

4. Click Import.

5. In the resulting Import XML dialog box, click Options to expose a Transform button and the additional options shown in Figure 7.13.

FIGURE 7.13   Add the transform.

6. Click Transform.

7. In the resulting Import Transform dialog box, click Add and use the Look in control to select RegionalOrders.XSL.

8. Click Add to import RegionalOrders.XSL and return to the previous dialog box, which now displays RegionalOrders in the list of available transforms.

9. Select RegionalOrders (it should be selected by default), and then click OK twice. The resulting tables are shown in Figure 7.14. As you can see, the transform limited the data that Access 2003 imported.

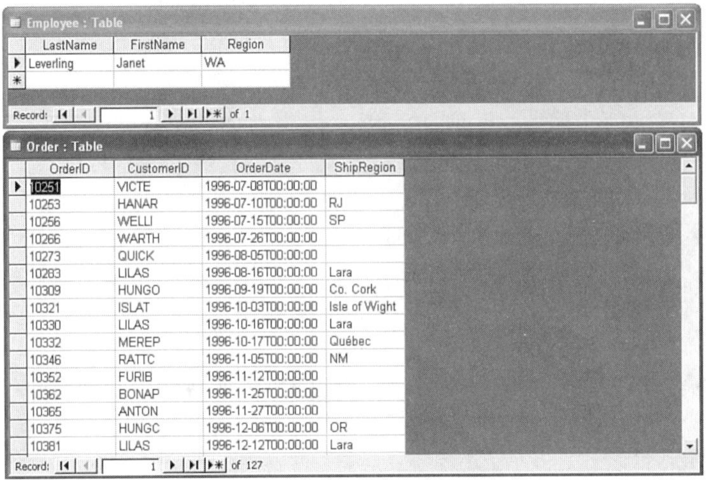
Employee : Table

LastName	FirstName	Region
Leverling	Janet	WA

Record: 1 of 1

Order : Table

OrderID	CustomerID	OrderDate	ShipRegion
10251	VICTE	1996-07-08T00:00:00	
10253	HANAR	1996-07-10T00:00:00	RJ
10256	WELLI	1996-07-15T00:00:00	SP
10266	WARTH	1996-07-26T00:00:00	
10273	QUICK	1996-08-05T00:00:00	
10283	LILAS	1996-08-16T00:00:00	Lara
10309	HUNGO	1996-09-19T00:00:00	Co. Cork
10321	ISLAT	1996-10-03T00:00:00	Isle of Wight
10330	LILAS	1996-10-16T00:00:00	Lara
10332	MEREP	1996-10-17T00:00:00	Québec
10346	RATTC	1996-11-05T00:00:00	NM
10352	FURIB	1996-11-12T00:00:00	
10362	BONAP	1996-11-25T00:00:00	
10365	ANTON	1996-11-27T00:00:00	
10375	HUNGC	1996-12-06T00:00:00	OR
10381	LILAS	1996-12-12T00:00:00	Lara

Record: 1 of 127

FIGURE 7.14 The transform limits the data Access 2003 imports from the XML file.

You can also limit the data that's exported using a transform. We'll use the same specifications as the last example and transform the data directly into HTML using the following code:

```
<?xml version="1.0" encoding="UTF-8"?>
<xsl:stylesheet xmlns:xsl="http://www.w3.org/1999/XSL/Transform" version="1.0">
<xsl:output method="html" version="4.0" indent="yes" />

<xsl:template match="dataroot">
      <html>
            <body>
                  <table border="1">
                        <xsl:apply-templates select="Employees"/>
                  </table>
            </body>
      </html>
</xsl:template>

<xsl:template match="Employees">
   <tr>
         <td><b><xsl:value-of select="FirstName"/></b></td>
         <td><b><xsl:value-of select="LastName"/></b></td>
         <td><b><xsl:value-of select="Region"/></b></td>
  </tr>
  <tr>
```

```
            <td colspan="3">
                <table cellpadding="5">
                    <tr>
                 <td>Order ID</td>
                 <td>Order Date</td>
                    </tr>
                    <xsl:apply-templates select="Orders"/>
                </table>
            </td>
    </tr>
</xsl:template>

<xsl:template match="Orders">
    <tr>
            <td><xsl:value-of select="OrderID"/></td>
            <td><xsl:value-of select="OrderDate"/></td>
            <td><xsl:value-of select="ShipRegion"/></td>
    </tr>
</xsl:template>
</xsl:stylesheet>
```

We named the previous XSL file `RegionalOrdersExport.XSL`. To apply the transform, follow these steps:

1. Open Northwind, open the Employees table, and select an employee. Or, just select the table in the Database window.

2. Select Export from the File menu.

3. Select XML from the Save As Type control's drop-down list, enter a name for the new XML file, and click Export All.

4. Click More Options.

5. On the Data tab, check the Orders table, click the Current Record option, and then click Transforms.

6. Click Add and use the Look in control to locate `RegionalOrdersExport.XSL`.

7. Select `RegionalOrdersExport.XSL` and click Add to return to the Export Transforms dialog box.

8. Click OK to return to the Export XML dialog box.

9. Replace the XML file's default name, using the HTML extension—we'll use `RegionalOrders.HTML`, as shown in Figure 7.15.

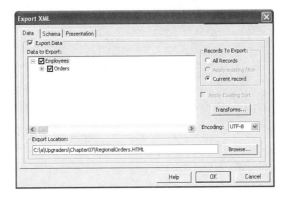

FIGURE 7.15   Create an HTML file.

10. Click OK. (You must explicitly specify the HTML extension.) Figure 7.16 shows the exported HTML file in Internet Explorer.

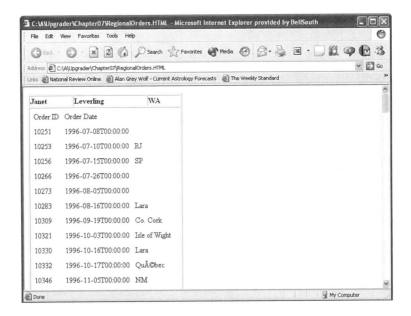

FIGURE 7.16   The exported data is browser-ready.

EXPERT ADVICE

ReportML is an XML dialect that describes the structure of a form, report, or data access page, including events and properties. ReportML uses Access-specific tags to specify the properties and inserts the actual setting within the tag. A transform converts the XML file into HTML, which is never an exact replica of the original report.

Changes to Security

One of the first changes you'll probably notice when you start working with Access 2003 is the macro security warning dialog box. It's shown in Figure 7.17 and appears if the database (or project) you're opening contains unsafe macros or Visual Basic for Applications (VBA) code.

FIGURE 7.17   Access joins other Office applications by securing macro and code bearing files.

EXPERT ADVICE

Depending on the last service pack installed on your system, you might see another warning regarding unsafe expressions. To avoid seeing this message each time you open a database created with an earlier version of Access, download Microsoft Jet 4.0 Service Pack 8 from
`http://v4.windowsupdate.microsoft.com/en/default.asp`.

You're probably wondering what *unsafe* means. According to Microsoft, unsafe expressions contain methods or functions that could be exploited by malicious users to access your system's files and resources.

SharePoint Integration

The capability to collaborate with a SharePoint site was added to Access 2002, but that feature has been improved for Access 2003:

- You can export Access data to a SharePoint list.
- You can import SharePoint data into Access.
- You can link SharePoint data to Access.

Exporting a Table or Query to a SharePoint List

Exporting a table or query to a SharePoint list creates a static list—there's no connection between the list and Jet or SQL Server. It's a one-time effort that you have to repeat if you need to update the list from an existing Access or SQL Server table. To export data to a SharePoint list, do the following:

1. Select the table or query in the Database window and select Export from the File menu. (Or, right-click and select Export.)

2. Select Windows SharePoint Services() in the Save As Type control to launch the Export to Windows SharePoint Services Wizard.

3. Enter the URL (on the SharePoint site) where you want to export the data, as shown in Figure 7.18. Enter a list name and description if you don't want to use the table or query's name and description.

FIGURE 7.18   Tell SharePoint where to publish the list.

4. Click Finish. Figure 7.19 shows the exported SharePoint list.

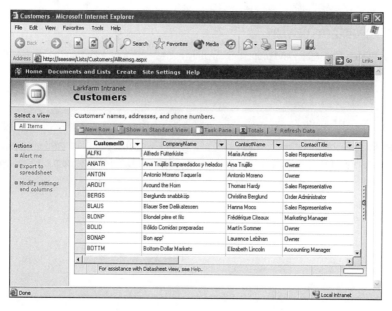

FIGURE 7.19   Export Access data to SharePoint.

Importing SharePoint Data into Access

Importing SharePoint data into Access requires a few more clicks, but it is still very easy. To import SharePoint data into Access, do the following:

1. In your database, select Get External Data from the File menu and then select Import.

2. Select Windows SharePoint Services() from the Files of Type control's drop-down list to launch the Import from Windows SharePoint Services Wizard.

3. Enter the URL (the SharePoint site) where the data currently resides, and click Next.

4. Select between importing a list or a view.

5. If the list contains a lookup column, specify whether the imported data should contain the displayed data or the stored data.

6. If you retrieve the stored values, you must specify whether you want to create linked or imported tables.

7. Click Finish to import the SharePoint data into Access.

UPGRADERS BEWARE

Review the resulting tables and properties carefully. Access assumes a lot about the imported data. Make sure those assumptions meet your needs before using the data.

 EXPERT ADVICE

Linked data lets you store the data in SharePoint and work with that data from inside Access. Use the same process to link as you use to import, except select Get External Data from the File menu and then select Linked Tables (instead of Import) .

What's New in FrontPage 2003

FrontPage 2003 is no longer part of any Office suite, but it shares common Office components and paradigms. For that reason, FrontPage 2003 is a good choice for the Web developer who is already steeped in Microsoft technology. Also, because FrontPage was a part of previous versions of Office 2003, many Office users will already be maintaining their Web sites with FrontPage. That's why we're devoting an entire chapter to a product that's really not part of the suite anymore—you might decide to upgrade separately from Office 2003.

Changes to the User Interface

FrontPage 2003 has probably received the most comprehensive makeover of all the applications. There are a number of new features and enhancements. We'll review the most relevant and productive of these, beginning with the interface changes.

- New and rearranged menu items
- New task panes
- New views of your Web site
- New toolbars

The New Menus

FrontPage 2003 has more menus than any of the Office applications, which equates to a lot of changes in this upgrade. Beginning with the File menu, there are four renamed items. For starters, the word *site* is used consistently instead of *Web*, so Open Site, Close Site, and Recent Sites replace Open Web, Close Web, and Recent Webs, respectively. Similar to the other applications, File Search replaces the Search command.

Read Chapter 2, "Shared Office Features," to learn more about the changes made to the File menu's Search command.

The Preview in Browser item isn't new to the File menu, but instead of displaying a dialog box, it now displays a submenu of resolution choices, as shown in Figure 8.1. The Import item isn't new, nor is importing a Web site, but the Import Web Site Wizard is new and provides a number of new options for making the import process less troublesome. Select Import from the File menu and then click Import Site in the resulting Import dialog box to launch the new Import Wizard.

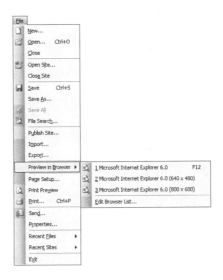

FIGURE 8.1   The Preview in Browser menu lets you choose a preview resolution.

The Edit menu has five new items: Go to Bookmark, Go to Function, Quick Tag Editor, Code View, and Intellisense. You'll learn about the last three in other sections of this chapter.

The View menu also has several new items:

- **Remote Web Site**—Displays a remote Web site next to the local version
- **Ruler and Grid**—Displays rulers and grid points in Design view
- **Tracing Image**—Lets you use an artistic mock-up of your Web site as a visual guide
- **Quick Tag Selector**—Provides a new toolbar at the top of the document window that's available in Code, Design, and Split views
- **Page Size**—Lets you view a page in a variety of resolution setups

Three items have been removed from the View menu: the Views Bar, Folder List, and Navigation pane. Other than these rearrangements of the user interface, there are no significant changes to the View menu for 2003.

The Insert menu has two new items: Layer and Interactive Button. Use layers to hold page elements when overlapping, nesting, and showing or hiding elements. The new Interactive Button feature replaces the Hover Button of prior versions.

The Format menu loses the Dynamic HTML Effects item but gains three new items: Behaviors, Layers, and Dynamic Web Templates. The Behaviors and Layers items open their respective new task panes.

Dynamic Web templates are new to FrontPage 2003. Select the Format, Dynamic Web Template menu to work with a dynamic template. The Theme and Style items aren't new, but now these items open their respective task panes instead of displaying a dialog box.

Look for five new items on the Tools menu:

- **Accessibility**—Checks your Web site for accessibility compliance.

- **Browser Compatibility**—Checks your site or a page for specific browser compatibility.

- **Optimize HTML**—Cleans up your HTML code.

- **Packages**—Provides predesigned and packaged Web site solutions as a starting place—much the same way a template helps you build a page. (Available only with SharePoint Services.)

- **Save Web Part to**—On a SharePoint-enabled site, allows you to save a Web Part to a file or to the gallery of available Web Parts.

In addition, Tools on the Web is gone and Site Settings replaces Web Settings on the Tools menu.

The Table menu offers two new supporting items: Layout Tables and Cells, and Cell Formatting. The former opens the new Layout Tables and Cells task pane. Use the Cell Formatting item to display the Cell Formatting task pane when you need to format table cells.

The entire Data menu is new, with 12 new items, as shown in Figure 8.2. We'll review the new data source features later in this chapter.

The Frames menu remains unchanged, but the Windows command has two new items: Open in New Window and Close All Pages, which are both fairly self-explanatory.

⇨ Like all the Office applications, FrontPage 2003's Help menu has had a major makeover. Read about the changes to the Help menu in Chapter 2.

FIGURE 8.2   The entire Data menu is new.

The New Task Panes

Most of FrontPage 2003's new task panes are associated with new features. You'll learn more about the feature-specific task panes throughout this chapter. For now, we'll just list them:

- **Layout Tables and Cells**—This lets you insert dynamic tables. Select Layout Tables and Cells from the Table menu.

- **Cell Formatting**—This is a subpane of the Layout Tables and Cells used for formatting individual or groups of cells. Select Cell Formatting from the Table menu.

- **Theme**—Themes aren't new, but the Theme task pane is. Select Theme from the Insert menu.

- **Layers**—These are tags used to create elements that occupy the same space. Select Layer from the Insert menu.

- **Behaviors**—These let you insert and manipulate behaviors from one spot. Select Behaviors from the Insert menu.

- **Data Source Catalog**—This displays your site's data sources. Select Insert Data View from the Data menu.

- **Find a Data Source**—This lets you connect to a data source to publish live data on your site.

- **Data View Details**—This displays the actual data from a data source, before you insert it into a page. Select a data source in the Data Source Catalog task pane and then select Show Data.

- **Conditional Formatting**—These are format values in a Data View component based on specific conditions. Select Conditional Formatting from the Data View Options menu.

- **Web Parts**—These are XML-driven data access components for supporting interactive data. Select Insert Data View from the Data menu.

Several task panes are new to all or some of the Office 2003 applications. Read Chapter 2 for more information on the following new task panes: Getting Started, Help, Search Results, and Clip Art.

Two New Views

FrontPage is a design tool and, as such, FrontPage 2003 has several new views that help you work more efficiently and logically. The Views Bar to the left is gone, freeing up a lot of space for design work, as you can see in Figure 8.3.

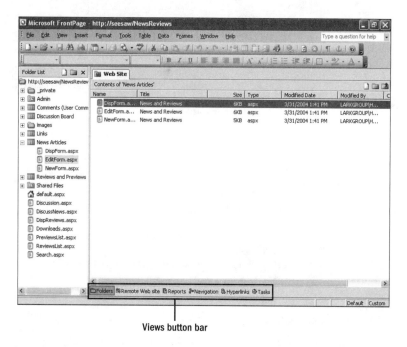

Views button bar

FIGURE 8.3 The Views button bar offers context-sensitive navigation.

As a result of this change, there's no common interface tool for accessing all the views. Site-specific views—Folders, Remote Web Site, Reports, Navigation, Hyperlinks, and Tasks—are still available via the button bar at the bottom of the screen. Not all views are available all of the time—context-sensitive views are available as you work.

Split View

Split view, shown in Figure 8.4, divides the screen between the Design and Code views. Consequently, you can see how code changes affect the overall design (or how design changes affect the HTML code) almost instantly. Any change made in one pane is reflected in the other. We'll work in this view almost extensively throughout this chapter, so you'll have plenty of time to get used to it.

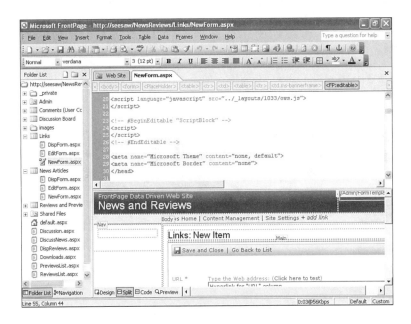

FIGURE 8.4   Split view allows you to view both code and design for a page.

Remote Web Site View

The Remote Web Site view is a new Folders view that displays your site next to the remote Web site, enabling you to compare the two sites side-by-side.

 UPGRADERS BEWARE

Before you can publish your Web site, you must specify a remote Web server type and a remote Web site location. You might need to contact your Web administrator or your Internet service provider (ISP) for the exact URL.

Two New Toolbars

Two new toolbars—Code View and XML View—are available. Figures 8.5 and 8.6 show the two new toolbars. Select Toolbars from the View menu to access either. Missing from the list of toolbars are the Navigation and Reporting toolbars.

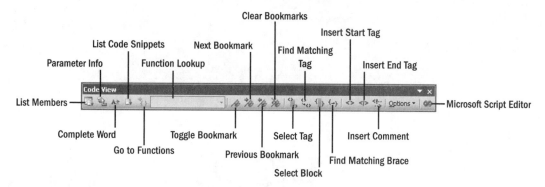

FIGURE 8.5   The Code View toolbar is new to FrontPage 2003.

FIGURE 8.6   The XML View toolbar is also new.

Introducing Scripting Behaviors

Behaviors are snippets of Jscript code that perform predefined tasks. They're ready to go and you just drop them right into your code. We could devote an entire chapter or two to just behaviors because they do so many things for you, from calling another script to configuring a complex element.

To take a quick peek, select Behaviors from the Format menu. Initially, the Behaviors task pane is empty because there are no behaviors. Click the Insert button to display the 16 behavior options shown in Figure 8.7.

 **EXPERT ADVICE**

Anytime you need to display a task pane, you can press Ctrl+F1 and then use the Other Task Pane control (the drop-down arrow at the top of the window) to access the exact task pane you want.

FIGURE 8.7   Work with behaviors via the new Behaviors task pane.

Selecting Popup Message displays a dialog box, where you'll insert a message, similar to Figure 8.8. When you're done, click OK. Figure 8.9 shows the message in the current page view (which happens to be Split view) and the task pane.

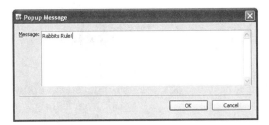

FIGURE 8.8   Enter a message into the Popup Message dialog box.

Curious about just what that behavior does? Click the Show Preview View button on the Buttons bar at the bottom of the screen to simulate loading the page. When you do, FrontPage 2003 displays the message shown in Figure 8.10. Click OK to clear the message and return to Split view.

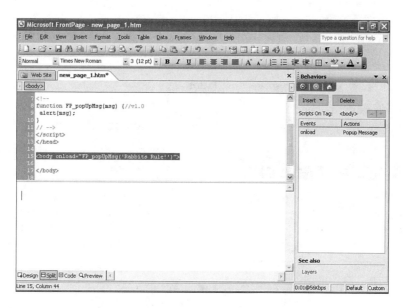

FIGURE 8.9   The new behavior is accessible via the task pane or Split or Code view.

FIGURE 8.10   Loading the page automatically displays this message.

 **MORE INFO**

FrontPage 2003 uses events and actions to implement behaviors. You can learn more about these events at `http://msdndhtml.frontpagelink.com`. Click the DHTML Reference and then click DHTML Events for the details.

Better Design and Graphic Tools

FrontPage 2003 offers a number of design and graphic features and enhancements that make working with just the right element easier:

- Layout tables and cells

- Dynamic Web templates

- Browser and resolution reconciliation

- Accessibility checking

Layout Tables and Cells

FrontPage 2003 introduces two new concepts: the layout table and the layout cell. Don't confuse layout tables and cells with the traditional multicelled table that organizes content. *Layout tables* are exactly what they sound like—tables that let you control the layout of a page. Everything on your page is arranged by the table. On the other hand, a traditional table is just one element, of perhaps many on the same page.

The layout table is the page framework, whereas the *layout cells* represent the individual regions that actually contain the content. Figure 8.11 shows one of the predesigned layout tables. You don't have to start from scratch. In fact, unless you have some very specific and unique requirements, you might never need to create a layout table from scratch.

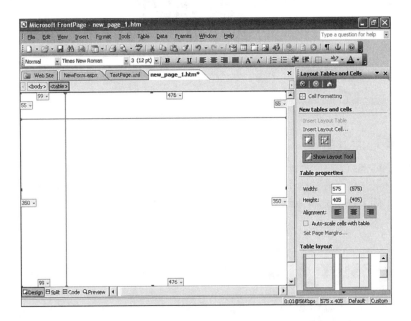

FIGURE 8.11 Use an existing layout table design.

Like most new features, FrontPage 2003 offers a task pane that makes working with these tables incredibly easy and intuitive. To display the Layout Tables and Cells task pane, select Table, Layout Tables and Cells.

The task pane has three sections. The first section, New Tables and Cells, offers links and tools for inserting a new layout table or layout cell. If you prefer to draw the table or cell yourself, click the Draw Layout Table or Draw Layout Cell button, respectively.

To learn the basics of using layout tables and layout cells, complete the following steps to begin creating the simple page shown in Figure 8.12:

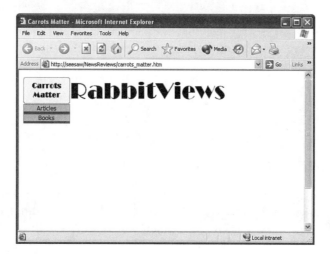

FIGURE 8.12   This page is based on a layout table.

1. Create a new blank page by clicking the New Normal Page button on the toolbar.

2. In Design or Split view, select Table, Layout Tables and Cells.

3. Click the third predesigned layout table in the Layout Tables section to insert a layout table.

4. Select any font and size you like on the Formatting toolbar and enter the text as shown in the upper-right section.

5. Select the upper-left corner of the page, and click the Cell Formatting link in the Layout Tables and Cells task pane to display the Cell Formatting task pane, which is shown in Figure 8.13.

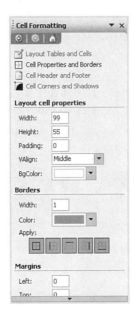

FIGURE 8.13   The Cell Formatting task pane lets you apply a format to a specific cell.

6. Select a color and border color—we selected yellow and hot pink, respectively. Then, click the four-cornered option, the first option in the Apply settings, to set the cell's color and border color. Click the Center alignment toolbar button, and select a font and size from the toolbar. Type `Carrots Matter` into the layout cell.

7. Click the Cell Corners and Shadows link in the Cell Formatting task pane. This displays a different set of choices inside the task pane. Select the default image, set the width and height to 10, and apply it to all four corners. The results are shown in Show Preview view in Figure 8.14.

8. Click the Save button to save this page.

With very little effort, you created a Web page with four distinct sections, a title, and one graphic element. Adding a layout cell let you easily and quickly customize the corner area. Layout tables and layout cells are both flexible and powerful, and this section barely scratches the surface.

For more in-depth information on this or any other topic on FrontPage 2003, check out *Special Edition Using Microsoft Office FrontPage 2003* (ISBN: 0-7897-2954-7), also published by Que.

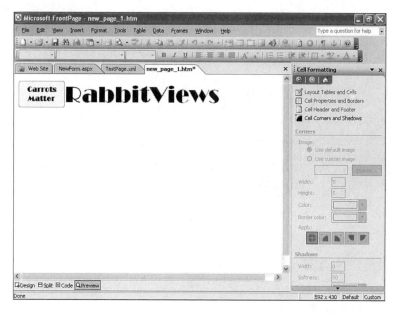

FIGURE 8.14 Add corners to the layout table.

Interactive Buttons

In the last section you started a simple page using one of the predesigned layout tables. Now, let's insert two interactive buttons into the layout cell and give them a task. Interactive buttons replace Hover buttons from earlier versions:

1. In Design or Split view, select the layout table section on the left, and select Interactive Button from the Insert menu.

2. Click the Button tab (the default) and select an item from the Buttons list.

3. Type **Articles** in the Text control and **ArticlesList.htm** in the Link control, as shown in Figure 8.15. Then click OK.

4. Repeat step 3 to add a second button using the text **Books** and the link **BooksList.htm**. (Refer to Figure 8.12 for the complete page.)

Clicking either button in Show Preview view returns an error because neither of the linked pages exists right now. In a real site, these two links would access pages that display a list of articles and books, respectively.

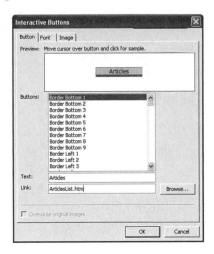

FIGURE 8.15   Select an interactive button.

Dynamic Web Templates

Templates aren't new to FrontPage 2003, but Dynamic Web Templates (.dwt files) are. These templates allow you to create any number of HTML pages that all share the same layout, with an exciting capability—you can edit the resulting page.

You decide which regions can be edited and which regions are protected. Content entered in an editable region can be changed; anything entered directly into the page can't. By doing so, you provide areas for others to add and edit content while maintaining the basic layout design from page to page. The result is a site of consistent design and layout components, with editable regions for entering unique content. If you change the template, you can propagate those changes to any linked template.

Dynamic Web Templates are useful when many people collaborate on the same site. Perhaps a designer controls the basic design, but others update content without changing layout.

Previously, you created a simple page with a few basic elements, which could easily serve as a Dynamic Web Template. To create a template from an existing page, simply select Save As from the File menu and select Dynamic Web Template (*.dwt) from the Save As Type control; then click Save. Name the new Dynamic Web Template **CarrotsMatter.dwt**. (You can also start with a blank HTML page. You don't have to work with a page in progress.)

The next step is to add an editable region. In this case, make the larger body section editable by right-clicking it and selecting Manage Editable Regions. Name the region, as shown in Figure 8.16, and click Add. Click Close to dismiss the dialog box and then close the new template page.

FIGURE 8.16 Name the editable region.

To illustrate using the Dynamic Web Template, open a new blank page and name it **ArticlesList**. Select Format, Dynamic Web Template, Attach Dynamic Web Template. Locate the Dynamic Web Template—CarrotsMatter.dwt in this case—using the Look in control, and then click Open. Click Close to confirm the update message.

FrontPage 2003 applies the template and displays the editable region. You can try editing the other areas of the page, but FrontPage 2003 won't let you change anything but the content in the list region.

Add content to the editable region by clicking inside the region and entering content. Figure 8.17 shows some content centered in the editable region, and with a font and size applied. Figure 8.18 shows the new page in Show Preview Mode. Clicking the Articles button accesses this new page, which you quickly created using a Dynamic Web Template that contained all the site's common layout elements.

Adding the content the way we just did probably isn't the way you'll typically approach the problem, but it is the quickest. Most likely, you'll add content and elements to editable regions, which the page author can then decide to publish or replace.

At this point, the new site doesn't have a home page or a page that lists books, so it's incomplete at best. Nor do we mean to suggest that the process used is the best or only way to create pages. Rather, this section was a simple example of applying a Dynamic Web Template to a page.

Browser and Resolution Reconciliation

One of the biggest challenges you'll face if you design sites for the public is compatibility. There are several browsers in use, and they don't speak the same language. FrontPage 2003 lets you test your site in various browsers and resolutions without changing a single setting.

You can even preview the site in multiple browsers simultaneously for the most accurate comparison possible.

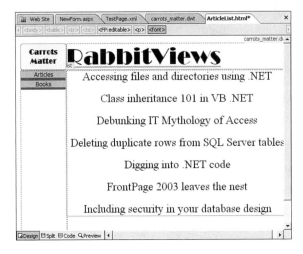

FIGURE 8.17   Edit the body region.

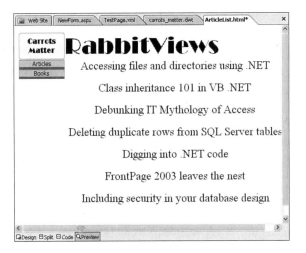

FIGURE 8.18   The new page has custom content.

To target a specific browser size, select Page Size from the View menu and then select the target browser size. If the target is smaller than the available space, FrontPage 2003 adds gray borders and displays a dotted line to indicate where the first screen ends.

Previewing the site in a specific browser is just as easy. Select Preview in Browser from the File menu. Then, select the target browser. Or, select several browsers for a simultaneous view.

 UPGRADERS BEWARE

By default, FrontPage 2003 works only with Internet Explorer. You have to install other browsers yourself. Select Preview in Browser from the File menu and select Edit Browser List. In the resulting dialog box, point to the browser's executable file.

Accessibility Checking

Accessibility compliance has never been easier. When you're ready, let FrontPage 2003 guide you to the most accessible site possible. From the Tools menu, select Accessibility. Then, click the appropriate options, and click Check. Use the returned suggestions, shown in Figure 8.19, to increase your site's accessibility. Click Generate HTML Report to save the suggestions to an HTML page.

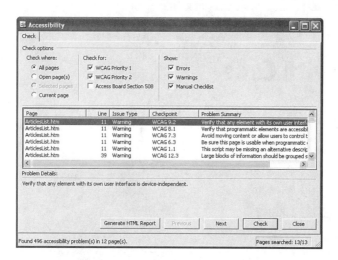

FIGURE 8.19   Work from the suggestions to ensure that your site meets the standards.

Other Layout Tools

The following are other new tools in FrontPage 2003 you'll want to explore:

- **Layers**—These work with multiple pieces of content that occupy the same space. Select Layer from the Insert menu to access this new option.

- **Positioning guides**—You can turn on guides such as Rules and a Background Layout Grid by selecting Ruler and Grid from the View menu. Then, select Show Grid or Show Ruler. This feature is especially helpful when you're trying to precisely position elements on a page.

- **Image Tracing**—This lets you work from a picture of your site. To apply Image Tracing, select View, Tracing Image, Configure. Enter the name of the picture file you want to trace. Use the Opacity slider control to adjust the image's transparency as required.

- **Cascading Style Sheets**—FrontPage 2003 uses CSS instead of HTML to apply themes. The files are smaller and easier to work with. (HTML themes still work in FrontPage 2003.)

- **Smart tags**—These keep you well-informed when importing graphics. Alter an imported graphic and then view the resulting smart tags for behavior and default specifics.

- **Editors**—Select the right editor for the content. To do so, select Options from the Tools menu and then click the Configure Editors tab for more options.

- **Macromedia Flash**—You can add content with a simple drag and drop. Select Picture from the Insert menu and then click Flash.

Working with Code

FrontPage 2003 is flexible enough to let you do most of your design work in Design view. However, some of you are more comfortable working directly with the code, and FrontPage 2003 has added many new features just for you. Use the following features to generate more efficient code:

- Quick Tag Selector
- Quick Tag Editor
- Optimize HTML

Quick Tag Selector and Editor

Use the new Quick Tag Selector to grab those hard-to-reach elements, such as nested tables. Simply click a tag to highlight the associated elements in Design view. In Code view, you see the highlighted code, whereas in Design view, the Quick Tag Selector is just below the page tab, shown in Figure 8.20.

Quick Tag Selector

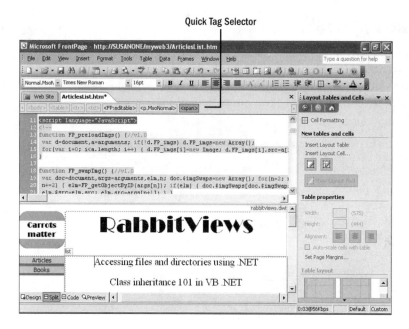

FIGURE 8.20 Quickly select elements.

To edit a tag, select it in Design or Code view. Open the Quick Tag Selector's drop-down list shown in Figure 8.21 and select Edit Tag to open the Quick Tag Editor toolbar shown in Figure 8.22. Use this new toolbar to modify the active tag. When you're done, click the green check mark to accept your changes or click the red X to cancel them. Either way, FrontPage 2003 closes the Quick Tag Editor toolbar.

FIGURE 8.21 Quickly edit a tag.

FIGURE 8.22 Use the Quick Tag Editor toolbar to edit a tag.

Optimizing HTML

Code can get ugly quick. Cleaning things up makes the code more readable and efficient. To optimize local HTML, select Optimize HTML from the Tools menu and then check the elements you want removed during the cleanup process. As you can see in Figure 8.23, FrontPage 2003 removes white space, nonessential tags, comments, and vector graphics.

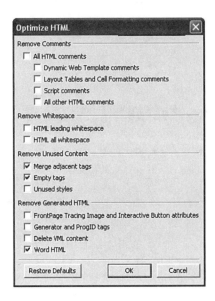

FIGURE 8.23   Clean up your code.

FrontPage 2003 extends this capability to your remote site. To enable this process, select Optimize Remote HTML from the Remote Web Site view. In the resulting dialog box, check the elements you want removed.

 **EXPERT ADVICE**

You don't have to remember to clean up the code every time you update the site. Check the Set As Default option in the Optimize Remote HTML settings and FrontPage 2003 will automatically optimize HTML every time the site is published.

Other New Coding Perks

Here are several other coding enhancements you'll want to try:

- Use Find and Replace to search HTML code for attributes or tags.

- Edit text files, such as JavaScript, XML, XSLT, and so on, in FrontPage 2003's editor.

- Let FrontPage 2003 write your code. Use IntelliSense for HTML, CSS, XSL, Jscript, VBScript, JavaScript, and ASP.NET. Enter the opening tag symbol (<) to display the AutoComplete drop-down menu. Select a tag and press the spacebar to insert the tag into your code.

SharePoint Services Integration

Collaboration is the buzzword throughout Office 2003, and FrontPage 2003 follows that trend. FrontPage 2003, Windows Server 2003, and Windows SharePoint Services create a powerful and flexible mix for integrating XML (and other) data into your Web site's content. Using these applications, you can integrate data through a variety of tools:

- Web Parts
- Data view
- XML
- Web package templates

Data Source View and Web Parts

Web Parts are FrontPage 2003's answer to publishing dynamic data. Specifically, Web Parts are XML-driven data access components. You might think of them as a complex data query. A page can have multiple Web Parts and those components can communicate and share data with one another.

 UPGRADERS BEWARE

Right now, Web Parts are still fairly limited because they're available only on SharePoint Services and SharePoint Services requires Windows Server 2003. In addition, SharePoint Services supports only one database, and that's Microsoft SQL Server (although you can use MSDE if the load on your SharePoint server is low).

The easiest way to experiment with SharePoint technologies in FrontPage is to start with a new SharePoint team site. Follow these steps to create a new SharePoint-backed site:

1. Select File, New.
2. In the New task pane, click the SharePoint Team Site hyperlink.
3. In the Web Site Templates dialog box, select the SharePoint Services tab.

4. Enter the base URL of your SharePoint server in the Specify the location of the new Web site text box and press Tab to retrieve the list of templates from the SharePoint server. Figure 8.24 shows the basic list of templates available on a Windows SharePoint Services server.

5. Select the Blank Site template and click OK.

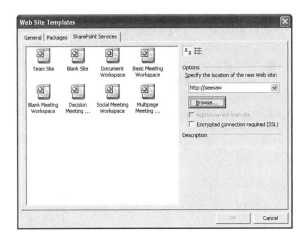

FIGURE 8.24   Creating a SharePoint-backed Web site.

Perhaps the best place to learn about Web Parts is the Data Source Catalog task pane, which is also new to FrontPage 2003. To display this task pane, select Insert Data View from the Data menu. Use the task pane to insert a Data view in a new, blank page on the Web site. Create a new page in the site and save it as `Data.aspx`.

Because a Data view populates a Web page dynamically, it's probably the most commonly used Web Part. The available data sources are as follows:

- **SharePoint Services lists**—Can contain any type of information. For example, you could store your customer list as a list in SharePoint and then display it on a Web page.

- **SharePoint Services libraries**—A collection of documents or pictures.

- **Database connections**—A configurable database connection. SQL Server and Oracle are available via the interface. You'll need connection strings to connect to other OLE DB–compliant data sources.

- **XML files**—Any XML files.

- **Server-side scripts**—Any server-side script data source, such as ASP.NET or ASP.

- **XML Web Services**—Any XML Web Service with a valid reference.

Initially, there's no data source. To initiate a connection, expand the appropriate data source link (for example, Database Connections) and click the Add to Catalog link. Doing so displays the Data Source Properties dialog box, which should be mostly empty at this point. Click the Configure Database Connection button to launch the Configure Database Connection Wizard. Enter the server name, select a security method, and enter a username and password, if required. Click Next when you're ready to continue. The wizard doesn't let you continue if the connection information you provide isn't correct, so it's difficult for a mistake to make it to the actual configuration properties.

Identify the database to which you're connecting by selecting it from the Database control's drop-down list. The Table, View, or Stored Procedure list updates accordingly. Select an item from this list or click the Use Custom Query option, shown in Figure 8.25; then click Finish.

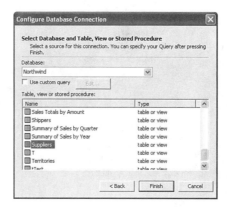

FIGURE 8.25   Identify the data source.

The resulting Data Source Properties dialog box displays the appropriate configuration settings, as shown in Figure 8.26.

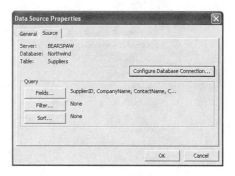

FIGURE 8.26   The Data Source Properties dialog box displays data source information.

Click OK to add the new connection to the Data Source Catalog, as shown in Figure 8.27. Click the data source to display options for working with the new data (see Figure 8.28).

FIGURE 8.27   The Data Source Catalog task pane displays the new connection.

FIGURE 8.28   Use the data source menu to access the data.

After creating the data source, select Insert Data View from the data source's drop-down menu. This inserts a table containing the specified data on the current page. It also displays the Manage View Settings list in the Data View Details task pane, as shown in Figure 8.29. This provides you with a handy way to work with live data directly in your FrontPage Web site.

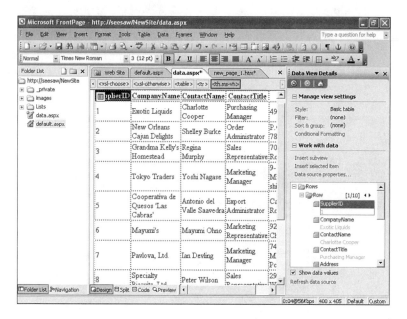

FIGURE 8.29 Inserting a data view in a Web page.

Displaying XML

XML originated as a data-sharing technology for Web developers. FrontPage 2003 lets you access XML files similarly to the other Office 2003 applications, but you use Web Parts to interact with those files because FrontPage 2003 treats XML data as a data source.

 UPGRADERS BEWARE

Your site must be hosted on a server running Windows SharePoint Services to work with XML data in FrontPage 2003.

Inserting XML data on a Web page in FrontPage 2003 is similar to inserting any other kind of data. The XML data needs to be stored on the SharePoint server; for this exercise, we exported a copy of the Customers table from the Access 2003 Northwind sample database to a file on our SharePoint server. To display this data in FrontPage, follow these steps:

1. In the Data Source Catalog task pane, expand the XML files node and click Add to Catalog.

2. In the Data Source Properties dialog box, select the Source tab.

3. Click the Browse button and locate the XML file.

4. Click OK to add the new data source to the Data Source Catalog.

5. Click the new data source and select Insert Data View from the drop-down list.

Figure 8.30 shows the result: tables created from XML data, with the same management tools available for database data.

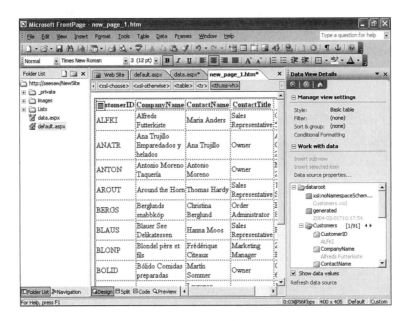

FIGURE 8.30   XML data on a Web page in FrontPage 2003.

Web Package Templates

A *Web package* is a collection of files that integrate with SharePoint Services to provide a complete Web-based solution. For instance, you might export a SharePoint Team Services site to a FrontPage Web package and then transfer the entire site to a new location using FrontPage 2003.

Select Packages from the Tools menu and then click Export to create a package. Use the resulting dialog box, shown in Figure 8.31, to add files to the package.

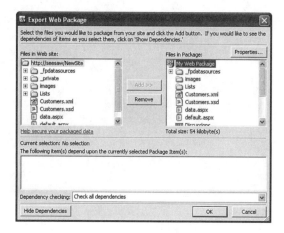

FIGURE 8.31   Create a Web package.

To install a Web package, select Packages from the Tools menu and select Import to display the Import Web Package dialog box shown in Figure 8.32. Uncheck the items you don't want to install (if necessary) and click Import.

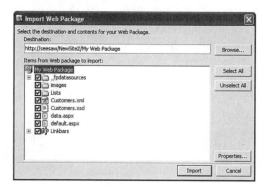

FIGURE 8.32   Importing a Web package.

After you import the package, you'll find that all the files in the package have been added to the current Web site.

What's New in Publisher 2003

Changes to the User Interface

L ike all the Office 2003 applications, Publisher has a new look. Colors are softer and icons and other common controls are rounder. You can learn more about these changes in Chapter 2, "Shared Office Features."

The New Menus

The File menu has only two changes: Publish to the Web replaces the previous Save As Web Page item, and File Search replaces the former Search item.

⇨ Read Chapter 4, "What's New in Word 2003," to learn more about the changes made to the File menu's Search command.

In previous versions, you couldn't move a page. You had to insert a new page and then move the content. Publisher 2003's Edit menu simplifies the process by offering a Move Page item. Select the page you want to move and then select Move Page on the Edit menu to display the Move Page dialog box shown in Figure 9.1. Select the appropriate option, and click OK.

There are no changes to the View menu. However, Connect Text Boxes replaces the Connect Frames item on the Toolbars submenu.

IN THIS CHAPTER

- The new look and feel
- New publication types
- Layout and graphics improvements
- Catalog merge
- New Web wizards and tools
- Improved productivity
- Commercial printing features

FIGURE 9.1   Move a page.

Two new commands on the Insert menu make quick work of adding elements to a page.
Select Insert, Duplicate Page to insert an exact copy of the current page. Quickly add a navigation bar to an existing page by selecting Insert, Navigation Bar to display the Design
Gallery, as shown in Figure 9.2. After selecting a bar option, click Insert Object. In the resulting dialog box, name the new bar, select the appropriate placement options, and click OK. In
response, Publisher 2003 inserts a navigation bar similar to the one shown in Figure 9.3.

 MORE INFO

Navigation Bars, and the associated menu items, are available only when you're working on a Web
publication.

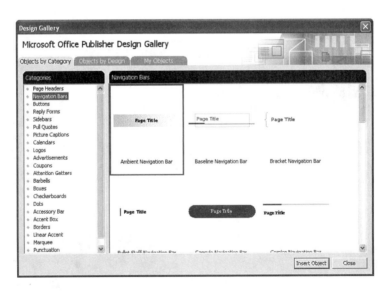

FIGURE 9.2   The Design Gallery automatically opens to the Navigation Bar choices when you select Insert, Navigation Bar.

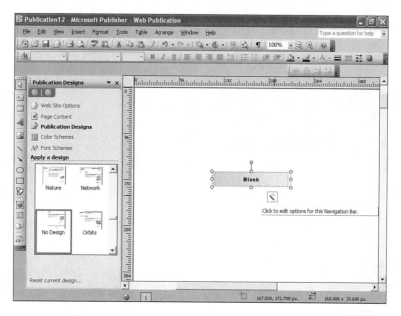

FIGURE 9.3   Add a navigation bar to a page.

There are lots of changes to the Format menu. The Paragraph and Bullets and Numbering items replace the previous Line Spacing and Indents and Lists items, respectively. Both new items offer more formatting options. Quick Publication Options replaces the original Web Site Options command.

You'll also find Page Content on the Format menu. Page Content is a completely new command that displays the new Page Content task pane. AutoFit Text is still around, but Do Not AutoFit replaces the None option on that command's submenu.

⇨ Similar to Navigation Bars, Page Content applies only to Web publications.

Two commands on the Tools menu are replaced: Mail and Catalog Merge and Web Page Options replace Mail Merge and Tools on the Web, respectively. One new command, Research, is now available. You can access the Graphics Manager directly from the Tools menu instead of the Commercial Printing Tools submenu (which was on the Tools menu). Both open corresponding task panes.

There are no changes to the Tables menu. However, the Cell Diagonals command isn't visible unless you're working on a print publication. Similarly, the Text Wrapping command on the Arrange menu is visible only when you're working with a print publication. That's the only change you'll find to the Arrange menu.

⇨ Like all the Office applications, Publisher 2003's Help menu has had a major makeover. Read about the changes to the Help menu in Chapter 2.

The New Task Panes

All Office 2003 applications have a number of new task panes, and Publisher 2003 is no exception to that rule. The following is a list of all the task panes:

NEW • Help

- Search Results—Replaces Search

- Clip Art—Replaces Insert Clip Art

NEW • Research

- Clipboard

NEW • New Publication

NEW • Find and Replace

NEW • Graphics Manager

NEW • Design Checker

NEW • Apply Master Page

NEW • Background

- Publication Designs

NEW • Web Site Options

NEW • Page Content

- Styles and Formatting

- Font Schemes

- Color Schemes

- Mail and Catalog Merge—Replaces Mail Merge

> ⇨ Several task panes are new to all or some of the Office 2003 applications. Read Chapter 2 for more information on the following task panes: Help, Search Results, Clip Art, and Research.

Figure 9.4 shows the New Publication task pane. Use the options in this task pane to start a new publication. The New from a Design list offers a number of template publication types. Or, open a new blank publication, a Web page, or an existing publication using the appropriate link at the bottom of the task pane.

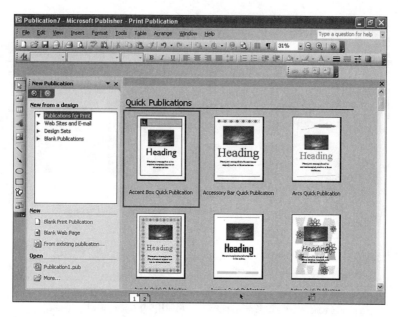

FIGURE 9.4   The New Publication task pane is the place to start.

⇨ Look for more in-depth information on the Graphics Manager, Design Checker, Apply Master Page, Publication Designs, Web Site Options, and Mail and Catalog Merge task panes later in this chapter.

Use the Background task pane shown in Figure 9.5 to quickly apply a predefined background scheme to a publication, the current page, or a range of pages.

The color bar at the top of the task pane lets you keep several colors handy. Click the More Colors link to update the colors. Use the scrollbar to view the many background schemes available from the list of backgrounds. Click the More Backgrounds link to create your own effects. Click the Background Sound link to display the Web Page Options dialog box so you can specify a sound file.

The Styles and Formatting task pane provides a one-step location for creating and applying styles. Select a style from the list of existing styles in the Pick Formatting to Apply list shown in Figure 9.6. You can also import styles or create new ones.

The Font Schemes and Color Schemes task panes, shown in Figures 9.7 and 9.8, respectively, make those scheme options easier to access.

FIGURE 9.5   Select a background from the Background task pane.

FIGURE 9.6   Control formatting from the Styles and Formatting task pane.

FIGURE 9.7   Fonts are easy to apply from this new task pane.

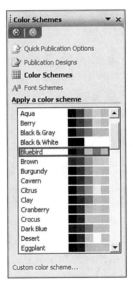

FIGURE 9.8   Quickly select a color scheme from this new task pane.

New Publication Types

Publisher has always provided a number of publication types in a variety of formats. Often, you can just drop in a few text and graphic elements to customize the publication and then print. Publisher 2003 adds several new publication types to increase your options.

New Design Sets

Publisher 2003 has 10 new master design sets. To access them, select New from the File menu to open the New Publication task pane. Select Design Sets in the New from a Design list and then click Master Sets. The following sets are new:

- Arrows
- Bounce
- Brocade
- Color Band
- Marker
- Modular
- Perforation
- PhotoScope
- Simple Divider
- Straight Edge

Publisher 2003 adds a new design set, Personal Stationery. This set includes eight new styles, each containing an address label, letterhead, and a matching envelope. You can create a coordinating address or business card by choosing the same design in the business card set (Publications for Print). To access these designs, click Design Sets in the New Publication task pane. Then, click the Personal Stationery Sets option. You'll also find new design sets for CD/DVD labels and more greeting and invitation cards.

When working with an existing publication, use the Publication Designs task pane shown in Figure 9.9. Several predesigned publication sets can help you get started. Browse through the many design options in the Apply a Design list. Then, tweak the elements as required to get just the look you need. It's a lot quicker than creating the entire look from scratch.

Use the Color Schemes and Font Schemes options to customize the design before applying it. Or, click the Reset Current Design option to cancel the most recent design application.

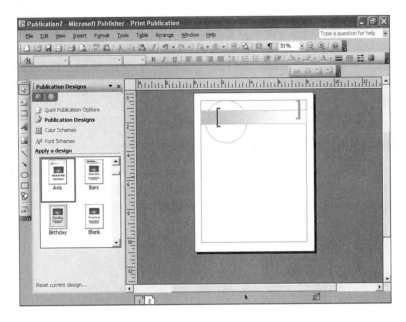

FIGURE 9.9   Select a predesigned publication design.

The new E-mail Wizard helps you create professional-looking email messages. In the New Publication task pane, click the Web Sites and E-mail option; then click the E-mail option to display a number of new email publications:

- Newsletter
- Letter
- Event/Speaker
- Event/Activity
- Product List
- Featured Product

Double-click any item to launch the wizard and create the new email publication.

The Web Sites item still launches a wizard, but three new Web site wizards are available: 3-Page Web Site, Product Sales, and Professional Services. In addition, one builder is provided: Easy Site Builder. Or, you can display the new Web Site Options task pane and work from the options shown in Figure 9.10.

UPGRADERS BEWARE

Publisher's use of the terms *wizard* and *builder* is somewhat idiosyncratic: A *wizard* creates a publication with no user interaction, whereas a *builder* prompts you to make choices to customize the publication.

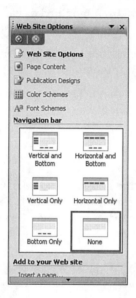

FIGURE 9.10   Select a predesigned Web site design.

Layout and Graphics Improvements

New and enhanced layout and graphics features give you more control over your design and more flexibility for asserting that control:

- Improved Graphics Manager
- Improved Design Checker
- Use of multiple master pages
- Improved layout guides

The Graphics Manager

Publisher 2000 introduced the Graphics Manager to help commercial printers manage the graphics in a publication. The new and improved Graphics Manager isn't just for print shops anymore. New features include the ability to do the following:

- List linked pictures that have been modified or whose links are broken by selecting the appropriate option from the Show control's drop-down list.

- Convert linked pictures to embedded pictures by right-clicking the file in the Select a Picture list and selecting the appropriate Save As option.

- Locate a specific picture by right-clicking the file in the Select a Picture list and selecting the Go to This Picture option.

- Replace a picture by right-clicking the file in the Select a Picture list and selecting the Replace This Picture option.

In addition, Publisher 2003 uses the new Graphics Manager task pane shown in Figure 9.11 instead of a dialog box, as in earlier versions. Check the Show Thumbnail option to display thumbnail graphics instead of filenames in the Select a Picture list. Use the Sort by control to determine how the graphics are listed.

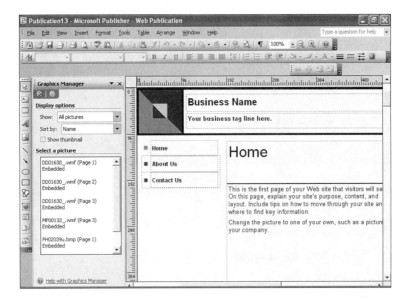

FIGURE 9.11   The Graphics Manager makes learning about and controlling the graphics in your publication or pages easy.

The Design Checker

Run the Design Checker frequently against your design to determine and then correct (many) problems before they work their way through your publication. After displaying the Design Checker task pane, click the Design Checker Options button at the bottom of the pane to customize the check by setting options in the resulting dialog box shown in Figure 9.12.

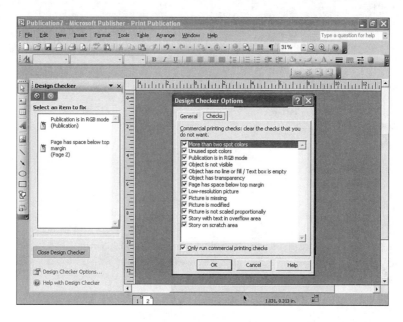

FIGURE 9.12   You can customize the design checker options. In this figure, we've limited the checks to commercial print checks only.

The Checks tab has the majority of options, and they're all checked by default. Most of the options listed in Table 9.1 are new, and a few are specific to both print and nonprint publications. Click the Only Run Commercial Print Checks option to narrow the list of options Publisher 2003 checks.

TABLE 9.1   Checks Tab Options

Option	New	Print
More than Two Spot Colors	Yes	Yes
Unused Spot Colors	Yes	Yes
Publication Is in RGB Mode	Yes	Yes
Object Encroaches Nonprinting Region	Renamed	No
Object Partially off Page	No	No

TABLE 9.1   Continued

Option	New	Print
Object Is Not Visible	Yes	Yes
Object Has No Line or Fill/Text Box Is Empty	Yes	Yes
Object Has Transparency	Yes	Yes
Picture Does Not Have Alternative Text	Yes	No
Page Cannot Be Reached from First Page	Yes	No
Page Does Not Have Links	Renamed	No
Page Has Space Below Top Margin	Renamed	Yes
Low-resolution Picture	Yes	Yes
Picture Is Missing	Yes	Yes
Picture Is Modified	Yes	Yes
Picture Is Not Scaled Proportionately	Renamed	Yes
Story with Text in Overflow Area	Renamed	Yes
Story on Scratch Area	Yes	Yes

The results of the check are listed in the Select an Item to Fix control. Each item has a list of drop-down options, as shown in Figure 9.13. Select Explain to display the associated Help item. The fix text will be unique to the problem.

FIGURE 9.13   Fix an item.

 **EXPERT ADVICE**

Both the Graphics Manager and Design Checker lend increased support to the commercial printing features.

The New Apply Master Page Task Pane

Earlier versions of Publisher support only one master page, although you can have a right and left version in a two-page spread. A *master page* is a background that you define and then apply to some or all of the pages in a publication. You can change the master page at any time, but its purpose is to treat design elements as a set that can be applied or removed in one quick, easy process.

Publisher 2003 lets you work with multiple master pages in the same publication. Create several and then select from the available pages when applying a design to a specific page or a group of pages.

Click the View Master Pages option at the bottom of the Apply Master Page task pane shown in Figure 9.14 to view all the available pages. To apply a page to the publication, select the master page from the Select a Master Page drop-down list.

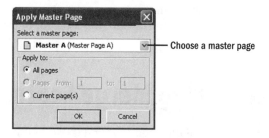

FIGURE 9.14   Apply a master page to the publication.

More Layout Guides

Layout guides help you divide a page into sections. The three tabs of the Layout Guides dialog box contain a mix of old and new options, as shown in Figure 9.15. The Baseline Guides options are new and help you align text across multiple columns. Access these guides by selecting Layout Guides from the Arrange menu.

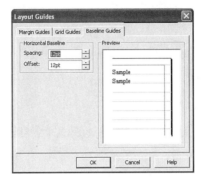

FIGURE 9.15   Use the new layout options.

A Few More

A few more improved design and graphic features deserve mention:

- **The new Line and Paragraph Breaks tab**—This lets you define paragraph spacing and eliminate widows and orphans. Select Paragraph from the Format menu.

- **Empty picture frames**—You can use these as placeholders. Select Picture from the Insert menu and then select Empty Picture Frame.

The New Catalog Merge Feature

Do you have data in an application that you'd like to use in a publication or Web page? Use the new Catalog Merge Wizard to merge that data with your publication.

By definition, a *catalog merge* is the process of combining data from an external data source with a template to create pages that display multiple records per page. You can then add the merged pages to an existing publication or create a new publication. This is a great option for creating a product catalog, phone directory, contact address book, or any kind of publication that list multiple items of the same type on a single page (or over several pages).

To get started, select Mail and Catalog Merge from the Tools menu and then select Mail and Catalog Merge Wizard from the resulting submenu. Or, display the Mail and Catalog Merge task pane, shown in Figure 9.16.

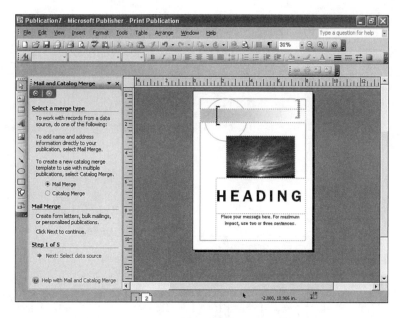

FIGURE 9.16   Use the Mail and Catalog Merge task pane to grab information from an existing external data source.

Click the Catalog Merge option in the middle of the pane to update the instructions that walk you through the process of selecting a data source and then selecting the appropriate data:

1. Click the Step 1 link and then click Browse to locate the spreadsheet or database that contains the data you want to merge. Figure 9.17 displays tables and queries in the Northwind database, the sample database that comes with Access.

FIGURE 9.17   Find the data source.

2. If you're using a database, select the actual table or query and then click OK. If you're merging with a spreadsheet, select the sheet or range.

3. At this point, you can use the AutoFilter controls (the arrows at the top of each column) to limit the records, as shown in Figure 9.18. To sort the records, click the

appropriate column heading. When you have just the records you want in the order you want, click OK.

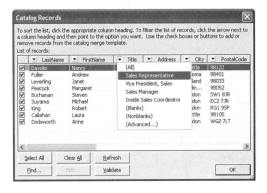

FIGURE 9.18   Filter the records you merge.

4. Click the Step 2 link and identify each field you want to merge. To do so, click the field's drop-down arrow and select Insert As Text or Insert As Picture, as shown in Figure 9.19, accordingly.

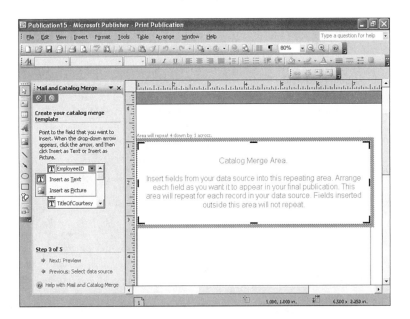

FIGURE 9.19   Identify the fields you want to merge.

5. Click the Step 3 link to preview the results. Browse or edit the records while previewing. Eliminate a record by clicking the Exclude This Record button.

6. Click the Step 4 link to complete the merge. At this point, you can create a new publication or add the merged pages to an existing publication. Figure 9.20 shows the first page in the new merged publication. Each field comprises its own text box.

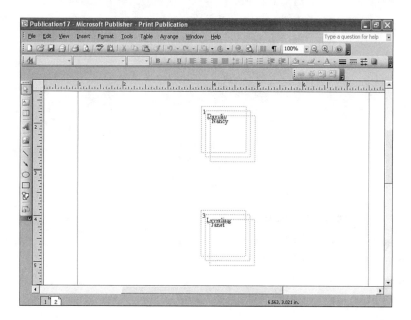

FIGURE 9.20   Merge external data with a publication.

New Web Wizards and Tools

You've already read brief descriptions of a few of the new Web site wizards and tools. In this section, we'll take a broader look at new features and improvements for working with Web pages and sites.

The Easy Web Site Builder

Publisher 2003's new Easy Web Site Builder lets you specify common goals for a new Web site and builds a generic site with the necessary pages. Select File, Web Sites and E-mail; then select Easy Web Site builder. Or, click Web Sites and E-mail in the New Publications task pane, click Web Sites, and then click Easy Web Site Builder.

Double-click one of the dozens of new site designs to launch the builder. Check the goals that apply to your new site to add the appropriate pages to your site, as shown in Figure 9.21. When you're done, click OK and Publisher 2003 customizes your Web site with the just the right pages.

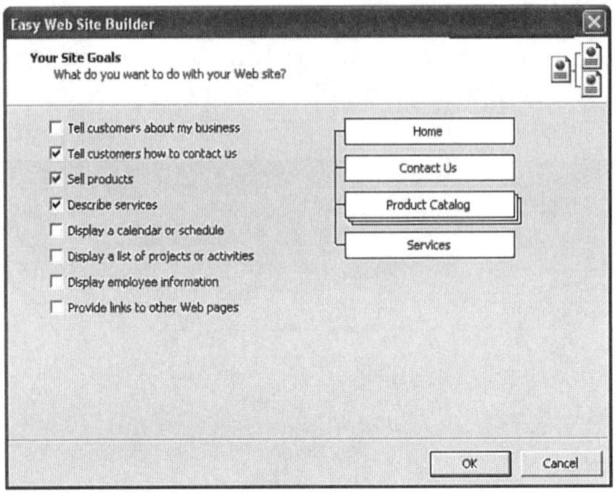

FIGURE 9.21   Select the goals that best describe your site's needs.

Other new Web wizards include the following:

- **3-Page Web Site**—This wizard generates a three-page Web site that includes a home page, an About Us page, and a Contact Us page.

- **Product Sales**—Use this wizard to generate a four-page site that includes a home page, an About Us page, a Contact Us page, and a Product List page.

- **Professional Services**—Produce a five-page site that includes a home page, an About Us page, a Contact Us page, a Product List page, and a Service List page.

New Web Site Page Types

Publisher 2003 adds a number of new publication types, including several new Web page types. You can add any of the new or improved pages listed in Table 9.2 to your Web site. To access any of these new page types, select Page from the Insert menu to display the Insert Web Page dialog box shown in Figure 9.22.

TABLE 9.2   New Publication Types

Page	Description	New/Improved
About Us	Tells visitors about your company or organization	New
Blank	A blank page	New
Calendar	A monthly calendar and list of events	New
Contact Us	Provides contact information	New

TABLE 9.2 Continued

Page	Description	New/Improved
Employee	Displays employee detail lists with links	New
Event	Promotes a specific event	New
FAQ	Lists frequently asked questions	New
Forms	Generates orders, responses, and sign-up forms	Improved
General Information	Describes an item or activity	New
General List	Creates a list of items or activities	New
Home	Creates the first page visitors see	New
Job List	Lists current job openings	New
Legal	Describes legal information or policies specific to your company or organization	New
News Articles	Presents news items	New
Photos	Includes photos and details with links	New
Products	Includes a product list with details and links	New
Project List/Resume	Displays a project list and details with links	New
Related Links	Lists your sites links or links to other sites	New
Services	Lists service list with details and links	New
Special Offer	Advertises a sale or special offer	New

FIGURE 9.22 Insert predesigned Web page types.

For Good Measure

There are a number of new and improved features that you'll notice as you begin to work with Web sites and pages:

- Look for the new globe icon in the Status bar (to the left) to indicate you're working in Web mode.

- Select only those pages that you've changed when uploading to a remote site.

- Use the Web Site Options task pane or dialog box to quickly access a number of options.

- Add and remove navigation bar links and add secondary bars.

Improved Productivity

Some new and improved features will make you more efficient and, in general, make your publishing tasks easier:

- New Page Sorter

- Improved Find and Replace

- Enhanced zooming

Page Sorter

Use this new feature to move, add, delete, and rename pages. You'll find the feature very familiar if you're already using other Office 2003 applications.

Use the drag-and-drop Page Navigation icons on the Status bar to move pages. You can also rename, duplicate, delete, and insert a page or apply a master page by right-clicking a page and selecting the appropriate option. (Renaming an individual page in a non-Web publication isn't particularly useful, but you can do so.)

Improved Find and Replace

Publisher 2003's Find and Replace feature has been improved. You can use the new Find and Replace task pane shown in Figure 9.23 for easier accessibility. In addition, you can run a Find and Replace task on multiple text boxes, multiple stories, or the entire publication.

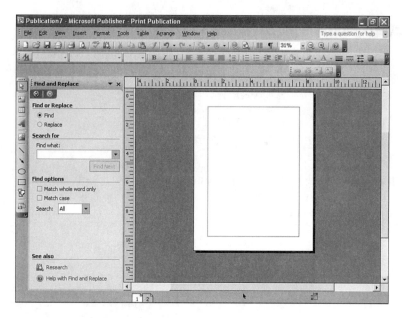

FIGURE 9.23   Find and Replace is now easy to initiate via one of the many new task panes.

Enhanced Zooming

Publisher 2003 improves zooming in two ways. You can zoom to 800%—earlier versions went only to 400%. In addition, Publisher 2003 now supports additional zooming control for Magellan mouse users. Use the fourth mouse button to zoom into a specific area of a publication, and use the third mouse button to pan across the workspace.

More Powerful Commercial Printing Features

Publisher has always supported commercial printing tasks, but this version offers more powerful and flexible features.

New CMYK Support

Publisher 2003 provides more accurate CMYK values for gradients and graphics that have been scaled or rotated. This capability is known as CMYK composite PostScript, and its support means you can get a larger range of color variation and contrast from a commercial printer.

Improved Print Separations

New print settings let you create separations from the Print dialog box, which is a more logical and convenient selection. From the Print dialog box, you can do the following:

- Convert spot colors to process colors.

- Convert process colors to spot colors.

- Convert RGB to CMYK or spot colors.

To access these new settings, select Tools, Commercial Printing Tools and then select Color Printing. Or, select Print from the File menu and then click the Advance Printing Settings button in the bottom-left corner.

Introducing Microsoft OneNote 2003

So far, we've been dealing with the new features in Office on an application-by-application basis. But some new features can't be discussed that way because they're a part of entirely new applications. This version of Office introduces two new applications: Microsoft OneNote (the subject of this chapter) and Microsoft InfoPath (which we cover in Chapter 11, "Introducing Microsoft InfoPath 2003").

IN THIS CHAPTER

- Getting to know OneNote
- Taking notes with OneNote
- Finding and organizing notes
- Working with audio notes
- Sharing notes with other applications

Getting to Know OneNote

Class notes, meeting notes, to-do lists, phone numbers, grocery lists…life is filled with little bits of text that don't warrant a heavy-duty application such as Microsoft Word. But if you store all these things in individual files or put them on sticky notes on your monitor, they're hard to keep track of. That's the premise behind OneNote, which is designed to give you a single place to keep all your notes.

 UPGRADERS BEWARE

OneNote isn't included with all versions of Microsoft Office 2003. See Appendix A, "Office 2003 Version Guide," for details on buying OneNote.

What Is OneNote?

Figure 10.1 shows the default view of OneNote when you first launch it (although we've rearranged the toolbars a bit so you can see all the buttons). Microsoft has promoted OneNote as an ideal application for the Tablet PC, but you can use OneNote on either a desktop PC or a Tablet PC. If you're working on a Tablet PC, you can use the Tablet PC Input panel to enter data (just as you can with any other Tablet PC application). We've chosen to leave the Input panel out of our screenshots to allow more room for OneNote itself.

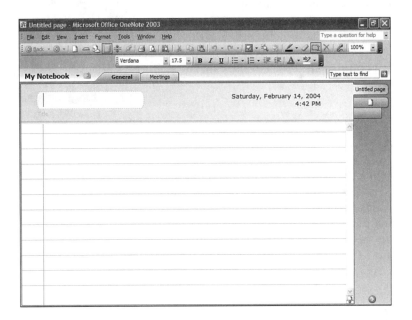

FIGURE 10.1   When you first launch OneNote, it displays a notebook with two tabs and lined paper.

A little later in this chapter, we'll explore this user interface in some detail. But first, let's take a little space to introduce this new application. It's all very well to say that OneNote is a new addition to the Microsoft Office system, but that doesn't tell you what it is or what it's good for. The name itself tells you a little about what this program is: It's a single repository to hold all your notes, both written and audio. Because it's a Microsoft Office application, it also features a user interface that you'll likely find comfortable and familiar (although, as you can see in Figure 10.1, there are some idiosyncrasies here as well).

Why OneNote?

Any computer user certainly already has ways of taking notes. You can store notes in Outlook (although our experience has been that practically no one does so), in Word documents, or in simple text files, on a legal pad, or on sticky notes on your monitor—just to name a few of the alternatives. So, why should you switch to using OneNote for this task? Here are some of the features OneNote offers to entice you to switch:

- Storage of notes on your computer where they're less likely to get lost

- Freeform note-taking that lets you write (or draw pictures) anywhere on the page

- A multiple-level hierarchical system for organizing notes

- Input by either handwriting or typing

- A system for fast note entry (called Side Notes) through an icon in your task tray

- Automatic, continuous saving of whatever you enter

- Audio notes that can be synchronized with written notes

- Integration with Outlook, SharePoint, and other applications

If you frequently find yourself having problems organizing the miscellaneous information in your life, take a look at OneNote as your next assistant.

Taking a Quick Tour of OneNote

OneNote is designed so you can get up and running with it easily, without even reading the help file. In this section of the chapter, we'll show you just how easy it is to get started, by covering these basics:

- The OneNote user interface

- Taking a note

- Writing a note

- Adding pictures to a note

- Taking a Side Note

- Saving the notebook

Getting Oriented

OneNote offers a variety of user interface widgets to help you navigate around your notes. OneNote offers a rich hierarchy that you can use as much or as little as you please:

- A notebook can contain folders or sections.

- A folder can contain other folders or sections.

- A section can contain pages.

- A page can contain notes.

In addition, the user interface includes standard Office features such as toolbars and task panes.

Toolbars

Most of the tools you'll use in OneNote are contained on the Standard and Formatting toolbars. Figure 10.2 shows the buttons on the Standard toolbar, and Figure 10.3 shows the buttons on the Formatting toolbar.

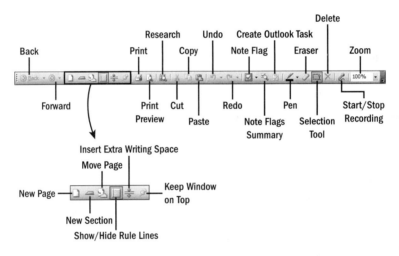

FIGURE 10.2   The Standard toolbar.

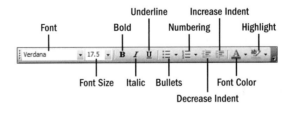

FIGURE 10.3   The Formatting toolbar.

As you can see, the tools on the Formatting toolbar are familiar from other Office applications, whereas some of the tools on the Standard toolbar are unique to OneNote. You'll learn more about using these tools as the chapter unfolds.

Sections, Folders, Pages, and Tabs

A OneNote notebook is more than just a simple heap of notes. Figure 10.4 shows some of the user interface widgets that let you organize your notes more efficiently.

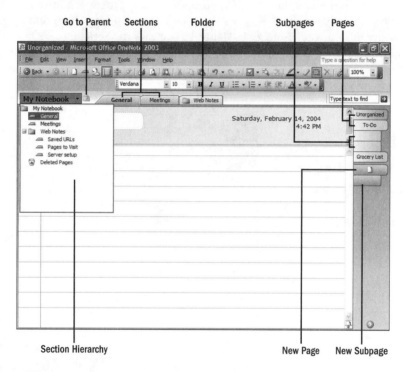

FIGURE 10.4   OneNote offers a variety of ways to group and organize your notes.

The section hierarchy (which is displayed when you click the My Notebook area) and the Go to Parent button let you navigate among all the folders and sections in your notebook. At any given time, the tabs across the top of the work area show the sections and folders in the current folder; folders can also be nested.

When you select a section by clicking its tab, that section comes visually to the front of the section list (like the General section in Figure 10.4). At that point, the tabs on the right side of the screen show the pages in the section. Longer tabs are pages, and shorter tabs are subpages. The differences are that subpages do not have a name of their own and they are associated with their parent page, so if you move or copy the parent page to another section, folder, or notebook, the subpages move with their parent page. You can add new pages or new subpages by clicking the lowest two tabs on the right side of the screen. To name a page, type a name in the title area in the upper-left corner of the page. Subpages do not have their own names.

Task Panes

Like the rest of the Office applications, OneNote includes task panes to make finding specific functions easier. Many of these are shared with the other Office applications. Such task panes as Help, Research, and Search Results are common to many Office applications. Others are distinctive to OneNote. Figure 10.5 shows the Page List task pane, which offers a fast way to navigate to any page in your notebook. Figure 10.6 shows the Set Language task pane, which you can use to customize the handwriting recognition used by OneNote. You can explore these and other task panes by pressing Ctrl+F1 to open the task pane area and then selecting from the drop-down list at the top of the task pane.

FIGURE 10.5   The Page List task pane provides easy navigation.

Taking Your First Note

To take notes with OneNote, you can click anywhere and start typing. There's no need to worry about making space on the page or taking notes in any particular order. As you type, OneNote shows a bar indicating the width of the note; you can either grab the right side of the bar and drag it to resize the note's width or drag the note to any other point on the page with the mouse. Figure 10.7 shows a new note being entered.

FIGURE 10.6   The language chosen in the Set Language task pane also determines which dictionaries are used during spell check.

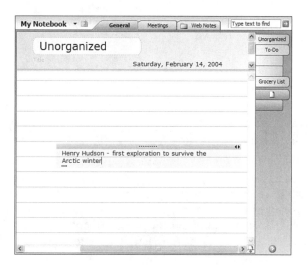

FIGURE 10.7   Typing a note into OneNote.

If you click inside an existing note and type more text, OneNote adds the text to the existing note. If you click elsewhere on the page and type, OneNote creates a new note. You can move notes around independently or merge them by dragging one of the notes and dropping it on top of the other.

Writing in the Notebook

You can also take notes in OneNote by handwriting. To do so, click the Pen tool on the Standard toolbar and then write anywhere on the notebook. Figure 10.8 shows a notebook with an ink note, added by using a drawing stylus on a Tablet PC.

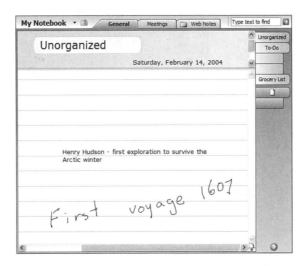

FIGURE 10.8   Note created by writing instead of typing.

EXPERT ADVICE

You don't have to have a Tablet PC to create handwritten notes. On a desktop PC, you can click the Pen tool and then use your mouse to write notes. Most people, though, have trouble creating recognizable letters using the mouse, so this probably isn't worth the effort. If you want to turn handwritten notes into text, though, you need a Tablet PC.

By default, OneNote stores your handwritten notes as *ink*. That is, the exact picture of your letters is retained as part of the notebook. You can also convert your handwriting to regular text. To do so, select the Selection tool on the Standard toolbar and then select the handwritten note. Right-click and select Convert Handwriting to Text. Figure 10.9 shows the result of converting part of the handwriting from Figure 10.8 to text. As you can see, OneNote isn't perfect, but it does a pretty good job of recognizing most handwriting.

FIGURE 10.9   Converting a handwritten note to text.

Drawing in the Notebook

Of course, you can also draw in your notebook. Just select the Pen tool and scribble anywhere. You can use the drop-down arrow next to the Pen tool to select from a variety of pen colors and widths. Figure 10.10 shows a notebook with some pen-based embellishment.

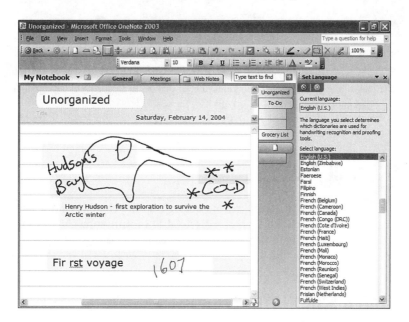

FIGURE 10.10   Drawing in a notebook.

Adding Other Content

If you have an image in another application—such as a bitmap image open in Paint—you can also copy that image and paste it into a OneNote notebook.

You can also paste data copied from other Office applications. Depending on what you paste, you might get a Smart Tag with choices when you perform the paste operation. If you're pasting text from a Word document or an Excel worksheet, for example, you can choose to use the source or destination formatting, to paste just the text, or to paste the text as a picture.

OneNote also has special handling built in for Web content. If you paste a URL, OneNote automatically makes it a live hyperlink to the Web page. If you copy a graphic or text from a Web page open in Internet Explorer, OneNote includes a link back to the original page when you paste the content.

Saving the Notebook

Saving your notebook is simple: You don't have to. OneNote automatically and continuously saves your changes. OneNote automatically makes a daily backup copy of your notes as well, just in case the notebook gets damaged.

 MORE INFO

You can adjust some of the save and backup properties in the Options dialog box, available by selecting Options from the Tools menu. You can change the location of the main or backup copies of your notebook on the Open and Save page, and you can change the frequency of backups and the number of backups to keep on the Backup page.

Taking Quick Notes

One of the goals of OneNote is to make note-taking fast and easy. Sometimes loading an entire application is too much work when you need to capture something immediately. For example, you might be on the phone and need to make note of a phone number. For those times, OneNote provides the Side Notes feature.

Launching a Side Note

When you install OneNote, it adds an icon to the notification tray area on your Windows taskbar, as shown in Figure 10.11.

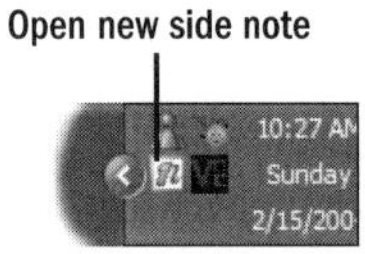

Open new side note

FIGURE 10.11   The side note icon.

 **EXPERT ADVICE**

The side note icon won't appear until the first time you reboot your computer after installing OneNote.

To create a new side note, click the side note icon in the tray area. This opens a small note-taking window, as shown in Figure 10.12. Type (or write, or draw) your note, and then click the Close icon to close the side note window. The side note automatically is saved to your notebook.

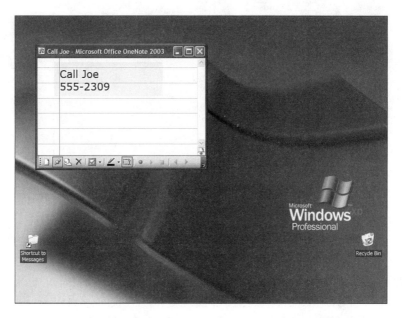

FIGURE 10.12   Taking a side note.

 **EXPERT ADVICE**

The side note feature is slower to launch the first time you use it because it's loading parts of OneNote into your computer's memory. If you know you're going to need to take side notes, you might want to launch and then close the side note window when you start your day, just to get it ready.

The Side Notes Section

When you close a side note, it is added to a Side Notes section in your notebook, as shown in Figure 10.13. OneNote automatically creates this section the first time you close a side note.

OneNote adds each side note to the Side Notes section as its own page, with a page title composed of the first few words of the side note. Of course, you don't have to keep the side notes in that particular section. You can cut and paste them to any page or section in your notebook.

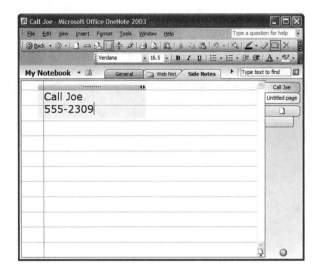

FIGURE 10.13   The Side Notes section of a notebook.

 **EXPERT ADVICE**

You might start to take a side note and then change your mind and decide you'd rather work with the full OneNote interface. In that case, just maximize the side note window. It will turn into the full OneNote window.

Working with Notes

OneNote isn't as powerful as, say, Word. But it does offer a reasonable variety of features for managing your notes. In this section, we review some of the basic features for working with notes:

- Spell-checking
- Flagging notes
- Finding notes
- Printing notes

Checking Spelling

As you probably expect, OneNote can check the spelling of your notes. Select Spelling from the Tools menu to spell-check the current page of your notebook. OneNote implements spell-checking as a task pane, which you can see in Figure 10.14 (we wish the other Office applications did this).

FIGURE 10.14   Spell-checking in OneNote.

OneNote also flags misspelled words on-the-fly with the same red squiggly underline that Word uses.

 UPGRADERS BEWARE

Spell-check checks only the current page; there's no way to tell it to check an entire section or your entire notebook. Also, only typed text is checked. You can incorrectly spell as many words in your hand-written text as you like, and OneNote will never complain about them.

Flagging Notes

OneNote includes a flexible system for flagging notes so you can find important notes later. To flag any note, select the note and then click the Note Flag button on the Standard toolbar.

You can click the drop-down arrow next to the Note Flag button to choose between different flags. By default, OneNote includes these flags:

- To Do

- Important

- Question

- Remember for Later

- Definition

When you add a flag to a note, the icon for that flag is displayed to the note and the flag's formatting is applied to the note. At any time, you can select Note Flags Summary from the View menu to see all the flags in your notebook. The summary opens as a task pane and lists all the flagged notes. Click any flagged note to jump directly to that note in your notebook.

You can also customize your flags by selecting Note Flags from the Format menu and then selecting Customize My Note Flags from the submenu. This opens the Customize My Note Flags task pane. OneNote supports nine flags. Select the flag you want to customize and click the Modify button. You can customize these features for each flag:

- The display name of the flag

- The symbol to display with flagged notes

- The font color to use for flagged notes

- The highlight color to use for flagged notes

 **EXPERT ADVICE**

If you use the To Do flag type, OneNote draws an empty check box next to the note. Later, you can click that box to place a check mark in it, marking a finished to-do item.

Finding Notes

To search for text in OneNote, type the text in the search box and click the Find arrow. This highlights the first instance of the search text in your notebook and changes the search box to a control that shows, from left to right

- The search term

- The number of matches and arrows for moving between them

- The View List control, which opens the entire list as a task pane

- A close button, which returns to the search box

Figure 10.15 shows the controls both before and after doing a search.

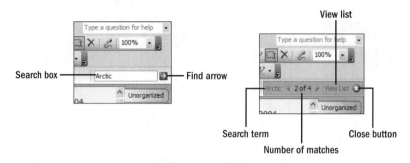

FIGURE 10.15 Searching in OneNote: Before (above) and after (below) searching.

 UPGRADERS BEWARE

The search facility searches through all the pages in your notebook, but it does not search handwritten text. If you think you'll ever need to search handwritten notes, you should convert them to text after each note-taking session.

Printing Notes

To print your notes from OneNote, select Print from the File menu. By default, this prints the entire contents of the current page group (the current page and all its subpages). You can narrow this to just the current page, or expand it to the current section, by selecting Print Preview from the File menu and selecting an appropriate value in the Print Range drop-down list. Figure 10.16 shows the Print Preview dialog box.

 UPGRADERS BEWARE

OneNote is oddly incompatible with the rest of Office when it comes to setting up your print job. If you look for page settings in the Print dialog box (where applications such as Word and Excel display them), you'll only be confused.

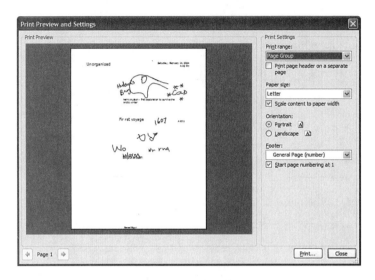

FIGURE 10.16   Setting up a print job in OneNote.

Working with Lists and Outlines

Another set of devices that OneNote offers for organizing your notes is lists and outlines. These are similar to the list and outline features in Word, but (especially with outlines) there are some new twists.

Creating Lists

Lists in OneNote can be either bulleted or numbered. To create either type of list, create a note, pressing the Enter key to separate items on the list. Then select all the list items and click either the Bullets button or the Numbering button—both of which are located on the Formatting toolbar. Each of these buttons has a drop-down arrow to let you choose between different bullet and numbering styles. For even more choices, click the More item at the bottom of either list of styles to open an appropriate task pane.

To remove bullets or numbering from a list of items, select the list and then click the Bullets or Numbering button a second time to toggle the feature off.

Creating Vertical Outlines

A *vertical outline* is probably what you think of as an outline, if you've used outlines in Word. It's a set of lines arranged in a hierarchy, just like the outlines you might have done for essays in school. To create an outline in OneNote, follow these steps:

1. Type the first item at the top level of your outline and press Enter.

2. To add another item at the same level, type it and press Enter.

3. To add another item at a deeper level, press Tab, type the item, and press Enter.

4. To add another item at a higher level, press Shift+Tab or Backspace, type the item, and then press Enter.

5. Select the entire outline and click the Numbering button on the Formatting toolbar.

Figure 10.17 shows a vertical outline in OneNote.

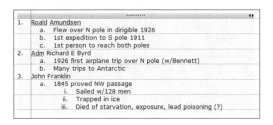

FIGURE 10.17   A vertical outline is simple to create in OneNote.

![Expert Advice icon] **EXPERT ADVICE**

To expand or collapse a level in a OneNote outline, double-click the paragraph selector that appears when you hover the mouse to the left of an item, as shown in Figure 10.18.

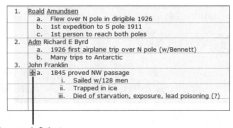

Paragraph Selector

FIGURE 10.18   Double-click the paragraph selector to expand or collapse a level in an outline.

Creating Horizontal Outlines

OneNote supports a second type of outline, the *horizontal outline*. There's no direct equivalent to this in other Office products, but it resembles a table. To create a horizontal outline, follow these steps:

1. Type the item you want to use as the first row of the first column of the outline and press Tab.

2. Type the rest of the entries for the first row, pressing Tab between each column.

3. At any time, you can press Enter to start a new row in the current column.

4. At any time, you can press Shift+Tab or Backspace to move to the previous column.

You can apply bullets or numbering to a horizontal outline, although the results tend to look odd. You can also collapse rows back to their initial columns by double-clicking the paragraph selectors. Figure 10.19 shows a horizontal outline.

Roald Amundsen	Norwegian	1872-1928
Richard E. Byrd	American	1887-1972
John Franklin	British	1786-1847
Matthew Henson	American	1866-1955
Henry Hudson	British	1565-1611

FIGURE 10.19   A horizontal outline in OneNote.

Managing Notebooks, Sections, and Pages

Like the other Office applications, OneNote allows you to rearrange, create, delete, and customize its files. If you're an experienced Office user, you should be able to figure out most of this functionality just by doing what seems right, but in this section we document some of the commonly useful OneNote operations.

Working with Notebooks

Notebooks are the main containers for notes in OneNote. OneNote creates the My Notebook notebook by default, but you're not limited to that single notebook. OneNote doesn't include any provision for renaming a notebook, but you can do it if you're sneaky enough.

To rename a notebook, follow these steps:

1. Close OneNote.

2. Locate the folder on your hard drive that corresponds to the notebook. For the default notebook, this is `My Documents\My Notebook`.

3. Rename the folder itself to anything you want—say, **My First Notebook**.

4. Launch OneNote. At this point, OneNote detects that the `My Notebook` folder is missing and re-creates it as a blank notebook.

5. Select Options from the Tools menu.

6. Select the Open and Save page of the Options dialog box.

7. Select the My Notebook path and click Modify.

8. Browse to your renamed folder and click Select.

9. Click OK to close the Options dialog box.

10. Close and restart OneNote. At this point, your renamed notebook is the current notebook.

By repeating these steps, you can create multiple OneNote notebooks, each in its own folder on your hard drive. But to switch between notebooks, you need to use the Options dialog box. The real lesson of this effort is that OneNote prefers to manage your notebooks for you.

Working with Sections

OneNote offers much better support for working with sections than it does for working with notebooks. Among other things, you can create, rename, rearrange, close, and delete sections.

To create a new section, follow these steps:

1. Right-click the tab for any existing section and select New Section.

2. Alternatively, select New from the File menu and then click Section in the New task pane.

To rename a section, follow these steps:

1. Right-click the tab for the selection and click Rename.

2. Type a new name on the tab and press Enter.

UPGRADERS BEWARE

Because section names are translated directly into filenames, a section name cannot include characters that are illegal in a filename, such as /, \, <, or >.

To move a section, follow these steps:

1. Right-click the tab for the section and select Move.

2. In the Move Section To dialog box (shown in Figure 10.20), click the section that should be directly ahead of the selected section in the notebook.

3. Click Move.

FIGURE 10.20   Moving a section within your notebook.

You can also open and close sections; each section is stored in its own disk file. To close a section, right-click the tab for the section and select Close. To open a section, select Open from the File menu, browse to the section, and click Open. OneNote sections are stored as files with the extension .one.

To permanently delete a section, right-click the tab for the section and select Delete. Click Yes in the confirmation message box. This deletes the section from your Notebook and deletes the underlying disk file from your hard drive.

 MORE INFO

A deleted section is moved to your computer's Recycle Bin, so you can still recover it if deleting it proves to be a mistake.

Working with Pages

OneNote also offers plenty of tools for working with pages. You can create, customize, flip through, move, extend, and delete pages.

To create a new page, click the New Page tab (which you saw in Figure 10.4) that's attached at the right side of any section. Alternatively, select New from the File menu and then click New Page.

You can also create pages based on *stationery*. In OneNote, stationery is a combination of page size and visual styles, and possibly preexisting content. To create a new page based on stationery, follow these steps:

1. Select New from the File menu.

2. Expand one of the categories in the Change Stationery area.

3. Click the stationery that corresponds to the page you'd like to create.

Figure 10.21 shows a new page based on the Meeting Minutes 2 stationery.

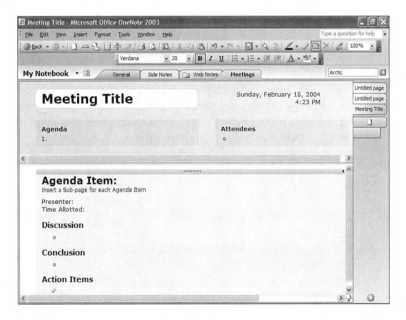

FIGURE 10.21 Stationery gives you a way to create a page with some starting content.

 UPGRADERS BEWARE

OneNote does not give you any way to change the stationery for an existing page.

You can create your own stationery by following these steps:

1. Create a new, blank page.

2. Add whatever content you like to the page. This content will be part of your stationery.

3. Select New from the File menu.

4. Click the Save Current Page As Stationery link at the bottom of the New task pane.

5. Supply a name for the new stationery and click Save.

To quickly flip through all the pages in a section, click the section tab to make it the current section. Then hold your primary mouse button down and move it down the page tabs. As you cross each tab, that page becomes the current page. Release the mouse tab when you find the page you're looking for.

To move a page within the current section, click the page tab and drag it sideways in either direction. A small triangle appears next to the page. Now you can drag the page up or down to its new location.

To move a page to a different section, right-click the page and select Move Page To; then select Another Section. Select the target section in the Move or Copy Pages dialog box (which also lets you create new sections and folders), and then click either Move or Copy.

Sometimes you'll want to make more room on a page to hold additional notes. There are two ways to do this. To add more room at the bottom of the page, click the Scroll Down by Half Page icon at the bottom of the vertical scrollbar, shown in Figure 10.22. To add more space in the middle of a page, click the Insert Extra Writing Space toolbar button on the Standard toolbar. Then click and drag on the page to create extra space. Text and images below the spot where you click are moved down to make more room.

Scroll Down by Half Page ─────────

FIGURE 10.22   Click the Scroll Down by Half Page icon to add more room at the bottom of a page.

Adding Audio

Ever wish you had an audio copy of a lecture to review along with your written notes? With OneNote, you can get just that. And as a bonus, the audio and the notes can be synchronized, so you're not wasting time trying to match up your written notes with what was being said at the time.

Recording Audio Notes

To record an audio note, click the Start/Stop Recording button on the Standard toolbar. After a brief pause while it loads the necessary software, OneNote begins recording through the computer's microphone. The recording is attached to the current point on the OneNote page.

 EXPERT ADVICE

Microsoft recommends installing Microsoft DirectX 9.0a or later and Windows Media Player 9 or later to work with audio notes. Audio notes are stored as .wma files.

 UPGRADERS BEWARE

Recording can be an intensive process. Don't try to take audio notes if your computer has a slow processor or is low on RAM.

While it's recording, OneNote displays the Audio Recording toolbar, shown in Figure 10.23.

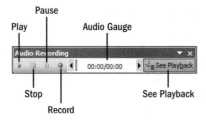

FIGURE 10.23   The Audio Recording toolbar.

To synchronize your audio notes with written notes, type or handwrite notes into your OneNote notebook as the audio recording is taking place. OneNote inserts a synchronization mark in the recording each time you start a new paragraph.

To end the recording, click the Stop button on the Audio Recording toolbar or click the Start/Stop Recording button on the Standard toolbar.

Playing Back Audio Notes

To play back an audio note, move the cursor next to the audio note in your notebook. This displays the paragraph selector and an audio note icon, as shown in Figure 10.24. Click the audio note icon to play back the note.

FIGURE 10.24   Visual cues indicate an audio note.

By default, OneNote selects the notes you typed while the recording is occurring. Each paragraph of notes is highlighted when you reach the appropriate point in the playback. If you just want to listen to the audio note without having the other notes highlighted, click the See Playback toolbar button on the Audio Recording toolbar to turn off this behavior.

Sharing Notes

Finally, OneNote offers a variety of ways to share your notes with other applications and people. You can email your notes through Microsoft Outlook, turn them into Outlook tasks, publish your notes, or use SharePoint to share them with a full suite of collaborative tools.

Emailing Notes

To share a note with another user by email, either select Email from the File menu or click the Email toolbar button on the Standard toolbar. OneNote displays new controls between your notes and the toolbars to let you enter the To, Cc, and Bcc addresses for your email, as well as a subject and introductory paragraph. Click Send a Copy to send the email.

When you send a note by email, OneNote makes a copy of the .one file for the current section and sends it as an attachment to the email. It also sends the current section as the body of the email. Thus, if the recipient has OneNote installed, she can open the section from your notebook in her own notebook. Otherwise, she can read the notes in her email client.

 UPGRADERS BEWARE

If you don't have Outlook 2003 installed on the same computer as OneNote, OneNote does not display the Email menu item or the Email toolbar button.

Turning Notes into Outlook Tasks

You can create Outlook tasks directly from OneNote, although really there's very little integration between OneNote notes and Outlook tasks. Click the Create Outlook Task button on the Standard toolbar to create a new task in Outlook. You'll see the regular Outlook Create

Task dialog box. OneNote fills in the title of the task from the current paragraph in your notebook, but it's up to you to copy any other necessary information to the task.

Publishing Notes

Finally, you can share your notes by publishing them, either to a Web page or to a SharePoint workspace.

Publishing a Web Page

To turn a section from your notebook into a Web page, first make the section active and then select Publish Pages from the File menu. Give the Web page a name, accept the default Single File Web Page as the file type, and click Publish. This publishes the section, including any graphics, as a .mht file, which is a Microsoft format for including all the pieces of a Web page in a single file. Figure 10.25 shows a Web page generated from OneNote.

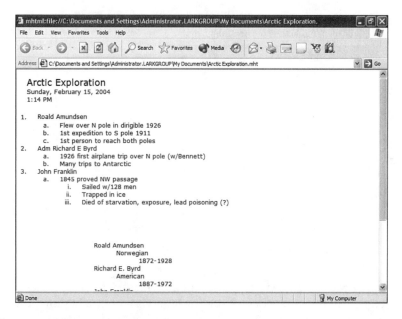

FIGURE 10.25   Publishing a OneNote section as a Web page.

 UPGRADERS BEWARE

You're not guaranteed perfect fidelity when turning a OneNote section into a Web page. In this particular case, for example, the format of the horizontal outline was changed to a vertical outline by the publishing process.

Turning a Section into a Shared Workspace

OneNote can store and retrieve sections from SharePoint, but the process is somewhat more complex than creating a shared workspace with Word, Excel, or PowerPoint. To store a OneNote section on a SharePoint server, follow these steps:

1. Create a document library on your SharePoint server (you might have to ask your network administrator to perform this step, depending on your security rights).

2. Make the notebook section you want to share active, and then select Save As from the File menu.

3. Enter the Web address of the SharePoint server (for example, http://seesaw for an intranet server named SEESAW) in the File Name box, and click Enter. This shows you a list of the document libraries on the server, as shown in Figure 10.26.

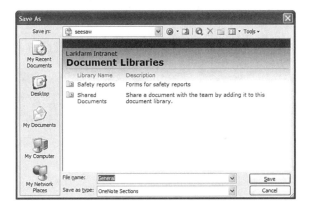

FIGURE 10.26   Selecting a SharePoint document library.

4. Double-click the library in which you want to store the document.

5. Enter a name for the document and click Save.

When you follow these steps, OneNote saves the .one file for the current section to the Document Library and then reopens it from the library. Figure 10.27 shows the result. Note the little arrow on the tab for the General section, indicating that it was opened from SharePoint. OneNote automatically opens the Shared Workspace task pane when you open a section from a document library. As other users open the same section, they show up as members of the shared workspace.

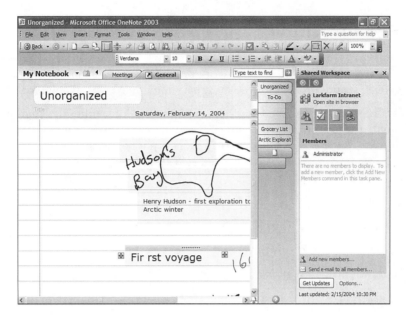

FIGURE 10.27   OneNote with a shared workspace.

Improvements in OneNote SP1

The beta version of OneNote Service Pack 1 offers a number of improvements and bug fixes. Keep in mind, that this section is based on a beta and not the SP1's final release. Things might change from the beta to the final release. In addition, you must download and install SP1 to take advantage of the improvements in this section.

The SP1 improvements to OneNote include

- Improved importing from Pocket PC, digital cameras, and electronic pictures
- Ability to record and play video notes
- Screen croppings included in notes
- Ability to integrate with Outlook and SharePoint
- Ability to publish notes to a Word document
- Better readability with resizeable page tabs and named subpages

Pocket PC Integration

A lot of people use some type of Pocket PC to keep up with information collected while on the run—in the car, attending a ceremony or event, waiting at the doctor' office, and so on—the places we all spend time but for the most part don't take along a laptop or tablet PC.

The problem is getting notes from your Pocket PC to OneNote without reentering them, which is inefficient. Fortunately, OneNote SP1 can copy information from a Pocket PC or smart phone when you dock the Pocket PC (or smart phone). Each note on the Pocket PC becomes a separate page in OneNote's Copied Pocket PC Notes section. This process can copy all types of content:

- Handwritten text

- Typed text

- Text converted from handwriting to typed text

- Hand-drawn diagrams and pictures

- Audio recordings

To copy notes from your Pocket PC to OneNote, first connect the Pocket PC to your desktop computer and launch OneNote. Then select Tools, Copy Notes from Pocket PC, Copy Now. This creates the Copied Pocket PC Notes section (if it doesn't already exist); then copy each note from the Pocket PC to a separate page in the section.

You can also set up OneNote to skip the manual step so it copies new notes from the Pocket PC every time you dock the Pocket PC. To do so, select Tools, Copy Notes from Pocket PC, Copy Automatically. After the notes are in OneNote, you can copy them to another OneNote page or section.

 UPGRADERS BEWARE

Unfortunately, there's no way to copy changed notes from OneNote back to the Pocket PC.

Including Video Notes

You learned how to record and play audio notes previously in this chapter in the "Recording Audio Notes" section. SP1 users can also record video notes—if they have a digital video camcorder or Webcam attached to their computer.

To record video notes, select Record Video from the Record button's drop-down list (on the Standard toolbar). Doing so displays the Audio and Video Recording toolbar shown in Figure 10.28. A few new tools appear on SP1's version.

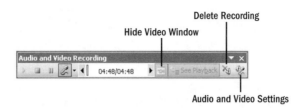

FIGURE 10.28   The SP1 version of this toolbar offers a few new tools.

Just as OneNote synchronizes audio notes with text notes, OneNote synchronizes video notes as you enter notes on the page. To clarify a text note, simply hover the mouse over the note in question. OneNote displays a speaker icon. To play the note's associated video, click the icon.

You can also replay the entire video by clicking the Play button on the Audio and Video Recording toolbar. Or, click the date stamp in the speaker icon. Select the new See Playback button on the Audio and Video Recording toolbar to highlight associated sections of notes as OneNote plays the video.

Including Screen Clippings

If you're like most of us, you probably spend a lot of time gleaning information from the Internet so this next addition will probably come in handy. OneNote SP1 lets you capture a snapshot of any view for pasting into your OneNote as an image. It's an interesting and useful new feature.

Suppose you're taking notes on sites that review technology products that might be useful to you and your staff. While viewing http://www.larkware.com, you note that this site reviews new products almost daily. You could spend time reentering a number of the comments and links, or you can simply snap a shot of the site and include it right in your notes. To accomplish the latter, follow these steps:

1. Using your browser, open http://www.larkware.com.

2. Return to OneNote and select Screen Clipping from the Insert menu.

3. OneNote returns you to the last window your browser pointed to (in this example, it would be larkware.com) and displays a crosshair cursor. Using this cursor, drag a rectangle over the portion of the screen you want to capture, as shown in Figure 10.29.

4. When you release the mouse, OneNote returns you to the OneNote window and automatically embeds the captured information in the current page as a bitmap graphic. Figure 10.30 shows the results.

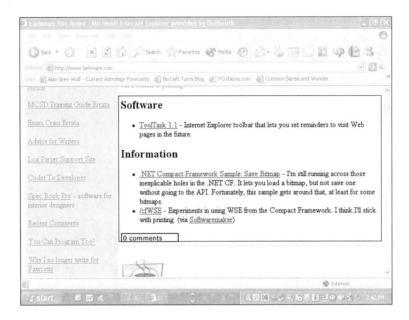

FIGURE 10.29   Use the crosshair cursor to enclose the information you want to embed in OneNote.

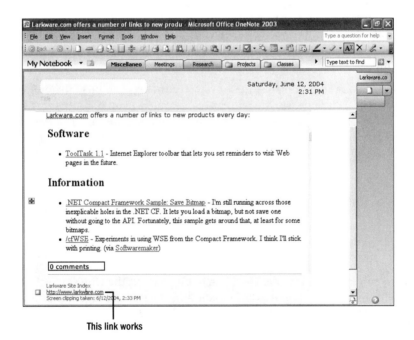

This link works

FIGURE 10.30   OneNote embeds the captured information as a bitmap.

The links embedded in the actual bitmap are lost, but the site link at the bottom of the clipping is intact. In OneNote, you can click that link to launch your browser and return to larkware.com.

Digital Camera Import

You can now insert a picture directly from a digital camera to a OneNote note. Select Insert, Picture, From Scanner or Camera. The Insert Picture from Scanner or Camera dialog box lets you choose any image-capture device currently attached to your computer. Pick the device and click OK to add the image to your note.

Additional Importing Capabilities

Earlier, you learned how to quickly copy information from a Pocket PC into OneNote. OneNote SP1 lets you import text files and other generic image file types. To do so, simply select Document As Picture option from the Insert menu. When OneNote displays the Choose Document to Insert dialog box, navigate to the graphic file you want to insert and then click Insert. OneNote inserts the file into the current page. At this point, you can take notes around or even right on top of the picture, as shown in Figure 10.31. Just click where you want to add a note and start typing.

FIGURE 10.31   Take notes right on top of an inserted picture.

If an inserted document is going to change frequently and it's important that you have the latest information, you might want to link to the file instead of just inserting it. When this is the case, drag the file from the desktop into OneNote. (You might want to resize the OneNote window first so you can see both the application window and the desktop.) OneNote displays the Insert File Options dialog box when you drop the file into OneNote (see Figure 10.32). Select an option, and click OK.

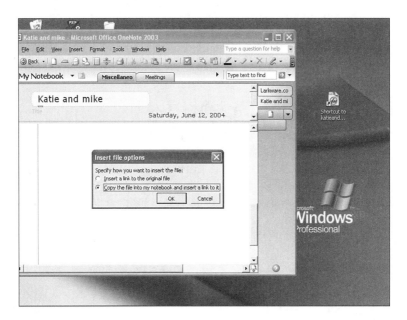

FIGURE 10.32   Choose between linking and copying and linking the information into OneNote.

Selecting Insert a Link to the Original File inserts just a link, as shown in Figure 10.33. Click the link to open the latest version of the document. Selecting the Copy the File into My Notebook and Insert a Link to it option copies the file to your OneNote section folder and inserts a shortcut link to the copied file. Use this option when the file might not always be accessible to you. Clicking either link opens the file in its native application (as long as you have access to the appropriate application).

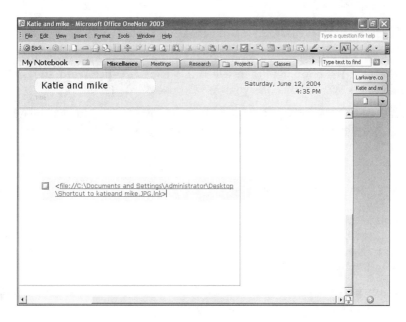

FIGURE 10.33   Insert a link to the original file.

Improved Office Compatibility

OneNote SP1 can take advantage of many Office features, even if OneNote SP1 is the only Office application you have installed. You can

- Create Outlook 2003 tasks, appointments, and contacts from inside OneNote by selecting the appropriate note and then clicking the Outlook button on the Standard toolbar.

- Import Outlook 2003 meeting details into a OneNote page by clicking Choose Outlook Meeting Details from the Insert menu in OneNote. In the resulting Insert Outlook Meeting Details dialog box, select the meeting to automatically add the meeting details to the current notes.

- Share your notebook with a SharePoint team (read more about this later in this chapter in "Real-Time Shared Notebooks").

- Publish a notes page to Microsoft Office Word 2003 (read more about this later in this chapter in "Publish to Word").

Publishing Your Notes to Word

You can quickly publish notes to a Word 2003 document by pulling down the File menu, selecting the Send To option, and then selecting Microsoft Office Word. In response, OneNote launches Word and copies your note into a Word file.

If you don't want to launch Word right away, select Save As from the File menu. Select Microsoft Word Document (.doc) from the Save As Type control's drop-down list, and then click Save.

Sharing Notebooks via SharePoint

Thanks to SharePoint Team Services, you can share your notes with other team members and see their comments and additions immediately. To do so, select Shared Session on the Tools menu. At this point, you can choose between inviting members to join a shared session and joining an existing shared session.

When you initiate a shared session, you identify the note page you're sharing and then invite participates via an email message similar to the one shown in Figure 10.34. When sharing a notes document, all participants can add notes or drawings to the file (as long as the participants have OneNote SP1). All participants see changes made by all other participants immediately.

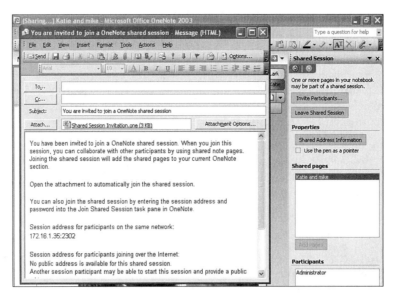

FIGURE 10.34   Invite team members to participate in a shared session with your OneNote notes.

Password Protection and Encryption

Protecting sensitive information stored in OneNote is easy. Simply select Password Protection from the File menu to display the Password Protection task pane, shown in Figure 10.35. Click the Set Password button to begin the process of protecting personal, sensitive, and business data that needs to remain confidential.

FIGURE 10.35   Use this task pane to protect sensitive data.

While you're working in a password-protected section, that section remains unlocked for the period of time you specify (10 minutes is the default). If you move from the section or close OneNote, the protected section is locked. To gain access to that section again, you must know the correct password. Protected sections are searchable and shareable only if you unprotect them first.

 UPGRADERS BEWARE

OneNote passwords are case sensitive. In addition, audio and video records cannot be password-protected. These notes are actually stored in separate files, so even if a password-protected section includes a video or audio recording, those notes are not protected.

Resizable Page Tabs

In the initial version of OneNote, the title area at the top of a new page was limited. If you entered a title that was too long for the allotted area, OneNote truncated the title. OneNote SP1 doesn't limit the title text. Figure 10.36 shows how OneNote can even push a title to the next line in an effort to accommodate the entire title.

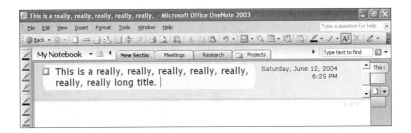

FIGURE 10.36   OneNote SP1 doesn't limit a page's title text.

Named Subpages

Subpages don't have names in the initial version of OneNote. As a result, the subpage tab to the right of the page is always blank. As you might expect, finding data using the default subpage tabs can be difficult. OneNote SP1 offers a bit of an improvement in that it usurps the first bit of text entered and displays that text in the tab, as shown in Figure 10.37.

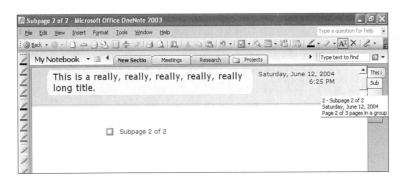

FIGURE 10.37   OneNote SP1 displays identifying text on subpage tabs.

Introducing Microsoft InfoPath 2003

Like OneNote, Microsoft InfoPath is a new member of the Microsoft Office family. Unlike OneNote, though, InfoPath is primarily directed at the corporate market. In this chapter, you'll learn the basics of InfoPath, which should help you evaluate whether its XML-oriented functionality could be useful in your own organization.

 UPGRADERS BEWARE

InfoPath isn't included with all versions of Microsoft Office 2003. See Appendix A, "Office 2003 Version Guide," for details on buying InfoPath.

Getting to Know InfoPath

Microsoft bills InfoPath as the application that "streamlines the process of gathering information by enabling teams and organizations to easily create and work with rich, dynamic forms." But what does that mean? In this section, we'll discuss some of the features of InfoPath and show you how it can be used to both design and fill out forms.

EXPERT ADVICE

Keep in mind that InfoPath is aimed at two distinctly different audiences. First, it's used by developers to design forms. But then InfoPath is also used to fill out those same forms. If you think of InfoPath as including both a design piece and a data entry piece in one package, it might be less confusing.

What Is InfoPath?

At the end of the day, InfoPath is a pretty face on top of industry-standard XML. By now you've seen how XML functionality has been added to many of the applications that make up Microsoft Office 2003, but InfoPath is different. Rather than adding XML support to some other functionality, InfoPath is all about XML in the first place. It uses a variety of XML standards, including

- **XML**—Specifies the overall structure of the files InfoPath uses

- **XSLT**—Provides a way to display XML files in different formats

- **XML Schemas**—Describes a database structure in XML

- **XPath**—Is an XML-based query language

 MORE INFO

You won't need to know the details of the various XML standards to use InfoPath, but if you'd like to find out more, a good place to start is the World Wide Web Consortium's site at http://www.w3c.org.

But unlike some other products that require you to edit XML at a low level, showing you all the angle brackets and other markup that make up the XML, InfoPath is designed to hide the complexities of XML from end users. It does this by providing a forms-oriented interface (similar to forms you might see in Access) on top of XML files. When you work with the design tools in InfoPath, you're specifying the XML you'd like to collect and the controls that will be used to collect it. When you fill in an InfoPath form, you're constructing an XML file.

InfoPath also enables a number of easy scenarios for working with its files:

- You can merge the information from many forms into a single form.

- You can email unfinished forms to another user for completion.

- You can export data to Excel for further analysis.

- You can integrate forms with a SharePoint forms library.

- You can submit data from a form to an Access or SQL Server database, or to a Web service.

- You can save InfoPath data to a read-only Web page or to an email message to share with a user who doesn't have InfoPath.

 MORE INFO

If you're a developer, you can extract the XML information from an InfoPath form to integrate with other business processes, such as Customer Relationship Management (CRM) or Enterprise Resource Planning (ERP). You can find further details by downloading the InfoPath 2003 Software Development Kit (SDK) from http://www.microsoft.com/downloads/
details.aspx?FamilyId=351F0616-93AA-4FE8-9238-D702F1BFBAB4&
displaylang=en.

Designing a Form

To give you an overview of InfoPath's workings, we'll build a form to collect warehouse inventory information. You might imagine this form being filled out on Tablet PCs by a team of workers moving through a warehouse to take the annual physical inventory. The warehouse is divided into a number of locations, each of which is identified by its floor and its section number. Within each section, there can be zero or more items, each of which has an item number, a count, and the date on which the inventory was taken.

To get started, launch InfoPath. By default, the application opens with the Fill Out a Form task pane displayed, as shown in Figure 11.1.

Before you can fill out a form, you need to design it. Select File, Design a Form, or click Design a Form in the task pane drop-down list, to open the Design a Form task pane shown in Figure 11.2. Then click New Blank Form to build your first InfoPath form.

Clicking New Blank Form does two things. First, it opens the Design Tasks task pane. Second, it actually creates a new form for you to work with; you can see this in Figure 11.3, which now has a white background in the working area instead of the default, empty gray.

As you can see in the task pane, five main design tasks are in InfoPath:

- **Layout**—Enables you to create devices such as tables and sections to organize your InfoPath forms

- **Controls**—Enables you to create controls such as text boxes and date pickers that can be used to enter data

- **Data Source**—Enables you to specify the structure of the form's data

- **Views**—Enables you to define multiple views of the same data

- **Publish Form**—Enables you to make your InfoPath form available to the users who will fill it in

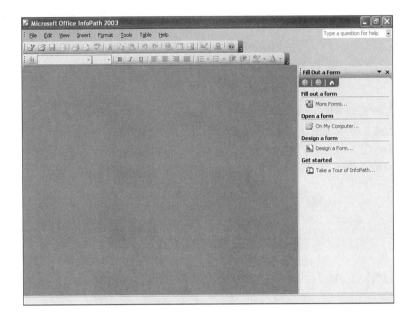

FIGURE 11.1   InfoPath defaults to Fill Out a Form mode.

FIGURE 11.2   The Design a Form task pane.

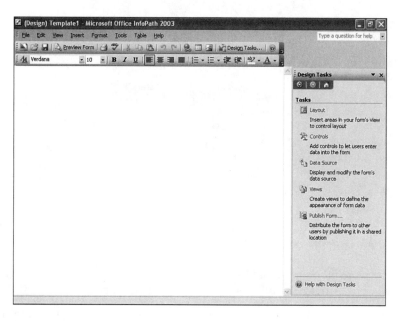

FIGURE 11.3 InfoPath with a newly created form open.

Each of these shortcuts in the Design Tasks task pane takes you to its own task pane, with shortcuts to the other design tasks.

Creating the Data Source

To continue, click the Data Source shortcut to open the Data Source task pane. This task pane shows you a single group named MyFields, which is the default root of the new InfoPath form's data. InfoPath data (like XML data) is arranged hierarchically into groups and fields. Follow these steps to build a data source with the structure we need for the inventory data:

1. Right-click the MyFields group and select Properties.

2. In the Field or Group Properties dialog box, change the name of the group to **inventory**. Click OK.

 **EXPERT ADVICE**

Microsoft uses camel case in naming groups and fields in the sample forms that ship with InfoPath. In *camel case*, you run all the words of a name together and capitalize all but the first word (if there are more words in the identifier). For example, `expenseReport`, `inventory`, and `reportsToName` are all camel-cased identifiers. We suggest you follow Microsoft's lead and use camel case in naming groups and fields.

3. With the Inventory group selected, click the Add button in the Data Source task pane. This opens the Add Field or Group dialog box, shown in Figure 11.4. Create a new group named **locations** and click OK.

FIGURE 11.4   Creating a new group in an InfoPath data source.

4. Use the same procedure to add another group as a child of the locations group. Name the new group **location** and check the Repeating check box for the group.

5. Add an element field as a child of the location group. Name the new field **floor** and set its Data Type to Text (String), as shown in Figure 11.5. Check the Cannot Be Blank check box for this field.

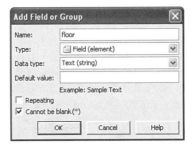

FIGURE 11.5   Creating a new field in an InfoPath data source.

 **EXPERT ADVICE**

Why use a text data type instead of a numeric data type for the floor element? Because, depending on the warehouse, a floor might have a designation such as L or B2 as well as a number.

6. Add a second element field as a child of the location group. Name the new field **section**, set its Data Type to Text (String), and check the Cannot Be Blank check box.

7. Add a new group as a child of the location group. Name the new group **items**.

8. Add a new group as a child of the items group. Name the new group `item` and set it to be a repeating group.

9. Add a new element field as a child of the item group. Name the new field `itemNumber`, set its data type to Text (String), and check the Cannot Be Blank check box.

10. Add a new element field as a child of the item group. Name the new field `count`, set its data type to Whole Number (Integer), and check the Cannot Be Blank check box.

11. Add a new element field as a child of the item group. Name the new field `inventoryDate`, set its data type to Date (Date), and check the Cannot Be Blank check box.

Figure 11.6 shows the completed data source structure. Note that the icons show you which groups repeat and which fields are required.

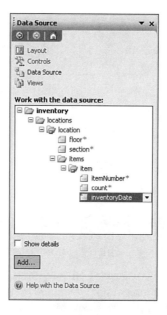

FIGURE 11.6   The finished data source is shown in the Data Source task pane.

 **EXPERT ADVICE**

If you explore, you'll find that you can create fields as either elements or attributes. This refers to two different ways to represent the data in XML. In most cases, you'll find that using elements for fields makes interoperating with other software easier.

Creating the Form

The next step is to create a form that lets users provide data that matches the data source that was just created. To do this, drag the locations node from the data source and drop it anywhere on the form design area. You'll have a choice of Section with Controls or Section when you drop the node. To generate the form, select Section with Controls as shown in Figure 11.7.

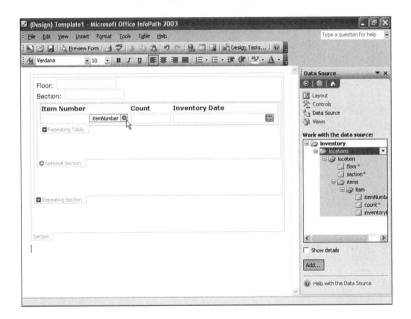

FIGURE 11.7   Laying out a form from a data source.

When you drag data to the form, InfoPath turns it into (in this case) a set of nested sections and layout tables, with controls where the user can enter data. As you move the cursor around over the form, tips show you which field or group is bound to each control.

You can use the mouse to move and resize controls, and you can use the Format menu or the Formatting toolbar to alter their appearance. Double-clicking a control opens a Properties dialog box that lets you set other details of the control, such as the ScreenTip to display when the user hovers his mouse over the control.

To save a local copy of the new form, select Save from the File menu. This opens a dialog box that gives you the choice of Save or Publish. Click Save a second time, assign a filename to the form, and use the .xsn (InfoPath Form Template) file extension.

Publishing the Form

Saving the form keeps a copy of the template on your computer but doesn't make it available to other users. To let other users fill in the form, you need to publish it. Follow these steps to publish the new form:

1. Select File, Publish.

2. Read the opening panel of the Publishing Wizard and click Next.

3. Select the To a Shared Folder on This Computer or on a Network option and click Next.

4. Browse to a location on your network that is accessible to users, assign a name to the form, and click OK. This returns you to the Publishing Wizard.

5. Assign a name to the form (such as **Inventory**), as shown in Figure 11.8, and click Next.

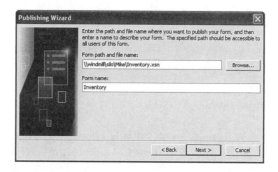

FIGURE 11.8   Identifying an InfoPath form on the network.

6. Verify that the path displayed is accessible to users and click Finish.

7. The last panel of the wizard lets you send email messages to users to tell them about the new form. When you're done with this, click Close.

At this point, you've designed and published your first InfoPath form. Now let's see how a user can fill it in.

Filling Out a Form

Select File, Close to close the copy of the form that's open in Design mode. Then select Fill Out a Form from the File menu to open the Fill Out a Form task pane. You should see a hyperlink for the new Inventory form as the first entry in the Fill Out a Form section of the task pane, as shown in Figure 11.9. Click the hyperlink to load the form.

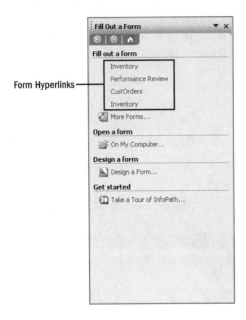

Form Hyperlinks

FIGURE 11.9 Click a hyperlink to fill out a form.

Figure 11.10 shows the new form as it will initially open. The downward-pointing arrow next to the Floor field indicates that this field is part of a repeating section; click the arrow to get a list of shortcut choices such as adding a new copy of the section or deleting an existing section. As you move your mouse around, you'll see similar arrows next to the sections representing the other groups in the initial data source.

Enter a floor number in the Floor text box (note that InfoPath has taken the camel-cased field and group names and turned them into proper case), and click Tab to move to the next field.

MORE INFO

If this is the first time you've used InfoPath, it will offer to turn on AutoComplete. AutoComplete remembers things you've frequently entered and offers to type them in again for you in the future.

Continue tabbing and you'll end up in the fields related to the item after you fill in the fields related to the location. Note the little calendar button next to the Inventory Date control; this lets you drop down a calendar, and you can select a date by clicking the calendar.

After using the drop-down arrows to the left of the sections to add another location and some additional items (you can also use the Ctrl+Enter shortcut to create more data entry controls in the current repeating section), your form might look like Figure 11.11.

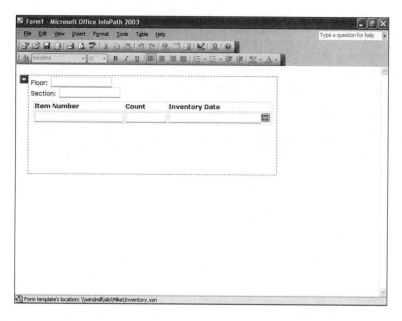

FIGURE 11.10   A blank InfoPath form, ready to fill out.

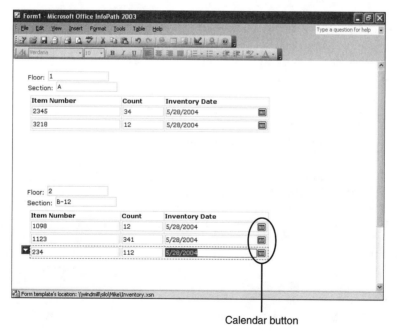

Calendar button

FIGURE 11.11   An InfoPath form with some data.

Saving a Form

When you're done entering data, select File, Save. You might expect this to overwrite the .xsn form template, but it doesn't. Instead, it lets you save the data you've entered as an InfoPath Form with the extension .xml (for example, Inventory.xml).

Sure enough, if you open the resulting file in a text editor (or a specialized XML editor such as XMLSpy, available from http://www.xmlspy.com), you'll find that it's a perfectly standard XML file. Here, for example, is the file that corresponds to the information in Figure 11.10:

```xml
<?xml version="1.0" encoding="UTF-8"?>
<?mso-infoPathSolution solutionVersion="1.0.0.2"
  productVersion="11.0.5531" PIVersion="1.0.0.0"
  href="file:///\\windmill\silo\Mike\Inventory.xsn" ?>
<?mso-application progid="InfoPath.Document"?>
<my:inventory xmlns:my="http://schemas.microsoft.com/office/
  infopath/2003/myXSD/2004-02-22T23:12:44" xml:lang="en-us">
  <my:locations>
    <my:location>
      <my:floor>1</my:floor>
      <my:section>A</my:section>
      <my:items>
        <my:item>
          <my:itemNumber>2345</my:itemNumber>
          <my:count>34</my:count>
          <my:inventoryDate>2004-05-28</my:inventoryDate>
        </my:item>
        <my:item>
          <my:itemNumber>3218</my:itemNumber>
          <my:count>12</my:count>
          <my:inventoryDate>2004-05-28</my:inventoryDate>
        </my:item>
      </my:items>
    </my:location>
    <my:location>
      <my:floor>2</my:floor>
      <my:section>B-12</my:section>
      <my:items>
        <my:item>
          <my:itemNumber>1098</my:itemNumber>
          <my:count>12</my:count>
          <my:inventoryDate>2004-05-28</my:inventoryDate>
        </my:item>
        <my:item>
          <my:itemNumber>1123</my:itemNumber>
```

```
          <my:count>341</my:count>
          <my:inventoryDate>2004-05-28</my:inventoryDate>
        </my:item>
        <my:item>
          <my:itemNumber>234</my:itemNumber>
          <my:count>112</my:count>
          <my:inventoryDate>2004-05-28</my:inventoryDate>
        </my:item>
      </my:items>
    </my:location>
  </my:locations>
</my:inventory>
```

This is where the true power of InfoPath lies. Although you never saw a single angle bracket, either when designing the form or when filling it out, the end result is an XML file that can be interchanged with any other application that understands XML.

Designing Forms

Now that you've seen the basics of InfoPath, we'll drill in a bit more on designing forms. Of course, we could write an entire book about InfoPath, so this coverage is necessarily a bit skimpy. But our hope is that by showing you some of the highlights, we can give you a glimpse of areas where further research will help in your own work.

 MORE INFO

If you need to delve further into the inner workings of InfoPath, check out Que Publishing's *Microsoft Office InfoPath 2003 Kick Start* for a more in-depth look.

Working with Data Sources

When you build a data source in InfoPath you're actually creating an XML schema (.xsd) file. InfoPath can also use an existing XML schema file as a data source. To do so, follow these steps:

1. Select File, Design a Form.

2. Click the New From Data Source link in the task pane to launch the Data Source Setup Wizard.

3. Select the XML Schema or XML Data File option. Click Next.

4. Browse to locate the schema file you want to work with. Click Finish.

MORE INFO

You'll learn a bit about other data file options later in the chapter, in the "Working with Databases" section.

As you saw earlier in the chapter, InfoPath makes its own best guesses when laying out your forms. But you can use the Data Source task pane to override the default choices InfoPath makes.

For example, in the inventory data source InfoPath chooses to use a Date Picker control to represent the inventoryDate field (as you saw in Figure 11.10). But you might prefer to let the user type the date directly into a text box instead. To accomplish this, right-click the inventoryDate field. The shortcut menu includes a variety of controls that can be used for data entry into this field. Click the control you want and InfoPath inserts that control on the form at the current cursor location.

 EXPERT ADVICE

If you've already let InfoPath create a control for a particular field, you can right-click the control on the form and select Change To if you'd like to use a different type of control.

 UPGRADERS BEWARE

You can also create new sections and controls on your form from the Layout or Controls task panes, but doing so adds fields to the data source rather than using the existing fields.

Working with Views

InfoPath enables you to create multiple views of a single form. Behind the scenes, a view applies an XSL transform to the data stored for a form. No data is lost when the user switches from one view to another, but the appearance of the data can be vastly changed.

Follow these steps to add a simplified view that shows locations only (and not item details) to the inventory form:

1. With the form open in Design view, switch to the Views task pane by selecting View, Manage Views.

2. Select the default View 1 view and click View Properties to open the View Properties dialog box, shown in Figure 11.12. Change the view name to **Full Details** and click OK.

3. Click the Add a New View hyperlink. In the Add View dialog box, name the new view **Summary** and click OK. A new, blank view now occupies the design surface.

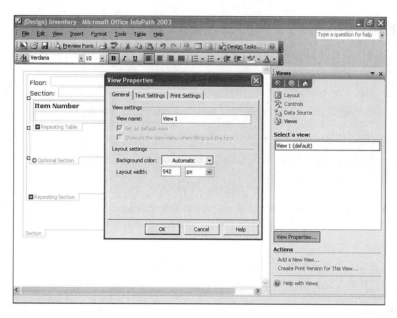

FIGURE 11.12 Modify properties for an existing view.

4. Click the Data Source hyperlink to switch to the Data Source task pane.

5. Drag the `floor` element from the Data Source task pane to the new view. This creates a repeating section for the location element, with a text box for the `floor` element nested inside the repeating section.

6. Drag the section element to the new view and drop it in the repeating section.

7. Save the form template and publish it to the same location you used earlier.

8. Double-click the `Inventory.xml` file you saved earlier. This opens it in InfoPath. You'll find that the View menu now includes entries for Full Details and Summary—the two views that were saved in the template. Select Summary from the View menu to display the summarized version of the form, as shown in Figure 11.13.

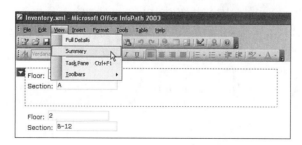

FIGURE 11.13 Displaying a nondefault view of the data.

Validating Data

As is the case with most other forms tools, InfoPath lets you validate the data the user enters. For example, in the inventory form we might want to limit the values entered to be between 1 and 1000. To do this, follow these steps:

1. Open the inventory form in Design view and navigate to the Data Source task pane.

2. Right-click the count field and select Properties.

3. In the Field or Group Properties dialog box, select the Validation and Script tab.

4. Click the Add button in the Validation section.

5. In the Data Validation (Count) dialog box, select Is Less Than in the middle box in the If This Condition Is True section. Select Type a Number in the third box, and type 1.

6. Click the And button to create a second row for the validation rule. Then click the drop-down arrow above And and change it to Or.

7. Set the second condition to Count Is Greater Than 1000.

8. Enter **Invalid Value** as the ScreenTip.

9. Enter **Count must be between 1 and 1000** as the message. Figure 11.14 shows the finished Data Validation (Count) dialog box.

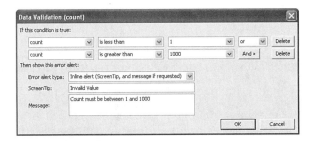

FIGURE 11.14   Creating a validation rule.

10. Click OK twice to apply the validation rule to the field.

11. Republish the form to its original location by selecting File, Publish and working through the Publishing Wizard as you did earlier.

To test the new validation rule, open the form in Fill Out a Form view. Enter an invalid value (such as **1278**) in the Count control and press Tab. InfoPath displays a dashed red border around the control to indicate that there's a problem, as shown in the top image of Figure 11.15. Hover the mouse pointer over the control to see a ScreenTip with the short error message, as shown in the middle image of Figure 11.15. Right-click the control and select Full Error Description to see the verbose description of the error, as shown in the bottom image of Figure 11.15.

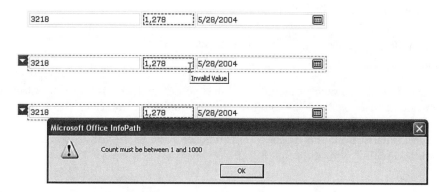

FIGURE 11.15   Validation rules in the user interface.

Publishing Forms

You've already seen that InfoPath forms can be published to a shared location on your network after you're finished designing them. You also have two other choices in the Publishing Wizard, as shown in Figure 11.16: You can publish a form to a SharePoint form library or to a Web server.

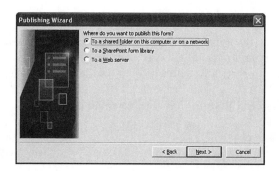

FIGURE 11.16   Publishing an InfoPath form.

Publishing to a SharePoint Form Library

If you choose to publish an InfoPath form to a SharePoint form library, follow these steps to complete the process:

1. Select between a new library (which is the recommended course of action) or an existing library. For this exercise, create a new library. Click Next.

UPGRADERS BEWARE

You should choose an existing SharePoint form library only if your template is compatible with any template that already exists in that library.

2. Enter the URL of the SharePoint site and click Next.

3. Enter a name and description of the form library and click Next.

4. The next panel, shown in Figure 11.17, lets you extract data from saved InfoPath forms and make them available as columns on the SharePoint site. Click the Add button to see a list of all the columns in the data source for your form. In Figure 11.17, we've added the first floor and first section from each form to the list. Click Finish when you're done selecting columns.

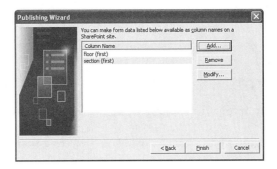

FIGURE 11.17   Adding InfoPath columns to a SharePoint site.

After you've published your form to a SharePoint site, users can fill out the form by navigating to the forms library and clicking Fill Out This Form. This opens the form in InfoPath, and saving the form automatically writes its data back to the SharePoint site. Figure 11.18 shows a SharePoint site with several instances of the Inventory form saved to it. Note the two columns of data from the form that are integrated directly into the SharePoint display.

Publishing to a Web Server

If you choose to publish an InfoPath form to a Web server, follow these steps to complete the process:

1. Enter the URL to use for the form on the Web server, and enter a friendly name for the form. Click Next.

2. If the public URL for the form is different from the one you entered in step 1, enter the public URL. Click Next.

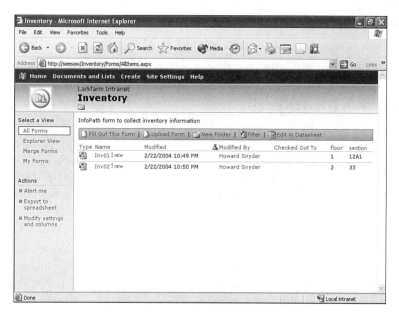

FIGURE 11.18   InfoPath forms in a SharePoint form library.

After you publish a form to a Web server, users can fill out the form by navigating to the URL that contains the form. The form is downloaded to the user's local computer, where she can fill it out using her own copy of InfoPath. At that point, it acts like any other InfoPath form opened from the local network. The filled-out copy is saved to the user's hard drive, not posted back to the Web server.

UPGRADERS BEWARE

Even when you publish an InfoPath form to a Web server, the user needs to have a copy of InfoPath installed on her own computer to fill out the form. There is no way to fill out an InfoPath form in a Web browser.

Collaborating with InfoPath

We'll conclude the chapter by reviewing some of the ways you can use InfoPath collaboratively, with other users or with other applications:

- Merging forms together
- Emailing forms
- Analyzing InfoPath data in Excel

- Working with databases
- Sharing data with non-InfoPath users

Merging Forms Together

If you have more than one form created from the same InfoPath template, you can merge their contents together into a single file. To do so, open any one of the forms in Fill Out a Form mode (which you can do just by double-clicking the saved form in Windows Explorer). Then select Merge Forms from the File menu. Browse to the other form you want to merge into the current form and click Merge. This extracts the data from the new form and inserts it into the current form. You can repeat the process as many times as necessary to merge all the data.

Merging forms is useful when multiple users are all working on the same project. For example, consider the warehouse inventory form we've been developing. If you had half a dozen workers with Tablet PCs all collecting inventory information in a single warehouse, you could use merging to consolidate their data into a single XML file.

As a forms developer, though, you might want to disable this facility. If you needed to track each worker's productivity individually, it probably wouldn't be a good idea to allow form merging. Fortunately, you can easily turn off this feature when you're creating the form template. To do so, select Form Options from the Tools menu. This opens the Form Options dialog box shown in Figure 11.19. Uncheck the Enable Form Merging check box to disable this feature for this template.

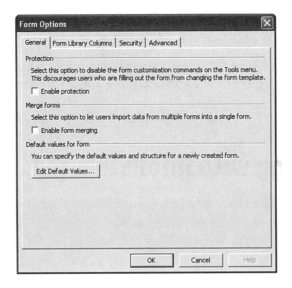

FIGURE 11.19   Setting options for an InfoPath form.

UPGRADERS BEWARE

Don't confuse Form Options with Options. The former menu item sets options for the current form open in the designer, whereas the latter sets options for InfoPath as a whole.

Emailing Forms to an InfoPath User

Some forms require the input of more than one user. A performance review form, for example, might have sections to be filled out by both the employee and the manager. In these cases, it can be convenient to transmit an InfoPath form by email for further processing.

When you're ready to pass an InfoPath form to another user, select Send to Mail Recipient from the File menu. This opens a set of mail controls at the top of the form, as shown in Figure 11.20. Fill in the form and click the Send button to send the message. You're returned to the form in InfoPath, while a copy is sent to the mail recipient.

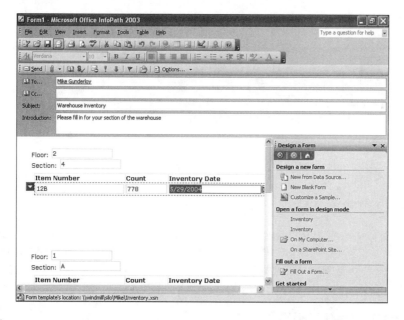

FIGURE 11.20 Emailing an InfoPath form.

The recipient gets an email that contains the form's current information in two formats. First, the body of the email is an HTML representation of the current data, which can be easily read in most email clients. Second, the .xml file for the form is sent as an attachment. If the recipient has a copy of InfoPath installed, he can open this attachment to continue editing the form.

Using InfoPath with Excel

With both InfoPath and Excel being XML-enabled, it should come as no surprise that you can use Excel to analyze data you've collected with InfoPath. Follow these steps to send your InfoPath data to Excel:

1. Select Export To, Microsoft Office Excel from the File menu to launch the Export to Excel Wizard. Click Next after reading the introductory panel.

2. Select the type of data (either the form fields only or the form fields and any lists displayed on the form) you want to export and click Next.

3. Select the specific data you want to export and click Next.

4. Specify any additional forms containing data to be merged with this form's data and click Finish.

Figure 11.21 shows the exported data in Excel. Each column is captioned with the name of the field and the XPath expression that locates the field within the data source. Note that the data is simply an Excel worksheet; it's not exported as an Excel list.

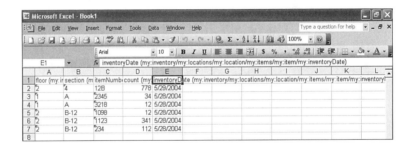

FIGURE 11.21   InfoPath data in Excel.

For more information on Excel lists, see Chapter 5, "What's New in Excel 2003." For more information on how to work with Excel and use the data you collected in InfoPath, check out Que Publishing's Business Solutions series book titled *Managing Data with Excel*.

Working with Databases

InfoPath has built-in hooks to make it work well with Microsoft Access and Microsoft SQL Server databases. You can easily design an InfoPath form that lets you query a database for existing data as well as enter new data into the database. Follow these steps to see an example:

1. Open InfoPath and select File, Design a Form.

2. In the Design a Form task pane, click the New from Data Source hyperlink.

3. Select Database (Microsoft SQL Server or Microsoft Access Only) and click Next.

4. Click Select Database to open the Select Data Source dialog box.

5. Browse to the Northwind sample Access database and click Open. This opens the Select Tables dialog box.

6. The Select Tables dialog box lists all the tables and queries in the database. Select the Customers table and click OK.

7. The Data Source Setup Wizard now displays the schema of the Customers table, as shown in Figure 11.22. You can choose which columns you'd like to display on the InfoPath form here.

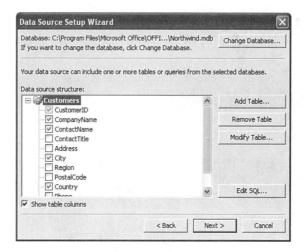

FIGURE 11.22   Choosing database columns in the Data Source Setup Wizard.

8. Click Add Table to open the Add Table or Query dialog box. Select the Orders table and click Next. Check the default relationship and click Finish to return to the Data Source Setup Wizard. This adds the Orders table as a child of the Customers table and lets you select fields from both tables to include on your form. Click Next.

9. Select the radio button marked Design Query View First and click Finish. InfoPath creates two different sets of fields (one for querying and one for display) and two views and displays the query view as shown in Figure 11.23.

10. Click Views and switch to the Data Entry view.

11. Click Data Sources to display the Data Source task pane. Expand the `dataFields` node of the data source and drag the `d:Customers` group to the blank view. Select Repeating Section with Controls to create the data entry view shown in Figure 11.24.

12. Publish the form to a convenient location.

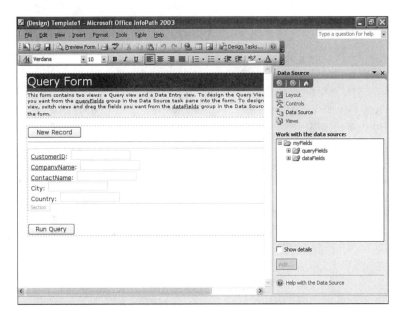

FIGURE 11.23   Automatically generated query view for a database.

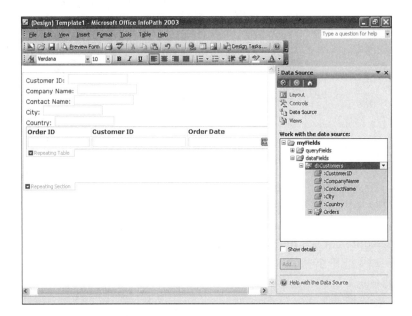

FIGURE 11.24   A data entry view for a database.

Now you're ready to see how the database-connected form works. Open the form in Fill Out a Form mode from the location where it was published. The form defaults to query view. Enter some data (for example, enter **Brazil** in the Country text box) and click Run Query. InfoPath looks for records that match your query criteria and then displays them using the data entry view, as shown in Figure 11.25.

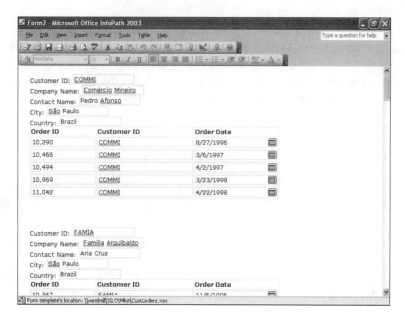

FIGURE 11.25   Records retrieved by a database query.

 **EXPERT ADVICE**

InfoPath returns only records that match all the data you entered in the query view. For example, if you specify Brazil for the country and São Paolo for the city, you get back only customers (and their orders) in that particular city and country combination.

Because returned records are displayed on the data entry view, you can enter data immediately after performing a query. Alternatively, you can click New Record on the query view to open the data entry view with no preexisting data.

When you've finished entering data, click the Save button on the Standard toolbar or select File, Save. InfoPath asks whether you'd like to save or submit the data. If you choose to save the data, it is stored in a .xml file, just like any other InfoPath data. But if you choose Submit, the data is sent back to the database. Thus, you can use InfoPath as a data entry front end for any Access or SQL Server database.

 EXPERT ADVICE

You can combine InfoPath's knowledge of databases with the capability to email InfoPath forms to easily enable remote data entry. First, create an InfoPath form based on the database and publish it to remote users. Have those users enter new data and email their forms back to the main office, where you can open them and then submit the data to the original database.

Using InfoPath with Web Services

InfoPath can also serve as a client for *Web services*. A relatively recent development in computing, Web services provide a standardized way to pass information between different applications over the Internet. Web services depend on a trio of XML protocols to function:

- **Simple Object Access Protocol (SOAP)**—Specifies the format for messages sent between a Web services server and its clients. SOAP provides a standardized way to encapsulate objects and documents within XML messages. These messages can travel to any point on the Internet and be interpreted by software on a variety of operating systems, making SOAP a sort of universal communications protocol.

- **Web Services Description Language (WSDL)**—Specifies the exact content of the SOAP messages that are understood by a particular Web service. The WSDL file for a Web service tells software how to interact with that particular Web service.

- **Universal Description, Discovery, and Integration (UDDI)**—Is the format for finding Web services by referring to a central directory. If you don't know where the WSDL file for a Web service is, you can look up that information in a UDDI server.

To get started with InfoPath and Web services, you need to find a Web service to use. Before you go hunting, you need to know the two major classes of Web services: document/literal and RPC. The technical distinction between the two isn't important for us (we won't have to look at the XML at all). What is important is that, as of InfoPath SP1, InfoPath can interact with only document/literal Web services.

As mentioned earlier, you can search for Web services in a UDDI directory, but that's not the only way. An easier way to find general-purpose Web services with interesting results is to use a public directory designed for human beings—instead of one designed for automated search. An excellent example of such a directory can be found at the XMethods Web site (www. xmethods.com). Although you can search the XMethods directory using UDDI, you can also browse it yourself, as shown in Figure 11.26. As you can see, the listings tell you whether a particular Web service uses RPC-style or document-style messages.

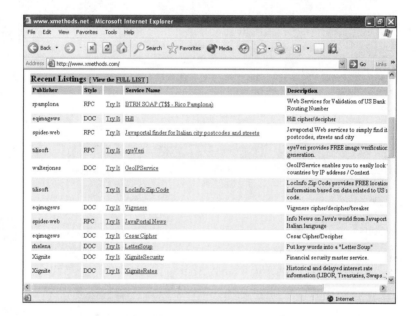

FIGURE 11.26 Locating a Web service to test.

When you find a Web service you want to use on the XMethods site, you can click the service name for more information (see Figure 11.27). In particular, you'll see a URL for the WSDL file associated with this service. We'll hook up InfoPath to retrieve information from the GeoIPService Web service shown here. GeoIPService is a fairly typical Web service. Given an IP address, it returns the country in which that IP address is located.

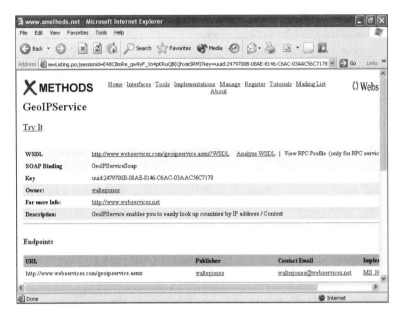

FIGURE 11.27   Details of a Web service.

Follow these steps to create an InfoPath data source that retrieves information from the GeoIPService Web service:

1. Launch InfoPath and select File, Design a Form.

2. In the Design a Form task pane, click the New from Data Source shortcut.

3. On the first panel of the Data Source Setup Wizard, specify Web Service as the type of the data source and click Next.

4. On the second panel of the Data Source Setup Wizard, specify that you want to receive data from the Web service and click Next. Some Web services also let you submit data, but in this case we'll only be asking the Web service to send us data.

5. On the third panel of the Data Source Setup Wizard (shown in Figure 11.28), enter the location of the WSDL file for the Web service you want to use. Note that you can also launch a UDDI search from this panel if you don't already know the WSDL location. Click Next.

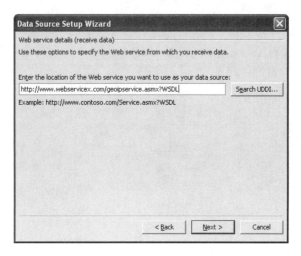

FIGURE 11.28   Connecting to a Web service.

6. InfoPath downloads the WSDL file and parses it to determine the SOAP messages the
   Web service will accept. The fourth panel of the Data Source Setup Wizard shows you
   all the operations the Web service can perform (see Figure 11.29). This information is
   retrieved from the WSDL file. Select an operation and click Next.

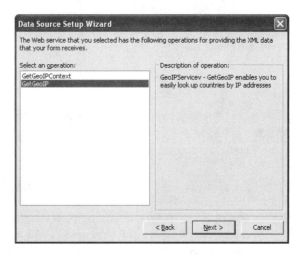

FIGURE 11.29   Selecting a Web service operation.

7. On the last panel of the Data Source Setup Wizard, select the option to design the
   query view first (this is the default) and click Finish.

When you create a data source based on a Web service, InfoPath determines the data you can send to the Web service in a query, and the data you will get back in response; however, it doesn't put any of that data on the form for you. Figure 11.30 shows the fields retrieved from the GeoIPService Web service's GetGeoIP operation.

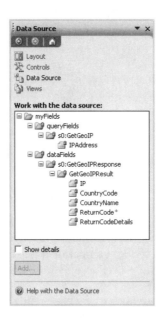

FIGURE 11.30   Query and data fields from a Web service.

 MORE INFO

The SOAP standard defines two types of messages: requests and responses. InfoPath maps all the fields from the SOAP request to the queryFields node in the data source and maps all the fields from the SOAP response to the dataFields node in the data source.

To continue designing the form for the GeoIPService Web service, drag the IPAddress field from the data source task pane to the query view of the form. This creates a text box control in which you can enter an IP address to query the service. Now drag the CountryCode and CountryName fields to the query view of the form. This creates two more controls that display the result of the Web service query.

 **MORE INFO**

When you're working with a Web service that returns only information, you only use the Query view of the form.

Use the Views hyperlink in the task pane to switch to the views task pane. Click the drop-down arrow for the Query view and set it to be the default view of the form.

Now you're ready to try calling the Web service from InfoPath. Click the Preview Form toolbar button. This opens the form in query view. Type an IP address and click the Run Query button to see the geographical location of that IP address, as shown in Figure 11.31.

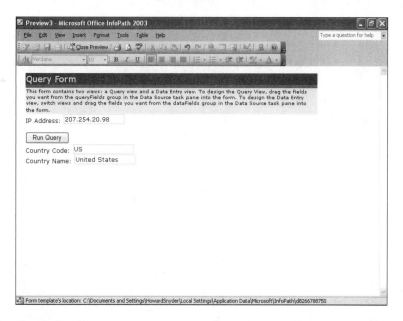

FIGURE 11.31   Calling a Web service from InfoPath.

Sharing Data with Non-InfoPath Users

Finally, there are two ways to share your InfoPath data with users who do not have InfoPath installed. You've already seen one of these: You can email InfoPath data. Although users without InfoPath won't be able to open the attached InfoPath XML file, they can still view the HTML representation of the data in the body of the email message.

MORE INFO

Actually, users without InfoPath can still open an InfoPath form, but they'll be able to view it only as an XML file, not as a form.

The other choice for sharing InfoPath data is to publish the data to a Web server. To do this, select Export To, Web from the File menu. This enables you to save your InfoPath form as a single-file Web page (.mht page). This is a Microsoft format that bundles both text and graphics in a single file. Figure 11.32 shows an exported InfoPath form open in a Web browser.

After you publish InfoPath data to a Web server, it's no longer tied to InfoPath. At this point, anyone can refer to the data without a copy of InfoPath; all they need is a Web browser.

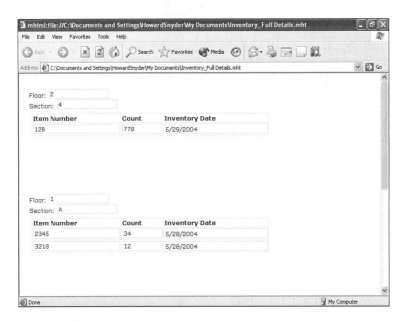

FIGURE 11.32   InfoPath data in a Web browser.

New Features in InfoPath SP1

Like OneNote, InfoPath gained many new features in the Service Pack 1 (SP1) release. SP1 can open forms created with the original InfoPath release (although the reverse is not necessarily true), and the new features are significant for both developers and users. Because of this, we recommend that you upgrade to SP1 whenever it's practical for your organization to deploy the new version.

End-user Changes

Some of the changes to InfoPath SP1 will primarily affect end users. Chief among these are a raft of new controls designers can use to create more functional and useable pages. For example, Figure 11.33 shows the new master-detail control, which is useful anytime the data contains a hierarchy (here one customer can have many orders). Adding this set of data-entry and display controls to a form is as simple as selecting Master-Detail when you drag the fields to the form.

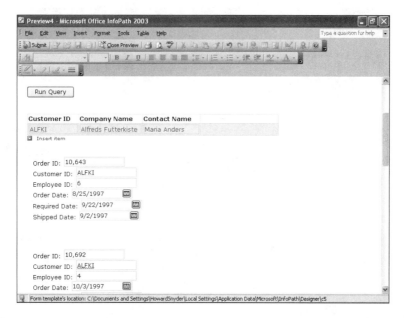

FIGURE 11.33 Master-detail controls in InfoPath SP1.

Here's a list of the other new control options you'll find in SP1:

- **ActiveX Control**—This control is a container for Microsoft ActiveX controls, which can display a wide variety of custom interfaces.

- **Choice Group**—An option control that lets you switch entire groups of fields at one time. For example, you could use a choice group to switch between home and office contact information for a customer.

- **File Attachment Control**—Allows users to upload a file when they submit an InfoPath form.

- **Repeating Recursive Section**—A section that can be inserted within and linked back to itself. This control is designed to enable the display of recursive information such as a bill of materials or an organization chart.

- **Scrolling Region**—This control lets you put other controls into a container with a vertical scrollbar. The scrolling region can help you conserve space, which is often a problem on InfoPath forms. Figure 11.34 shows an InfoPath form in which the detail section of a master-detail control has been enclosed in a scrolling region control. This control lets you scroll among the details, rather than displaying them all on the master form.

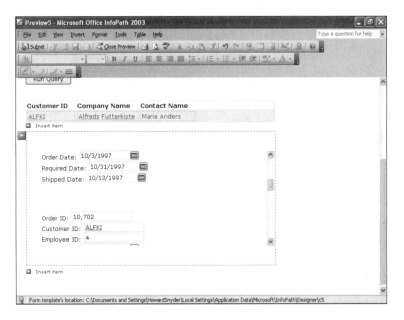

FIGURE 11.34   Scrolling region control in InfoPath SP1.

- **Vertical Label**—A label that displays text rotated 90°.

Another change that will have a direct impact on end users is the vastly improved support for digital signatures. When you're designing a form, you can select Tools, Form Options and then navigate to the Digital Signatures tab to see the choices shown in Figure 11.35.

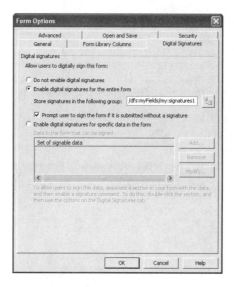

FIGURE 11.35   Digital signature options for an InfoPath form.

You can decide on a form-by-form basis whether to enable digital signatures. If you do want to enable digital signatures, you can enable them for the entire form or for only selected data. When they're enabled, you can use prompting to ensure that the user doesn't submit an unsigned form.

Digital signatures provide a way to ensure that a form hasn't been altered after it was submitted. By using digital signatures on sensitive data, along with optional signing comments, you can have a high degree of confidence that the data seen when you look at a saved form is the data the user intended to submit.

Designer Changes

Other changes in InfoPath SP1 have more impact on the form designer than on the end user.

For starters, InfoPath is now more tightly integrated with SharePoint. You already saw how you could publish InfoPath forms to a SharePoint library and save filled-out forms back to the library. But with SP1, you can also use a SharePoint list (data stored in SharePoint's native format) as a secondary data source for InfoPath. A secondary data source is one that provides data to help in filling out a form. For example, you can use a secondary data source to provide a list of choices for a drop-down list. To use a SharePoint list as a secondary data source, follow these steps:

1. Select a control that will display the data retrieved from SharePoint. For example, you might have a text box on a form that you use to enter a customer name. Right-click the control and select Change To, More. Select Drop-Down List Box from the Select a Control dialog box and click OK.

2. Right-click the control and select Drop-Down List Box Properties.

3. In the Drop-Down List Box Properties dialog box, shown in Figure 11.36, select the option to look up values in a data connection.

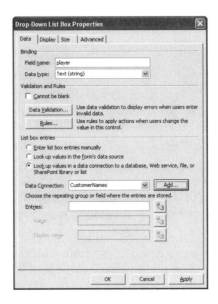

FIGURE 11.36   Properties of a drop-down list box.

4. Click the Add button to add a new data connection.

5. Select the SharePoint Library or List option in the Data Connection Wizard and click Next.

6. Enter the base URL of your SharePoint site and click Next.

7. Select the SharePoint list that contains the data and click Next.

8. Select the data fields you want to use and click Next. If you want, you can select different fields to display and to store.

9. Enter a name for the data connection and click Finish.

10. Back in the Drop-Down List Properties dialog box, select the new data connection as the data connection for the drop-down list. Choose the repeating group or field in the data that stores the selected data, and then click OK.

The three main advantages to using SharePoint lists as data sources for controls such as drop-down lists are

- Because SharePoint is accessible via HTTP, these lookup lists can be available in situations in which end users cannot connect to a corporate database.

- The data for the lookup lists is stored centrally, where it's easy to edit without needing to edit and republish InfoPath forms.

- You can use the same data for lists on many InfoPath forms, eliminating the chance that two different forms will disagree on something such as your list of customers.

Other changes that will primarily interest form developers include

- **Support for ADO.NET DataSets when requesting data from or submitting data to a Web service**—This makes InfoPath compatible with a wider variety of Web services built with Visual Studio .NET.

- **Support for filling out forms on a Tablet PC using ink**—InfoPath now smoothly translates ink to text in a control. There's also a new ink picture control that lets you prompt the user for raw ink (such as a graphical signature). The end result is stored in the XML file as base64-encoded text.

- **New security options that prevent the user from accessing data that isn't needed for the form**—This helps cut down the chance that a malicious form could damage the computer or steal data. It also helps guard your data against accidental data changes by locking out those who should not be reading the data in the first place.

- **Support for writing code in Visual Studio .NET that integrates directly with an InfoPath form**—This provides a much richer programming experience than the scripting support in the original release.

Overall, we think the layout, data, security, and Tablet PC improvements make a compelling case for installing Service Pack 1 if you're rolling out InfoPath in your own organization.

What's New in Rights Management

A s we mentioned in Chapter 1, "What's New in Office 2003," rights management (sometimes called Digital Rights Management [DRM]) is one of the areas where Office 2003 has added all-new functionality. This area of computing is evolving rapidly, so you should consider the Office 2003 implementation a first attempt to add value in a changing area. In this chapter we give you the information you need to evaluate Office 2003's approach to rights management and to decide whether it's right for your organization.

IN THIS CHAPTER

- **Understanding rights management**
- **Setting up rights management**
- **Rights management for documents**
- **Rights management for email**

 UPGRADERS BEWARE

You need to be using Windows Server 2003 as your server operating system for the Office 2003 rights management features to function. Depending on how quickly your organization upgrades its servers, this might limit your ability to deploy the rights management features. In addition, rights management is available only in some versions of Office 2003; see Appendix A, "Office 2003 Version Guide," for details.

Overview of Rights Management in Office 2003

In the context of computing, *rights management* refers to the ability of the creator of a document (or another file such as an email message or a digital music recording) to dictate what other users can do with the file. As the economy becomes ever more dependent on computers, this is a hot topic. Information creators (understandably) want to retain control over the files they release. For example, a publisher who produces books as electronic files rather than as paperbacks would like to prevent buyers from just making copies for all their friends.

Office 2003 implements some basic rights management functionality under the name of *Integrated Rights Management (IRM)*. The idea behind IRM is that you can assign rights to your documents without ever leaving Office. For example, if you're working in an Excel worksheet, you can specify a short list of users who can modify the worksheet and another list of users who can read the worksheet without modifying it. All other users are locked out entirely. In addition to protecting documents in Word, Excel, and PowerPoint, IRM also enables you to create email messages that cannot be copied or forwarded.

 MORE INFO

Other Office 2003 applications, such as Access or InfoPath, do not include IRM features.

IRM is dependent on a rights management layer for Windows Server 2003, called the Rights Management Service (RMS). RMS is a free add-on for Windows Server 2003 that helps you manage digital rights for an entire domain. To work with IRM, you need to have access to a server that includes RMS. Microsoft makes a trial server available over the Internet that you can test if you don't want to install your own RMS server.

 MORE INFO

In this chapter, we'll concentrate on the details of setting up and using rights management, rather than the technical innovations that make it possible. If you'd like to understand the underlying public key software, download the "Technical Overview of Windows RMS" white paper from

```
http://www.microsoft.com/windowsserver2003/techinfo/overview/
rmenterprisewp.mspx.
```

Setting Up Rights Management

Working with rights management in Office 2003 requires additional setup beyond simply installing Office 2003. You must have both a rights management server and a rights management client installed before you can use this technology. In this section of the chapter, we show you how to set up the various pieces of software involved:

- Microsoft's Trial IRM Service
- Windows Rights Management Services
- Windows Rights Management Client Software

Using Microsoft's Trial IRM Service

The easiest way to test rights management in Office 2003 is to use Microsoft's free trial IRM service. To do so, first install the rights management client (you'll find details later in this chapter, in the "Installing Windows Rights Management Client Software" section). Then open Word, Excel, or PowerPoint and either click the Permission button on the Standard toolbar or select Permission, Restrict Permission As from the File menu. This opens the Service Sign-Up dialog box shown in Figure 12.1.

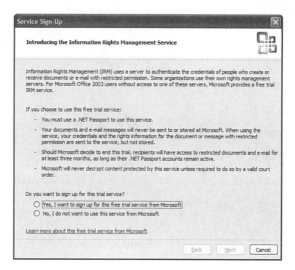

FIGURE 12.1 Signing up for the trial IRM service.

You need to have a .NET Passport to sign up for this service. Follow the instructions in the dialog box to connect to the service.

When you use the trial IRM service, your documents are sent to Microsoft to have rights management technology applied. Microsoft promises to keep the documents confidential unless presented with a valid court order, but you should still carefully consider whether you are comfortable with this method of working. Because it holds the certificates that serve as the key to the rights management scheme, Microsoft can technically decrypt any document signed with the IRM tools.

UPGRADERS BEWARE

If you're seriously testing rights management in Office 2003 for use as part of your corporate workflow, we recommend that you set up your own server rather than using Microsoft's trial service.

Installing Windows Rights Management Services

To get started, go to `http://www.microsoft.com/downloads/details.aspx?FamilyId=BE7FAE0C-2DB2-4F7F-8AA1-416FE1B04FB1&displaylang=en` and download Windows Rights Management Services 1.0. You should also ensure that your server has the necessary prerequisite software installed:

- Windows Server 2003 as the operating system

- The NTFS file system

- Microsoft Message Queuing (MSMQ)

- Internet Information Services (IIS) 6.0 with ASP.NET

- An Active Directory domain based on Windows 2000 SP3 or later

- Microsoft SQL Server 2000 or MSDE SP3 or later for logging

To install the software, run the downloaded executable. If any of the prerequisites is missing, running the download gives you a warning message. If this happens, you should cancel the installation, fix the missing prerequisite, and start again.

When you get everything set up, the Windows Rights Management Services Setup Wizard installs three things on your server:

- The Windows RMS components themselves

- The Windows RMS Administration Web site

- Windows RMS documentation

When you finish the installation, the Setup Wizard opens the help so you can read about the next steps.

 EXPERT ADVICE

We recommend reading at least the Quick Guide section of the help before proceeding any further. Although setting up Windows RMS is not as complex as some other tasks (such as Active Directory setup), there are a number of fine points to review.

The next step is to *provision* the Windows RMS server. Provisioning is the process of configuring the server so it can be used with RMS clients. The first Windows RMS server you set up becomes the root certification server for your organization.

To provision a server, do the following:

1. Select Start, All Programs, Windows RMS, Windows RMS Administration. This opens the browser-based administration tool shown in Figure 12.2. As you can see, if you have more than one Web site configured on the server, you can choose any one of these sites to host Windows RMS.

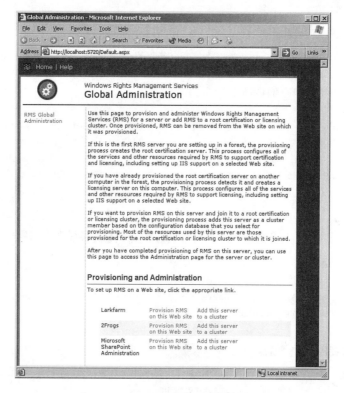

FIGURE 12.2   Starting the provisioning process for a Windows RMS server.

2. Select a Web site and click the corresponding Provision RMS on this Web Site link. This opens another Web page where you can specify the necessary information to provision the site:

   • The location of the database to use for configuration and logging

   • The domain account that will be used by the Windows RMS service

- The URL that will be used by client computers to reach the computer running the service

- Details that will be used to create the public and private keys for the service

- Any proxy settings required for the server to reach the Internet

- Details of any third party that should be able to revoke this server's certificate

3. Click Submit and Windows RMS is provisioned on the server. This includes a step in which the computer contacts Microsoft to generate appropriate keys.

 EXPERT ADVICE

You should create a user account in your domain specifically for the RMS service. The provisioning process takes care of adding the necessary permissions to this account. You might need your server administrator to perform this step for you.

After you've provisioned the service, the choices on the Windows RMS Administration Web page change, allowing you to administer RMS on your server. Before proceeding to client installation, you should load the Administration page and use the RMS Service Connection Point link to register the RMS server in your Active Directory. If you don't do this, clients won't be able to discover the RMS server.

Installing Windows Rights Management Client Software

The next thing you need to do is install the Windows Rights Management client software on each computer that will use the IRM functionality in Office 2003. Go to `http://www. microsoft.com/downloads/details.aspx?familyid=3115A374-116D-4A6F-BEB2-D6EB6FA66EEC& displaylang=en` and download the client software.

 UPGRADERS BEWARE

Some Microsoft documentation claims that you can also install the Rights Management client through Windows Update. In early 2004, this was not yet true.

Download and run the setup package to install the Rights Management client software. After the installation is finished, open Word, Excel, or PowerPoint and either click the Permission button on the Standard toolbar or select Permission, Restrict Permission As from the File menu. You should see the animation shown in Figure 12.3.

FIGURE 12.3   Registering a client with a rights management server.

This dialog box might remain on your screen for a considerable period of time. During this time, the rights management client is performing two tasks:

1. Contacting the rights management servers at Microsoft to issue the computer a unique activation certificate. This creates a digital "lockbox" on the computer where rights management information can be stored.

2. Contacting your own rights management server to issue a certificate to the current user. This certificate is stored in the lockbox and allows the user to perform rights management activities on this computer.

When your computer has successfully completed both steps, the Permission dialog box is shown. We'll discuss this dialog box in the next section, "Rights Management for Documents."

 UPGRADERS BEWARE

When you first try to use the Permissions menu item after installing the client software, you might receive the following error message: `This service is temporarily unavailable. Microsoft Internet Explorer may be set to Work Offline.` In Internet Explorer, verify that Work Offline on the File menu is not selected, and then try again. In our experience, this error almost always means that the server installation failed. Check the event log on the rights management server for error messages.

 EXPERT ADVICE

If you have trouble installing or configuring rights management on the client, go to `http://www.microsoft.com/downloads/details.aspx?FamilyId=11DE5515-55AC-4C20-B7EF-F6F05B8FA7D2&displaylang=en`, download the Administration Toolkit for Windows Rights Management Services 1.0, and install it on the offending computer. This toolkit contains several utilities and diagnostic tools that can help you pinpoint the cause of any failures.

Although you can install the Windows Rights Management client software by following the previous steps, you should be aware that this does *not* make your installation legal. The RMS server software is free, but you need to purchase a special client access license (CAL) for each computer that will serve as a rights management client. The price for this license is $37 for each computer, and it is not included in the purchase price of Microsoft Office 2003. In addition, if you want to allow users outside your own organization access to your rights management server via a public URL, you must purchase a Windows RMS External Connector License for $18,066.

Rights Management for Documents

After you've installed all the pieces, you're finally ready to test rights management in Windows. In this section, we show you how to set permissions for other users at a variety of levels.

Removing All Permissions

Start by opening a Word document, an Excel worksheet, or a PowerPoint presentation. Then select Permission, Restrict Permission As from the File menu. This opens the Select User dialog box, shown in Figure 12.4. This dialog box lists all the users who are authorized to work with rights management on this computer. Select your account and click OK.

FIGURE 12.4   Choosing a user for rights management.

Clicking OK opens the Permission dialog box, shown in Figure 12.5. Check the Restrict Permission to This Document check box to begin limiting the rights that other users will have when they work with your document.

 **EXPERT ADVICE**

The Permission button on the Standard toolbar takes you directly to the Permission dialog box. In this case, you don't need to select a user. Instead, it assumes that you want to work as the current user.

Add users with Read permission   Give all users Read access

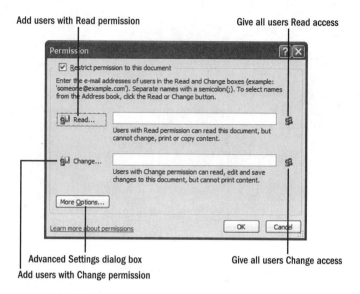

Advanced Settings dialog box   Give all users Change access
Add users with Change permission

FIGURE 12.5   Setting permissions for a document.

 UPGRADERS BEWARE

This dialog box includes four hidden buttons that don't appear until you move the mouse over them; the labels in Figure 12.5 show you where they are.

Click OK without making any other changes in this dialog box. This protects the document by removing all rights from every user except you, the document's author. When you click OK, Word opens the Shared Workspace task pane, displaying information on the document's right, as shown in Figure 12.6.

Save and close the document and then try to open it from another user's copy of Word 2003 (you'll need to install rights management for this user first, of course). When you open the document, you get a warning that permission is restricted, as shown in Figure 12.7.

As you can see, you must be able to connect to the managing server when working with a rights managed document. If you click Cancel in this dialog box, or the server cannot be reached at the indicated URL, the document simply won't open.

In this particular case, the document does not open even if you do contact the server because you're signed in with an account that has no permissions. Figure 12.8 shows the information message displayed by Word in response to opening a document to which you have no rights.

FIGURE 12.6   A document with restricted permissions.

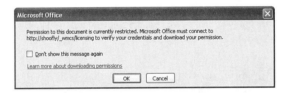

FIGURE 12.7   Prompt when opening a document with restricted permissions.

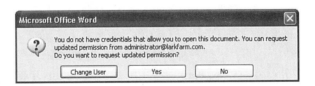

FIGURE 12.8   Prompt when permissions cannot be obtained.

You have three options when you receive this prompt:

- **Change User**—Click this to attempt to open the document again, supplying a different username.

- **Yes**—Click this to send email to the owner of the document, asking for the necessary permissions.

- **No**—Click this to abandon the attempt to open the document.

Granting Read Permissions

Now let's grant a user read-only access to a document:

1. Open a new document in Word and click the Permission button to open the Permission dialog box. Alternatively, you can open a document that is already protected and click the Change Permission link in the Shared Workspace task pane.

2. In the Permission dialog box, click the Read button. This opens the Select Users or Groups dialog box, shown in Figure 12.9.

3. Enter the name of a user on your network and click the Check Names button.

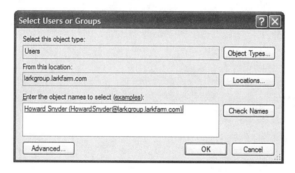

FIGURE 12.9   Granting rights to a user.

4. Click OK to return to the Permission dialog box. The user you selected is shown in the text box that lists users with read permission.

5. Click OK to apply the permission to the document.

When you attempt to open this document as another user who has read permission, the document opens. However, as Figure 12.10 shows, there are several indications that your rights to the document are restricted:

- The Permission icon appears in the status bar.

- The Shared Workspace task pane opens and displays the restricted permission icon.

- The title bar of the document includes the [read only] indicator.

- If you click the View My Permission hyperlink, you see a summary in the My Permission dialog box.

Although you can read this document, your ability to work with it is severely limited. Many menu items, such as Save As, are disabled by Word. You also can't copy content from the document and paste it in another application. Because the owner has granted you very limited permission, the IRM features in Office 2003 enforce all these limitations.

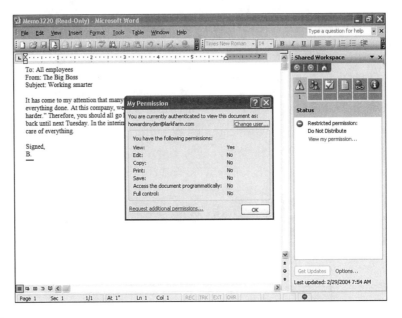

FIGURE 12.10   Permissions in a rights managed document.

 UPGRADERS BEWARE

There are limitations to how much software can protect your documents. For example, you could make a copy of this particular document by taking a screen shot and then using Optical Character Recognition (OCR) software to read it back from the graphical image. Or, you could use a digital camera to take a picture of your screen—or even write the contents of the memo down on a piece of paper.

Granting Change Permissions

Once again, open a document and navigate to the Permission dialog box. This time, add a user to the Change list. Then save the document and reopen it while logged in as that user. Figure 12.11 shows the permissions Word grants you in this case.

As you can see, being on the Change list for a document doesn't allow you to do anything you like with the document. In particular, you can't print copies of the original document (although you can copy the data from the document to a new document and print the new document). You also cannot alter the permissions for the document. So, just having change permission doesn't let you give access to the document to other users.

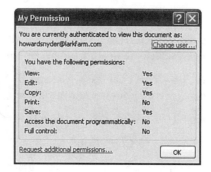

FIGURE 12.11   The change permission set is less restricted than the read permission set.

Understanding Advanced Permissions

If the built-in Read and Change permissions aren't enough for you, IRM offers much finer control of the rights you grant to any particular user. Open the Permissions dialog box and click the More Options button to open the advanced Permission dialog box, shown in Figure 12.12.

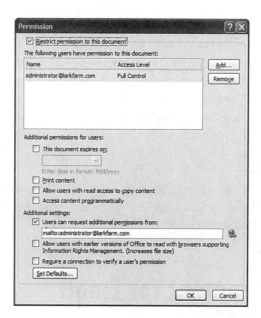

FIGURE 12.12   Setting advanced permissions adds another level of control to the document.

The controls in this dialog box are as follows:

- **Restrict Permission to This Document**—This lets you add new users to the permission list. For each user, you can select the Read, Change, or Full Control level of permissions.

- **This Document Expires on**—This enables you to specify an expiration date for the document. After that date, the document cannot be opened.

- **Print Content**—This enables users to print the document.

- **Allow Users with Read Access to Copy Content**—States the obvious.

- **Access Content Programmatically**—This allows programmatic access to the document (for example, from Visual Basic for Applications code).

- **Users Can Request Additional Permissions from**—You can change or disable the email address to use for requesting permissions.

- **Allow Users with Earlier Versions of Office to Read with Browsers Supporting Information Rights Management**—You can allow users with earlier versions of Office to read the document.

- **Require a Connection to Verify a User's Permission**—You can prevent caching credentials, so users have to connect every time they open the document.

 UPGRADERS BEWARE

Before users with earlier versions of Office can read a protected document, they need to install the Rights Management Add-On for Internet Explorer. The add-on requires either Internet Explorer 5.5 SP2 or Internet Explorer 6 SP1 and can be downloaded from `http://www.microsoft.com/windows/ie/downloads/addon/default.asp`.

 MORE INFO

The administrator of the Windows Rights Management Service can define additional sets of permissions besides Read, Change, and Full Control. Refer to the documentation installed when you set up the server for more details on creating these templates.

Rights Management for Email

Microsoft Outlook 2003 also ties in to IRM. When you compose an email message, you can specify that it's only for use of the recipient. To do so, create your email message as you always would. Before sending the message, however, click the Permission button on the Standard toolbar inside the message or select Permission, Do Not Forward from the message's File menu. This adds an explanatory header to the message before you send it, as shown in Figure 12.13.

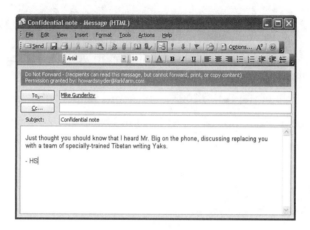

FIGURE 12.13   Here's an email message with rights management invoked that cannot be forwarded.

When the recipient receives the message, he must open it to verify his credentials (Outlook does not display the message in the preview pane until after it has been opened). Opening the message displays the same prompt to connect to the rights management server that you saw in Figure 12.7 (with some minor wording differences reflecting that the source of the prompt is a message rather than a document).

After verifying his credentials, the recipient can reply to the message or view it in the Preview Pane. But he still can't save, copy, or forward the message. Figure 12.14 shows a restricted message that has been opened by the recipient.

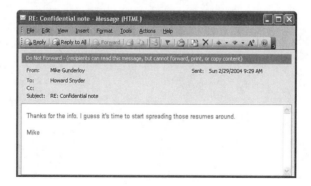

FIGURE 12.14   Reading a restricted message.

When you reply to a restricted message, your reply doesn't contain the original message text (because Outlook can't copy the original text). By default, the reply is set to restrict permissions in return.

Integrated Rights Management Summary

You might not be ready to use Office 2003's IRM support yet—or not ready to pay for it! But you should be aware of the key points that you've learned in this chapter:

- Some, but not all, of the Office 2003 applications support IRM.

- You need to be using Windows Server 2003 in your organization to use these features.

- You need to set up software on both the client and the server.

- After the setup, you can perform rights management activities directly from Office applications.

- Although it's not perfect, IRM does offer some protection for your critical documents.

Office 2003 Version Guide

Remember when OLE was the latest and greatest? The idea that you could use Word to compose a letter inside an Access form was revolutionary—and a bit mysterious. Since then, each new version of Office has exchanged a few grunts for true interactivity. Office is almost standing erect with this latest version, but the applications don't really talk to one another as the earlier trend seemed to imply they might. Office 2003 applications share data and collaborate with one another via SharePoint Services, XML data, and Windows Server 2003. Yes, OLE still exists, but it's on its way to being the Office tail bone—obsolete.

Never in its history has Office included so many applications and so much potential. Whether you're upgrading for a huge corporation or a small home business, you'll find an Office edition that's right for you.

Give Me the Works!

Eleven applications now comprise the Microsoft Office System 2003. Some of these applications are also available packaged into various suites. Those applications are

Access—A desktop relational database management system.

Excel—The best spreadsheet on the market.

InfoPath—Gather and share information across your organization using dynamic forms.

OneNote—Take, organize, and share notes, with support for both desktop and tablet PCs.

Outlook—An integrated solution for managing email, schedules, tasks, notes, contacts, and much more.

PowerPoint—Professional presentation software.

Project—Project management software.

Publisher—Desktop publishing software.

SharePoint—A set of technologies to support collaboration, both in Office and other applications.

Visio—Drawing and diagramming software.

Word—Word processing software with more bells and whistles than you could ever imagine.

 MORE INFO

You'll notice a couple of products here that we didn't cover in this book. Although they're members of the Office family, Microsoft Project and Microsoft Visio are aimed at particular niche markets rather than the regular Office user.

The Professional Enterprise Edition 2003

The Microsoft Professional Enterprise Edition 2003 offers the most but is available only through volume licensing. That means the suite isn't available through the regular retail channels. A volume license lets a company purchase and manage multiple software licenses. This is the edition most IT managers should consider.

> You can learn more about Microsoft's volume licensing or academic licensing programs at
> `http://www.microsoft.com/licensing/default.mspx`.

This edition comes with the following products:

- Access 2003
- Excel 2003
- InfoPath 2003
- Outlook 2003 (optionally including Business Contact Manager)
- PowerPoint 2003
- Publisher 2003
- Word 2003

The Professional Enterprise Edition also includes support for all the XML features we've discussed in this book, as well as for the digital rights management features we covered in Chapter 12, "What's New in Rights Management."

The Professional Edition

Microsoft Office Professional Edition 2003 offers the same products as the Enterprise version with one exception. InfoPath 2003 isn't in the Professional edition. Keep in mind that this version sells retail or preinstalled with a new computer with a single-user license. This is for the single user who wants the works but doesn't need to license several systems. It's also the highest-power version of Office available without purchasing a volume license.

The Professional Edition also includes support for all the XML features we've discussed in this book, as well as for the digital rights management features covered in Chapter 12.

The Small Business Edition

Microsoft Office Small Business Edition 2003 is available through retail vendors, preinstallation, or a volume license edition. All versions contain the following products:

- Excel 2003

- Outlook 2003 (optionally with Business Contact Manager)

- PowerPoint 2003

- Publisher 2003

- Word 2003

Notice that Access 2003, InfoPath 2003, and the collaborative tools aren't included in this package. The Small Business Edition also does not support the XML or digital rights management features.

The Standard Edition

Microsoft Office Standard Edition 2003 is available with a volume license, with an academic license, at retail, and preinstalled; it includes the following applications:

- Excel 2003

- Outlook 2003

- PowerPoint 2003

- Word 2003

The Standard Edition also does not support the XML or digital rights management features.

Student and Teacher Edition

Microsoft Office Student and Teacher Edition 2003 is a retail choice for students, teachers, and parents. The most popular products are included:

- Excel 2003

- Outlook 2003

- PowerPoint 2003

- Word 2003

In addition, you can install this version on three systems by purchasing only a single license. Although the Student and Teacher Edition includes the same products as the Standard Edition, student and teacher pricing is much lower than standard pricing.

⇨ To find an academic reseller, visit `http://www.microsoft.com/education/?ID=AERFind`.

The Basic Edition

Microsoft Office Basic Edition 2003 is a preinstalled version that comes with the following products with a single-user license:

- Excel 2003

- Outlook 2003

- Word 2003

The Basic Edition doesn't support any of the advanced features of Office, such as collaboration, XML, or digital rights management.

Individual Products

You can also order any of the Office products as standalone products. This is the only way to get a copy of OneNote 2003, and if you don't have a volume licensing agreement, it's also the only way to get InfoPath 2003.

Trial Software

If you're not certain just which products you need, consider sending for an evaluation kit. They're available worldwide for free (a small shipping fee applies). You can order a kit for the following applications:

- Office Professional Edition 2003
- FrontPage 2003
- InfoPath 2003
- OneNote 2003*
- Project Standard Edition 2003
- Publisher 2003
- Visio 2003*

 EXPERT ADVICE

The main thing to remember when contemplating a purchase is that the Professional editions support XML, IRM, and SharePoint functionalities at the development level. That means you can create, customize, and protect documents using these features. The other suites can use these files; they just can't originate them.

A Table's Worth a Thousand Words

The saying really applies to pictures, but in this case, a comparison table is almost as good. Table A.1 compares the four editions by the products available and licensing opportunities.

---

*Downloadable trials for these products are available at http://www.microsoft.com/office/trial/ default.mspx. *Live Meeting's* trial version is available only online via the same page.*

TABLE A.1   Applications Included in Each Office 2003 Suite

Application	Enterprise	Professional	Small Business	Standard Student and Teacher	Basic
Access 2003	✓	✓			
Excel 2003	✓	✓	✓	✓	✓
InfoPath 2003	✓				
Outlook 2003	✓	✓	✓	✓	✓
Outlook 2003 with Business Contact Manager	✓	✓			
PowerPoint 2003	✓	✓	✓	✓	
Publisher 2003	✓	✓			
Word 2003	✓	✓	✓	✓	✓
Supports Extensible Markup Language	✓	✓			
Supports Information Rights Management	✓	✓			
Supports Visual Studio Tools	✓	✓			
Licensing	Volume, academic	Volume, single-user retail, preinstalled, academic	Volume, single-user retail, preinstalled,	Single-user retail, academic	Preinstalled

System Requirements

Before you make any serious decisions, you should make sure the systems on which you plan to run Office 2003 can handle the version you want. Table A.2 lists each edition's suggested requirements.

TABLE A.2   System Requirements for Office 2003 Suites

Hardware	Professional	Small Business	Standard	Student and Teacher
CPU	Intel Pentium 233MHz or faster; Outlook 2003 BCM requires 450MHz or faster.	Intel Pentium 233MHz or faster; Outlook 2003 BCM requires 450MHz or faster.	Intel Pentium 233MHz or faster.	Intel Pentium 233MHz or faster.

TABLE A.2 Continued

Hardware	Professional	Small Business	Standard	Student and Teacher
Memory	128MB of RAM or greater; Outlook 2003 BCM requires 256MB of RAM.	128MB of RAM or greater; Outlook 2003 BCM requires 256MB of RAM.	128MB of RAM or greater.	128MB of RAM or greater.
Hard disk	400MB of available hard-disk space; Outlook 2003 BCM requires an additional 190MB of available hard-disk space.	400MB of available hard-disk space; Outlook 2003 BCM requires an additional 190MB of available hard-disk space.	260MB of available hard-disk space.	260MB of available hard-disk space.
Drive	CD-ROM or DVD.	CD-ROM or DVD.	CD-ROM or DVD.	CD-ROM or DVD.
Display	Super VGA (800 × 600) or higher resolution monitor.	Super VGA (800 × 600) or higher resolution monitor.	Super VGA (800 × 600) or higher resolution monitor.	Super VGA (800 × 600) or higher resolution monitor.
Operating system	Microsoft Windows 2000 with Service Pack 3 (SP3), Windows XP, or later.	Microsoft Windows 2000 with Service Pack 3 (SP3), Windows XP, or later.	Microsoft Windows 2000 with Service Pack 3 (SP3), Windows XP, or later.	Microsoft Windows 2000 with Service Pack 3 (SP3), Windows XP, or later.
Internet connectivity	Yes	Yes	Yes	Yes

 **EXPERT ADVICE**

Microsoft is always very optimistic about specifying the hardware requirements for its products. We'd suggest at least an 800MHz CPU and at least 256MB of RAM to make full use of Office 2003.

Outlook 2003's Business Contact Manager

B

The size of your business isn't a factor when it comes to organization. Whether you're a large or small business, you might find yourself so busy organizing details that you've no time left to actually take care of business. Outlook 2003's Business Contact Manager (BCM) might be just the tool you need to help you manage the following:

- Contacts

- Accounts

- Leads and other potential business

Businesses pay a lot of money for software and experienced personnel to manage data. If organizing and tracking your business is becoming more of a business than your actual product, try BCM. It takes some work initially to get everything up and running, but the time and effort might be your best investment this year.

 UPGRADERS BEWARE

BCM works with a single user to organize and manage contacts, accounts, product lists, and opportunities. This first release doesn't have PDA support or any of the collaborative capabilities shared by other Office 2003 applications.

What Is BCM?

BCM is a Component Object Model (COM) add-in for Outlook 2003. That means, after you install it, BCM runs with Outlook 2003.

 **EXPERT ADVICE**

COM is a Microsoft technology used to build component-based applications. These objects expose an interface that allows other applications or components to access their features. For example, ActiveX is based on COM.

Outlook is the perfect place for BCM because you're probably already dealing with most contact, account, and lead information through email contacts—no more switching back and forth between applications to update and manage all this information.

Installing BCM

The first step is to install Outlook 2003 and then BCM. We'll assume you have Outlook 2003 installed (you can't use BCM without Outlook 2003). To install BCM, do the following:

1. Close Outlook 2003 and insert the Business Contact Manager CD.

2. Click Next after reading the welcoming message.

3. Click the I Accept the Terms in the License Agreement option, and click Next.

4. Accept the default install location or click Change to choose another location. After determining the installation folder, click Next.

5. Click Install to begin the process, which might take a few minutes.

6. When the installation's complete, click Finish.

7. Reboot the system.

After installing BCM and rebooting, launch Outlook 2003 so you can configure BCM. The first time you launch Outlook 2003 after installing BCM, Outlook 2003 prompts you to choose between the current profile or a new database. Single users see the dialog box shown in Figure B.1. Most of you will click Yes. If your system accommodates multiple uses, BCM lets you create a new database for each user.

When the process is complete, the Navigation pane lists a new folder group called Business Contact Manager in the Mail Folders view, as shown in Figure B.2. Also notice the new toolbar shown in Figure B.3.

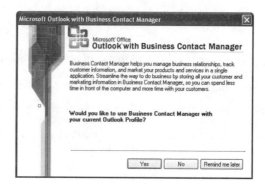

FIGURE B.1 Most likely you'll want BCM to use your existing profile.

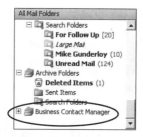

FIGURE B.2 BCM adds a new group folder to Outlook 2003.

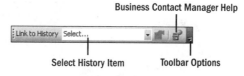

FIGURE B.3 BCM displays a new toolbar in Outlook 2003.

 **EXPERT ADVICE**

BCM appears to be contained in a Personal Folders file, but it's really stored in an MSDE database on your local system.

Using BCM

Outlook 2003's BCM helps you organize and efficiently manage business details:

- BCM contacts hold information about the people with whom you do business.

- BCM accounts store information about companies with whom you do business.

- BCM opportunities store information about potential sales and leads, enabling you to prioritize your choices.

Creating Contacts

BCM contacts are separate from the personal contacts you store in Outlook 2003's Contacts folder. (More than likely, you'll not want to confuse things by storing any personal contacts in BCM.)

Initially, there are no contacts in BCM and you have two options. You can import business contacts, or you can create them from scratch. To import contacts, do the following:

1. Launch the Business Data Import/Export Wizard by selecting File, Import and Export.

2. Select Business Contact Manager, click the Import a File option shown in Figure B.4, and then click Next.

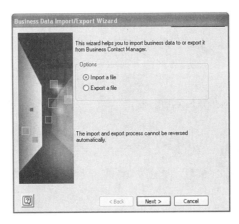

FIGURE B.4   Use the wizard to import records.

3. Identify the type of file you're importing. You can directly import the following file types:

- bCentral List Builder

- Act! 4.0, 5.0 database

- QuickBooks 8.0, 9.0 data

- Comma Separated Values (.csv)

- Access database (.mdb)

- Excel Workbook 11 (.xls)

- Business Contact Manager data

- bCentral Customer Leads

Select the appropriate file type item and click Next.

4. Click Browse to locate the file you're importing. Select the file and click Open. Then, click Next. Figure B.5 shows us importing employee records from the Northwind database (a sample database that comes with Access). BCM can create duplicates, but it doesn't merge existing information for duplicated items. Choose appropriately whether to import duplicates, and then click Next.

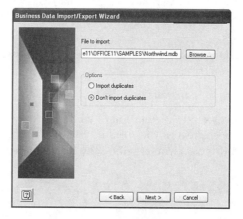

FIGURE B.5   Identify the data source.

5. The next pane displays items that are specific to the data source. Figure B.6 shows the Northwind tables. If you're importing from Excel, you'd identify a specific worksheet in a workbook. If you've previously imported records from the current data source, you might need to click the Clear button. Check the object that contains the data you want to import.

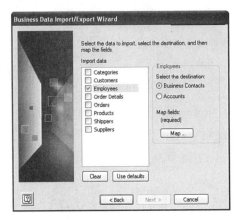

FIGURE B.6   Identify the specific data you want to import.

 **EXPERT ADVICE**

The wizard lets you import contacts and accounts at the same time when importing from the same data source. Check the object that contains data and then identify it as contact or account data. Repeat this process as many times as necessary.

6. After selecting the data, choose a destination for the imported records by selecting Business Contacts or Accounts.

7. Click the Map button to map your fields.

8. Drag each data source field to the appropriate BCM field. Figure B.7 shows four fields. Click OK. Within the context of the current task, *map* simply means to align data with an existing field. In this case, you're telling the BCM where to store the imported data.

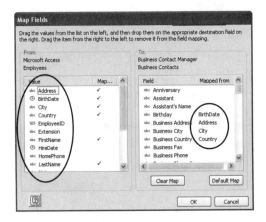

FIGURE B.7   Map the imported fields to a specific destination.

9. Click Next twice to import the records. The process might take a few minutes.

10. Click Close when the import is done.

 UPGRADERS BEWARE

When importing Excel data, BCM treats the first row of data as a header row. You might need to adjust the worksheet before importing to accommodate this behavior.

You can use Outlook contacts in Contacts folders in BCM. To set this up, do the following:

1. Open the appropriate Contacts folder and select the contacts you want to copy to BCM.

2. Select Edit, Copy to Folder.

3. Select the appropriate subfolder in the Business Contacts folder shown in Figure B.8; then click OK.

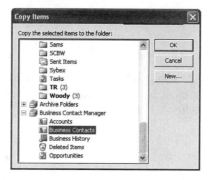

FIGURE B.8   Copy contacts from Outlook 2003 to BCM.

 UPGRADERS BEWARE

Right now, BCM doesn't synchronize updates between a BCM folder and an Outlook 2003 Contacts folder. If you change one, you have to update the other manually. Neither Outlook 2003 nor BCM automatically sees the change in the other and updates accordingly.

When you need to create new contacts in BCM, use the contact form shown in Figure B.9. A business contact has more available fields than the Outlook version. In addition, you can associate an account with a contact by clicking the ellipses button (…) next to the Account field.

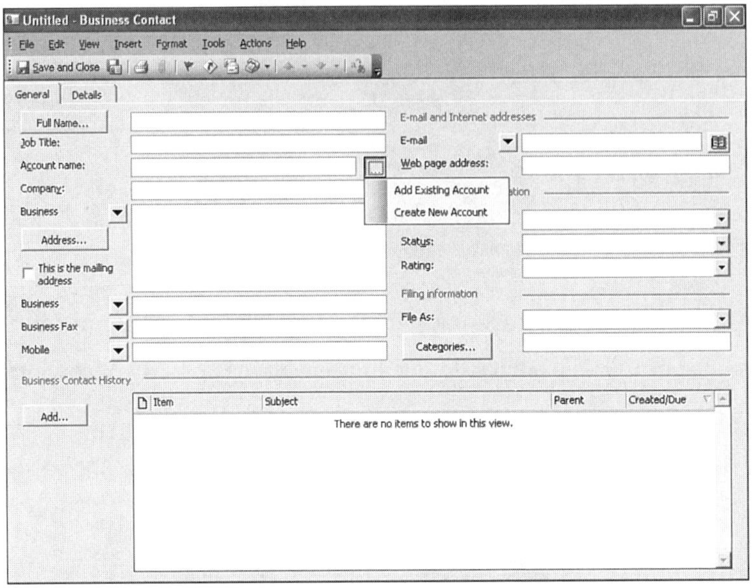

FIGURE B.9   Create new contacts directly in BCM.

The Details tab contains standard contact information, such as department, profession, important dates, and so on. New fields let you identify the source of the lead (initial contact), the method of contact, and when you last modified the record.

Creating Accounts

Accounts contain information about companies with whom you do business. You can associate any number of contacts with each account.

To import accounts, use the Import/Export Wizard as shown previously in the "Creating Contacts" section. Or, create a new account by selecting BCM's Accounts folder and following these steps:

1. Click the New drop-down list in the toolbar and select Account to display the blank form shown in Figure B.10. (Or, select File, New, Account.)

2. Enter a name for the account.

3. To create an association to a contact, click the ellipses button (...) next to the Primary Contact control. Save the record when prompted to. Select a contact from the Business Contacts dialog box, shown in Figure B.11, and click OK. (This step is optional.)

4. Click Add in the Business Contacts section to associate additional contacts with this account.

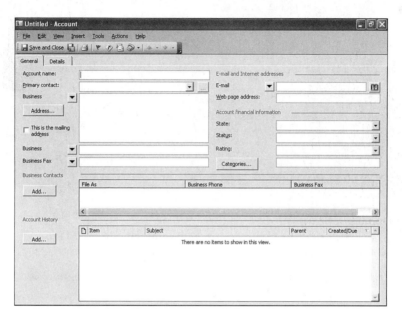

FIGURE B.10 Use this form to create a new account.

FIGURE B.11 Select a contact to associate with the new account.

5. To associate other items to the account, click Add in the Account History section and identify the transaction type in the form shown in Figure B.12. Continue appropriately to add the specific item.

FIGURE B.12   Link items to an account.

6. Click Save and Close when you're done.

Creating Opportunities

Opportunities are leads or other potential business-generating items. You can create an opportunity for a particular product or business by following these steps:

1. Click the New drop-down list on the toolbar and select Opportunity to display the Opportunity form shown in Figure B.13.

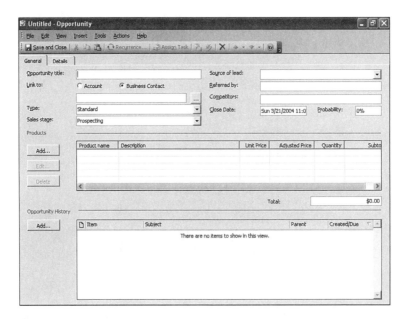

FIGURE B.13   Create new opportunities.

2. Enter the appropriate data; a few fields are filled in automatically, but you can change their default values.

3. To add an item to the history, save the opportunity, click Add, and identify the item you want to add.

4. Click Save and Close when you're done.

Linking Email

Linking emails to a contact or an account lets you quickly review the contact or account's entire email exchange—automatically. BCM configures every email folder for linking when you install it.

You can unlink a folder by selecting Link E-mail from the Business Tools menu and then selecting Auto Linking to display the dialog box shown in Figure B.14. Uncheck any folder you don't want automatically linked and click OK. Otherwise, this feature works on every email you receive (after installing BCM).

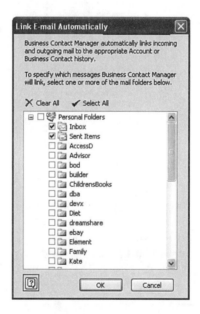

FIGURE B.14 Configure email links.

To link existing emails, select Link E-mail from the Business Tools menu, and then select Link Existing E-mail. (The resulting dialog box is almost identical to the one shown in Figure B.14.) Select the folders you want BCM to check for email messages to and from your accounts and contacts. Click Start to begin the search and link process, which could take a few minutes.

Using Views and Reports

BCM comes with a number of built-in views and reports that can help you manage contacts, accounts, and all those opportunities on which you want to act. You can also manage data through special views of the account, contact, and opportunities folders.

To view data in a particular format, select the folder to update the Current View list shown in Figure B.15, accordingly. Simply select one of the available views, which are all fairly self-explanatory.

FIGURE B.15   Choose a view.

To access a built-in report, select Reports from the Business Tools menu. Then, select the category you want to report. All the reports are self-explanatory, but customizing them can require additional input from you. We recommend that you experiment with the possibilities to learn what's available. Table B.1 lists the many reports by type.

TABLE B.1   Types of BCM Reports

Category	Report
Business Contacts	Business Contacts Phone List
	Business Contacts by Status
	Business Contacts by Rating
	Business Contacts by Category
	Business Contact History
	Neglected Business Contacts

TABLE B.1 Continued

Category	Report
Accounts	Account List with Business Contacts
	Quick Accounts List
	Accounts by Status
	Accounts by Rating
	Accounts by Category
	Account History
Opportunities	Opportunity Funnel
	Opportunity Forecast
	Opportunities by Product
	Opportunity History
	Past Due Opportunities
Other	Business Tasks List
	Source of Leads

Figure B.16 shows a phone list (after importing employee information from the Northwind database into the Contacts folder earlier). From this window, you can save, print, hide, or show groups; you can even modify the report. The modifications you can make are specific to each report.

Modifying a BCM Report

The phone list report is a standard report, and BCM doesn't care whether your contacts actually have phone numbers. There are a number of ways to customize one of these standard report formats, but before we get to that, let's review the Main Report toolbar, shown in Figure B.17.

The grouping is fairly obvious—it sorts contacts alphabetically and then groups each contact by the first character in their last names. To view the grouping categories, click the Show/Hide Grouping button on the Main Report toolbar. BCM opens a new window to the left, as shown in Figure B.18. You can use this window as a quick selection tool. Click any group heading in the grouping window and the report window automatically displays the appropriate group's heading (see Figure B.19). The phone list doesn't leave a lot of room for customization, so close it by clicking the Windows Close button in the window's title bar.

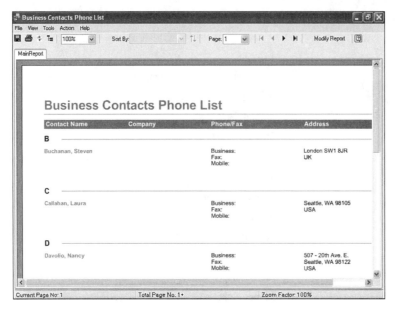

FIGURE B.16   Use BCM to create a simple phone list.

FIGURE B.17   Use this toolbar to customize BCM reports.

 **EXPERT ADVICE**

Select the Fit to Width option from the Zoom drop-down list to see the full width of the report (from left to right). This item is helpful when other windows, such as the grouping window, are open.

Sorting and Filtering Contact Data

Figure B.20 shows the BCM Accounts by Status report without any modifications. By default, the BCM sorts the accounts by name and groups by status. Select an option from the Sort by drop-down list to change the sort order. (Right now, only two accounts exist, so you won't see any actual change.)

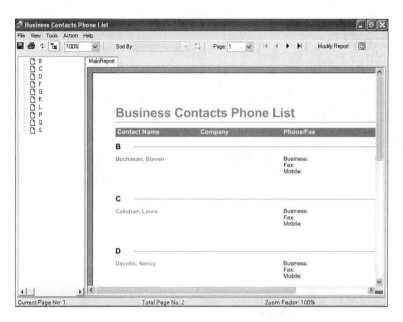

FIGURE B.18   Display a report's groups.

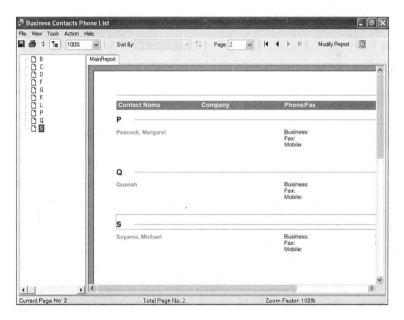

FIGURE B.19   Quickly display a different group.

Re-sort the account data

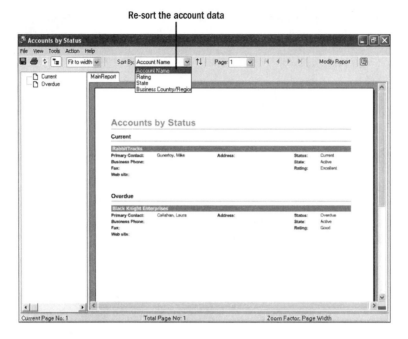

FIGURE B.20   The Accounts by Status report has a number of ways you can sort and modify the data.

Click Modify Report on the Main Report toolbar to open the Modify report dialog box, shown in Figure B.21. Most of the options on the General tab are disabled because they're not relevant to the available data or the report's purpose. After you add opportunities and create a history for your accounts, more of these options will be available.

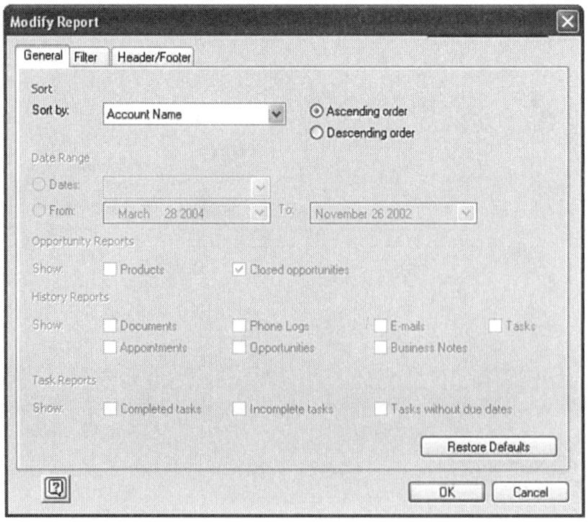

FIGURE B.21   Change the default settings to customize the report.

Click the Filter tab and then select Accounts, as shown in Figure B.22, to display the Accounts dialog box. Double-click those you want to include in the report. Doing so moves the selected account to the list on the right, shown in Figure B.23. When you return to the report, it includes only those accounts selected and moved to the list on the right.

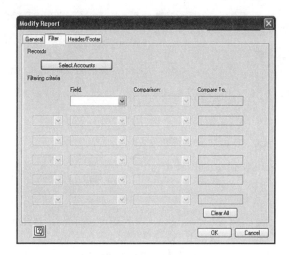

FIGURE B.22   The Filter tab gives you access to the Accounts dialog box.

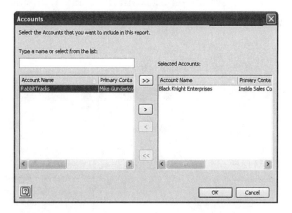

FIGURE B.23   Use the Accounts dialog box to choose accounts to appear on the customized report.

Click OK twice to return to the modified report shown in Figure B.24. As you can see, it contains only the Black Knight Enterprises account information.

Accounts by Status

Overdue

Black Knight Enterprises			
Primary Contact:	Callahan, Laura	Address:	Stat
Business Phone:			Stat
Fax:			Rati
Web site:			

FIGURE B.24   Only the filtered accounts make it to the report.

Customizing the Report

Besides manipulating the data by sorting and filtering, you can customize the report itself. Click Modify Report and then click the Header/Footer tab. By default, the report title is in the report's header and the page number and date created are in the report's footer. You can add your company's name to the report's header, as shown in Figure B.25. Click OK when you're done. Figure B.26 shows the resulting report, with the company name in the header. We've made only a few simple changes, but you can easily see how beneficial the BCM's reporting capabilities can be.

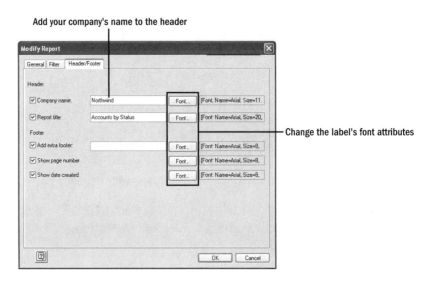

Add your company's name to the header

Change the label's font attributes

FIGURE B.25   Create custom headers and footers for a report.

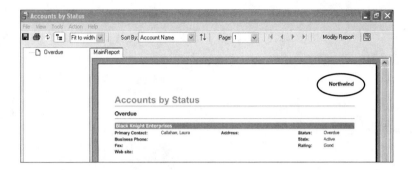

FIGURE B.26   Display additional information in the header or footer.

Saving a Report

Modified reports must be saved if you want to access them later. Select Save As from the File menu and name the report as you would any other document file. By default, BCM saves the report as a Word document (.doc). You have other options. Save a BCM report in the following foreign formats:

- Word document (.doc)
- Rich Text format (.rtf)
- Excel worksheet (.xls)
- Web page (.htm)

Backing Up and Restoring BCM

The BCM stores a lot of critical data—not necessarily critical in and of itself, but critical because of the number of ways you can manipulate and report that data. Back up BCM data frequently and regularly. To do so, complete the following steps:

1. Select File, Business Database, Backup to display the Database Backup dialog box shown in Figure B.27.

2. Click Browse to choose a location for the backup file.

3. If necessary (and recommended), enter a password to protect the backup file from unauthorized use.

4. Click OK to copy the database to the backup location. BCM lets you know when the process is complete.

FIGURE B.27   Specify a location and password for your backup file.

 **EXPERT ADVICE**

Be sure to write down the location of the backup file and the password and then store these references in a safe and secure location. It's easy to forget these details and if you can't remember the password, you can't restore the data—even if you can find the backup file. Depending on your organization's size and requirements, you might want to save the backup file to a disk and store it offsite in case of fire or some other type of disaster.

You might be lucky enough to never need a backup, but if and when you do, you'll be glad you've got it. If your database becomes corrupted, you can restore the backed-up database to the BCM by completing the following steps:

1. Close Outlook.

2. Click Start on the taskbar; then click Control Panel to open the Widows Control Panel window.

3. If the Mail icon isn't available in this first window, your system recognizes more than one user account. Click the User Accounts link.

4. In the resulting window, double-click the Mail icon to display the Mail Setup dialog box shown in Figure B.28.

5. Click the Show Profiles button to see whether more than one profile exists. If that's the case, select your profile and click Properties. If there's only one profile, click Cancel and double-click the Mail icon a second time.

6. Regardless of which Mail Setup dialog you're now working in, click Data Files to display the Outlook Data Files dialog box.

7. Select Business Contact Manager, as shown in Figure B.29; then click Settings to launch the Associate Database Wizard.

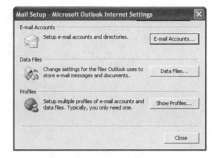

FIGURE B.28   You might have to restore the BCM backup to your profile.

FIGURE B.29   Select all the data files associated with your profile.

8. The wizard defaults to creating a new database. Accept that default, and click Next.

9. Enter a name for the new blank BCM database you're about to create, and click Next.

10. When the wizard is done, click Finish.

11. Click Close twice.

12. Launch Outlook so you can import data from the backup file.

13. Select File, Business Database, Restore to display the Database Restore dialog box shown in Figure B.30.

14. Click Browse to locate the backup file. You also might have to enter a password. Click OK to start the restoration

15. When the restore task is complete, launch Outlook.

FIGURE B.30   Start the restoration process.

 UPGRADERS BEWARE

Unfortunately, the restoration process is lengthy and prone to mistakes. What you're really doing is deleting the corrupted database and then importing the backup data. It's a plan with failure written all over it. We can only hope that Microsoft improves this process in the next version. This is far more difficult than it should be, even for a new feature.

The best way to learn the BCM is to simply use it. We believe you'll be surprised and pleased with how efficiently you can manage all your data. In addition, even though this add-in is somewhat limited, we believe third-party vendors will produce a number of support features that will expand the capabilities even further.

Index

Numbers

A

B

I

Picture, From Scanner or Camera, 223

Screen Clipping, 221

installations

BCM (Business Contact Manager), 292-293

Rights Management Add-On, 280

Web packages, 169

Windows Rights Management client software, 272-274

Windows Rights Management Services, 270-272

IRM (Integrated Rights Management). *See* **rights management**

integration

Exchange Server, 56

lists, Excel 2003, 102-105

Pocket PC, OneNote, 220

SharePoint

Access 2003, 140-141

alerts, 57

FrontPage 2003, 163-169

meeting workspaces, 57-58

Interactive Button command (Insert menu), 155

interactive buttons, FrontPage 2003, 155

Internet, online help searches, 24-25

J

JScript, behaviors (FrontPage 2003), 149-151

Junk E-mail menu, commands, 35

junk email, filtering, 49-50, 56

K-L

Large Messages search folder, 41

Layer command (Insert menu), 159

layers, FrontPage 2003, 159

layout cells, FrontPage 2003, 152-154

layout guides, 183

layout tables, FrontPage 2003, 152-154

Layout Tables and Cells task pane, 153

libraries, form (SharePoint), 245-246

licensing, 284

Line and Paragraph Breaks tab, 184

Line Spacing and Indents command. *See* Paragraph command

Link E-mail command (Tools menu), 301

linked tables, local, 128

linking

email, BCM (Business Contact Manager), 301

files, OneNote, 224

meeting requests, 30

Links tab (Shared Workspace task pane), 29

List command (Data menu), 102

List, Create List command (Data menu), 100

lists

control, sorting, 128-129

distribution (Outlook 2003), 49

Excel 2003, 92-93, 100-101

Favorite Folders, 39-40

integrating, Excel 2003, 102-105

OneNote, creating, 208

Lists command. *See* Bullets and Numbering command

loading XML files, 70-72

local linked tables, 128

locking files, 83

How can we make this index more useful? Email us at indexes@samspublishing.com

New Document task pane, 77

New Mail Message Using, Microsoft Office Word 2003 (HTML) command (Actions menu), 35

New Publication task pane, 174, 177

New Workbook task pane, 18, 87-89

New, Internet Fax command (File menu), 34

New, Key command (Edit menu), 52

New, Meeting Request command (File menu), 30, 57

New, Search Folder command (File menu), 34

New, Section command (File menu), 211

New, String Value command (Edit menu), 52

Note Flags, 205-206

notebooks

    managing, 210-211

    saving (OneNote), 202

    sharing, SharePoint, 226

notes

    audio, playing, 215-216

    emailing, 216

    flagging, 205-206

    handwritten, 200, 207

    Pocket PC, copying, 220

    printing, 207

    publishing, 217-218

    recording, 215

    saving, Outlook tasks, 216

    searching, 206-207

    side notes, 202-204

    spell-checking, 205

    taking (OneNote), 198

    video, 220-221

numbered lists (OneNote), creating, 208

O

Object Dependencies task pane, 123-125

objects

    ancestors, 124

    embedded, displaying (PowerPoint 2003), 118

Office. *See* Microsoft Office

Office 2003 XML Reference Schemas, downloading, 99

Office Clipboard command (Edit menu), 88

Offline Folders file, 56

one-line views, Outlook 2003, 37

OneNote

    audio, 214-216

    features, 194-195

    ink, 200

    lists, creating, 208

    notebooks, managing, 210-211

    notes

        emailing, 216

        flagging, 205-206

        printing, 207

        publishing, 217-218

        saving as Outlook tasks, 216

        searching, 206-207

        spell-checking, 205

    outlines, 209-210

    overview, 193-194

    pages, managing, 213-214

    sections, managing, 211-212

    side notes, 202-204

    stationery, 213-214

    user interface

        copying/pasting content, 201

        drawing, 201

T

How can we make this index more useful? Email us at indexes@samspublishing.com

How can we make this index more useful? Email us at indexes@samspublishing.com